Moses Harvey

Newfoundland as it is in 1894

A Hand-Book and Tourist's Guide

Moses Harvey

Newfoundland as it is in 1894
A Hand-Book and Tourist's Guide

ISBN/EAN: 9783337191696

Printed in Europe, USA, Canada, Australia, Japan

Cover: Foto ©Andreas Hilbeck / pixelio.de

More available books at **www.hansebooks.com**

Advertisements

G. KNOWLING.

WATER STREET, - - ST. JOHN'S, N. F.

Wholesale & Retail Dry Goods.

DRESSMAKING! MILLINERY! MANTLES!

HARDWARE !!!

Provisions and Groceries:

LARGEST STOCK! LOWEST PRICES!

SHIPS' STORES!

Cordage, Chains, Anchors, Glass, Paints and Oils, and all goods required for the Fisheries and Farming.

Building Material !!!

ALL KINDS OF MECHANICS' TOOLS!

No home should be without or no vessel should sail without a supply of BEECHAM'S PILLS. There is no better medicine known. We are sole Agents.

SPECIAL NOTICE.

Customers residing in Outports can save the trouble and expense of coming to St. John's, by sending order and money in registered letter or Post Office Order, as we give such orders the greatest attention and charge our lowest price.

G. KNOWLING.

Advertisements.

WM. H. DAVIDSON,

WHOLESALE AND RETAIL

FAMILY GROCER.

367 - - WATER STREET, ST. JOHN'S, - - 367

MANUFACTURER of Jams and Jellies made from native Fruits, which have received the approval of Her Majesty the Queen; and Sole Agents for

G. W. GOODWIN & SON,

"*IVY SOAP.*"

MANCHESTER, ENGLAND.

ALEX. OGSTON & SONS,

"SCOTCH SOAP."

ABERDEEN, SCOTLAND.

COX & CO.,

"*Anti Burton Ales and Stout.*"

LONDON, ENGLAND.

FORBES, MAXWELL & CO.,

"*Cordials and Fruit Syrups.*"

ABERDEEN, SCOTLAND.

The New HYDROLEINE CO., (Limited), Sanitary Washing Powders, Ashly-de-la-Zouch, England.

TERMS—Cash with orders or approved City references.

Advertisements.

ESTABLISHED 1823.

Thos. McMurdo & Co.,

Wholesale and Dispensing CHEMISTS.

FULL stocks of Drugs and Chemicals of all kinds always on hand. English and American Patents and Proprietory Goods of repute. Dry Paints, Stains, Varnishes, &c. Agricultural, Garden and Flower Seeds. Flowering Bulbs in their season.

☞ Careful and prompt attention to Outport orders.

Marine and Family Medicine Chests.

Water-St., - - St. John's, N. F.

CALLAHAN, GLASS & CO.,

Cabinet-makers,

Upholsterers,

—AND—

GENERAL HOUSE FURNISHERS.

DUCKWORTH AND GOWER STREETS.

Advertisements.

Bowring Bros.,

Shipping & General Merchants.

Water Street, St. John's, N. F.

Importers and Wholesale and Retail Dealers in all kinds of

Canadian & American Goods.

Our Departments are replete with the largest stocks in town of

Dry Goods, Hardware, Groceries,

Provisions and Ships'

Chandlery.

Agents for the Liverpool & London & Globe INSURANCE CO.

LLOYDS' AGENTS.

Advertisements.

JAS. BAIRD,

WATER STREET, - ST. JOHN'S,

GENERAL IMPORTER OF GOODS, GROCERIES, PROVISIONS, LIQUORS, &c., is now occupying his New Premises

BAIRD'S BUILDING

Where he invites inspection of his large stock. Codfish, Oil and Lobsters purchased at market rates. Wharfage and Storage accommodation. Premises all new and centrally situated.

J. F. CHISHOLM,

WATER STREET, - - ST. JOHN'S, NEWFOUNDLAND,

IMPORTER and Dealer in Stationery and Books of all kinds; Periodicals, Music, Charts and Nautical Works, Fancy Goods, Toys, Walking Sticks, Trout and Salmon Tackle, Pipes and Smokers' Sundries. Books, Periodicals, Music, &c., supplied to order promptly, at lowest cash prices. Orders filled with despatch.

ESTABLISHED 1858.

R. CALLAHAN,

——DEALER IN——

STOVES AND TINWARE,

Wholesale and Retail.

Plumbing and Gas Fitting.

384 & 386 WATER STREET, ST. JOHN'S, N. F.

Advertisements.

| James Angel. | Cable Address:
 "ANGEL," ST. JOHN'S.
 Telephone:
 DOCK, No. 48. STORE, No. 37. | A. D. Brown. |

JAMES ANGEL & CO.

ST. JOHN'S DRY DOCK.

The Largest Dry Dock on this side the Atlantic. Length, over all, 610 ft; width of entrance, 84 ft. 9 in.; Depth of water on sill at ordinary tides, 24 feet.

LARGE SHEDS for the storage of Freight. Every facility for Ship repairs. Vessels of any size requiring repairs without Dockage can be laid alongside our deep-water piers. An exclusive Lloyd's Surveyor resident in the port. Extensive Work Shops on Dock side fitted with machinery for the repairs of Hulls, Engines and Boilers.

We have had a long and varied experience in all kinds of Ship and Engine work. A large and efficient staff of Engineers, Boiler-makers, Ship Repairers, Coppersmiths, Blacksmiths and Ship Carpenters always employed and ready for any size job. Diver, with all appliances; Steam Pump and wrecking materials on the premises.

Ships' bottoms cleaned and coated with Anti-Fouling Compositions.

Dockage rates according to size of vessels and time on Dock, but always reasonable.

Castings in Iron or Brass to any weight. Ship Stores for deck or engine room always on hand at the Dock or at our Engineers' and Mill Furnishing Stores No. 7 Water Street West.

Friends and strangers are always welcome to examine the Dock, with its splendid Pumping House and Work Shops, where are carried on all classes of Engine and Foundry work and the manufacture of any requisite for the smallest fishing schooner to the largest steamship.

Late Shipping and Engineering Papers on fyle at our offices and shown with pleasure to those interested.

At our Engineers' and Mill Furnishing Stores are kept a large stock of Brass Goods for Engines and Steam Fittings; all sizes of Iron Pipe and Fittings; Belting, Oils, Steel Bar Iron. Every class of Goods in our line.

Machinery for Saw Mills; Hoisting Engines for Mines; Boilers for Land and Marine work made; and dealers in second-hand Machinery of every class.

Advertisements.

Goodfellow & Co.

GENERAL IMPORTERS AND COMMISSION MERCHANTS,

239, 241, 243, 245, 247,
Water Street, St. John's, Newfoundl'd.

—DEALERS IN—

Dry Goods, Hardware,

Provisions, Groceries, and Ships'

Chandlery.

Agents for the well-known firm of WM. HOUNSELL & Co., Bridprt, Line and Twine manufacturers.

In ne above departments a large and varied assortment of all classes of goods is kept which are sold at the smallest margin of profit. For all kinds of produce, such as FISH, OIL, HERRING, SALMON, LOBSTERS, FURS, we pay the highest prices. Having excellent facilities for doing business in our new premises, we guarantee satisfaction in all departments to those who may favor us with their patronage.

Advertisements.

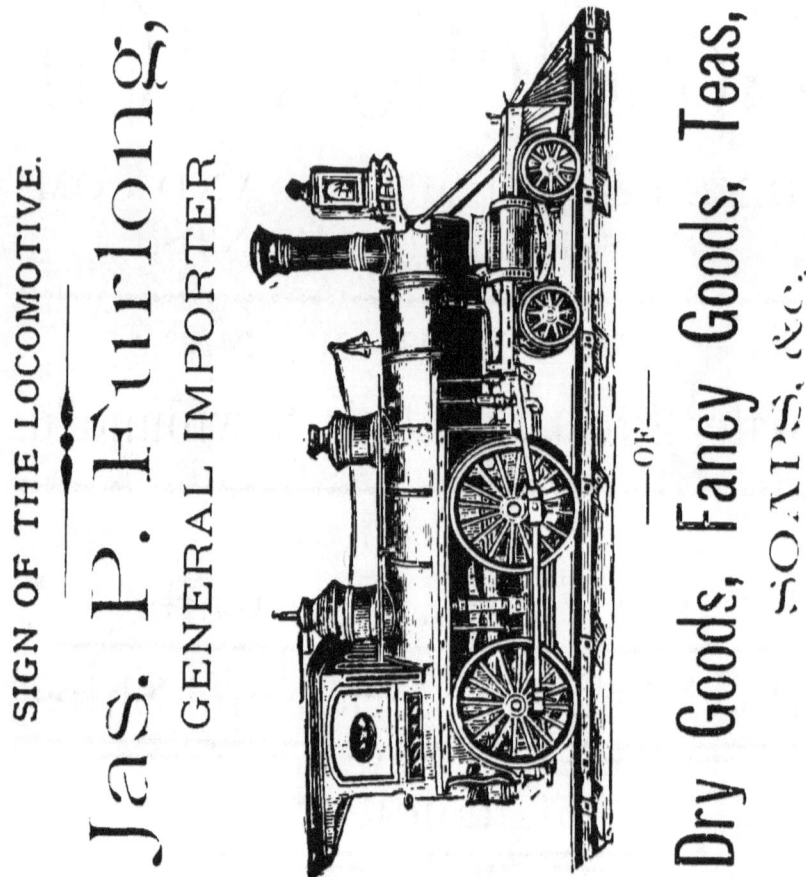

Jas. P. Furlong,
GENERAL IMPORTER
SIGN OF THE LOCOMOTIVE.
—OF—
Dry Goods, Fancy Goods, Teas,
SOAPS, &c.

THE ST. JOHN'S CONFECTIONARY, FRUIT AND FLOWER STORE!

FRED B. WOOD, Proprietor.

Manufacturer and Importer of

❖— CONFECTIONERY —❖

of superior quality.

AGENT FOR NFLD. OF THE NOVA SCOTIA NURSERY.

Choice Ice Cream, Soda Water with pure Fruit Syrups, and all kids of New Fruit in season.

CITY CLUB BUILDING, WATER STREET, ST. JOHN'S, N. F.

Advertisements.

S. E. GARLAND,

BOOKSELLER, NEWSDEALER, AND STATIONER.
Wholesale and Retail Dealer in Charts, Domestic and Fancy Glass, China and Earthenware, Jewellery, Tin, Wood, and other Toys, Trout and Salmon Tackle, Smokers' Requisites, and all kinds of Fancy Goods. *⁂* Used Newfoundland Stamps, second-hand Books bought and sold.

GARLAND BUILDING:
177 WATER STREET EAST, AND 296 WATER STREET, WEST.

FINE TAILORING.
Water-St., St. John's, N. F.

SNOW & CO.,
Harness and Trunk-Makers,
422 WATER STREET WEST, ST. JOHN'S, NEWFOUNDLAND.

A full stock on hand of
HARNESS, HORSE CLOTHING, STABLE WEAR.
REPAIRING A SPECIALTY.

WM. CAMPBELL,
(SUCCESSOR TO THE LATE HENRY DUDER),
BUTCHER.

Ships supplied promptly.   Ships' Stores on hand.
Satisfaction guaranteed.

350 - WATER STREET, ST. JOHN'S, NEWFOUNDLAND. - 350
One Door East of General Post Office.

BY
THE REV. M. HARVEY, LL.D., F.R.S.C.

Author of "Text-Book of Newfoundland History; Articles "Newfoundland," "Labrador," and "Seal Fisheries of the World," in Encyclopaedia Britannica; "Lectures Literary and Biographical; "Where are we and Whither Tending;" and one of the authors of "Newfoundland—The Oldest British Colony."

WITH COLOURED MAP.

ST. JOHN'S, N.F.
J. W. WITHERS, QUEEN'S PRINTER.
1894.

PREFACE.

In the following pages I have aimed at presenting, in a moderate compass, a comprehensive and trust-worthy account of Newfoundland as it is at the present time. In doing so it was necessary, of course, to refer to its history and to trace its progress in the past, so as to understand how it came to be what it is in 1894.

I have devoted a considerable portion of the volume to a description of the natural resources and capabilities of the Island. These have been largely overlooked or mis-represented; and, as a consequence, undervalued and neglected. The account given in these pages of the agricultural and mineral resources of the country and of its forest wealth, will be a surprise to many. I have endeavoured, however, in dealing with the subject, to secure strict accuracy of statement, and to be guided solely by facts and by the highest and best authorities. These natural resources, as I believe, are such as warrant us in predicting a bright and prosperous future for the Colony now that the construction of railways has opened its agricultural, mineral and forest lands, and prepared a way for enterprise and capital to turn them to profitable account.

I have also dwelt on the grand staple industry of the Colony—the fisheries,—and given a full account of their present condition and prospects in the future. The French Treaty Rights on certain portions of the shore and their effects on the Colony, have received due attention. Other topics dealt with are education, finances, trade and commerce, government, public institutions, population, and the general business of the country.

In the chapter for travellers and tourists I have dwelt on the fine scenery of the Island, and given such information and directions as are required for enabling them to see the country to the best advantage. There can be little doubt that, in the near future, Newfoundland is destined to hold an important place as a health-resort during its summer months, and as a country which presents rare attractions for the tourist and the sportsman. Numerous lines of steamers now render access to its shores easy, and the extension of its railway system and local steam communication place within reach of visitors from other lands all that is attractive and interesting in the beauty of its scenery.

A residence of over forty years in the Colony has given me opportunities of becoming acquainted with the country and the people. It will be a source of gratification to me if this little volume should aid in making the country better known and attracting to it that attention which it richly merits.

M. H.

St. John's, July, 1894.

CONTENTS.

CHAPTER I
HISTORICAL SKETCH.   PAGE

The Aborigines ; The Northmen ; The Coming of the White men ; The first fishermen ; Sir Humphrey Gilbert ; The French in Newfoundland ; Historic Misfortunes ; Unjust Laws ; Dawn of better days .   7

CHAPTER II.
PHYSIOGRAPHY AND TOPOGRAPHY OF THE ISLAND.

Geographical position ; Its mountain-ranges, rivers, lakes, etc. ; Geology ; Climate   ...   24

CHAPTER III.
ROADS AND RAILWAYS.

First roads ; Beginning of Railway construction ; Railway to Harbour Grace and Placentia ; The Great Northern and Western Railway —its route, character of the country traversed ; resources to be developed ; land, minerals, timber   43

CHAPTER IV.
AGRICULTURAL RESOURCES AND FOREST WEALTH.

Western Newfoundland ; Fertile Valleys ; Coal Fields ; Mineral Deposits ; Exploits, Gander and Gambo Valleys ; Value of Agricultural Products ; Prospects of Cattle and Sheep Raising ; Forests .   89

CHAPTER V.
MINERAL RESOURCES.

Rise and Progress of Mining Industry ; Copper Mines ; Gypsum and Marble ; Iron Pyrites at Pilley's Island ; Discovery of Asbestos ; Coal Areas   125

CONTENTS.

CHAPTER VI.

THE CROWN LANDS' ACTS.

Purchase of Land; Licenses of Occupation; Homestead; Licenses to cut Timber; Paper Pulp Act; Licenses to search for Minerals; Sheep Farming Regulations 134

CHAPTER VII.

THE FISHERIES.

Evolution of the Cod-fishery — its value and prospects; Seal, Herring, Salmon and Lobster Fisheries; Fisheries' Commission — its good work; Artificial Propagation of Marine Food-fishes; Great Success of Cod and Lobster Hatching; Bait Preservation — the Freezing Barrel; Refrigerators ... 146

CHAPTER VIII.

INTERNATIONAL TREATIES.

Their Effects; Treaty Rights of the French; The "French Shore." Disputes. Perils of the Situation; *Modus vivendi*; Legislative Action; Present Negotiations ... 176

CHAPTER IX.

CHARACTERISTICS OF THE PEOPLE—THE CLASSES AND THE MASSES.

Saxon and Celtic Elements; Mental and Moral Qualities, Capital and Labour; The Credit System; The Fishermen; Social Pleasures. 193

CHAPTER X

POPULATION.

Rate of increase—The Census of 1891; Numbers of Religious denominations; Agricultural returns; Employments of the people ... 205

CHAPTER XI

MODE OF GOVERNMENT.

Constitution—House of Assembly—Legislative Council—The Governor—Law Courts; Revenue; Trade; Finances; Shipping ... 222

CONTENTS.

CHAPTER XII.
EDUCATION.   PAGE
Schools Academies Colleges- Legislative Grants for Education ... 220

CHAPTER XIII.
Post Office Department ; Constabulary ; Light Houses ; Banks ; Newspaper Press   226

CHAPTER XIV.
SCENERY.
Attractions for Travellers and Tourists ; Likeness to Norway ; The Island as a health-resort ; Opinions of travellers on Scenery ; The weather ; London "Times" on Newfoundland   .. 233

CHAPTER XV.
DIRECTIONS FOR TOURISTS.
How to see the Country ; Routes of Travel ; Steamship Lines to England, Halifax, New York, Montreal ; Coastal Steamers ; St. John's—Objects of interest there, its streets, buildings, etc. ; Industries ; Drives and walks in vicinity of St. John's ; Signal Hill ; Quidi Vidi ; To Torbay ; Portugal Cove ; Petty Harbour ; Renews ; Excursions by Sea—Western Route to Bonne Bay ; Northern Route to Battle Harbour and Labrador ; Moravian Mission stations ; Grand Falls, Labrador ; Railway Excursions from St. John's to Harbor Grace, thence to Heart's Content ; Working of Cables—Instruments ; Repairing Cables ; New Cable of 1894 ; Heart's Delight—Scene of Joseph Hatton's "Under the Great Seal" ; Dildo Hatchery ; Placentia, its fine Scenery ; History ; Curiosities ; Relics, etc. ; Richard Brothers the Mad Prophet ; St. John's to Exploits ; Northern and Western Railway ; Stations and Distances ; Fishing ; Hotels in St. John's ; Trip to St. Pierre and Miquelon ; Description of the Islands   245

CHAPTER XVI.
SPORT IN NEWFOUNDLAND.
Wild Geese and Ducks ; Curlew, Plover, Ptarmigan Shooting ; Deer Stalking ; Salmon Fishing 291

APPENDIX.
No. 1—Erratum ; New Cable ; Stock Exchanges, London and New York, connected by Cable ; Table of Lengths of Cables. No. 2—Scenery ; Bay of Islands   ... 295

NEWFOUNDLAND AS IT IS IN 1894:

A HAND-BOOK AND TOURISTS' GUIDE.

CHAPTER I.
HISTORICAL SKETCH.

ABORIGINAL NEWFOUNDLAND.

SHOULD it be asked: Who were the very first human inhabitants of this large island; to what race or nation did they belong; and what were their appearance and habits; what plane of civilization had they reached? We are unable to answer these questions. History enables us to go back only to the arrival of the first European explorers, and to describe the inhabitants found by them in possession of the island some four hundred years ago. But it is quite possible and even likely that other races may have preceded the Red Indians who were occupants of the soil when the "pale faces" first trod these shores, and these may have disappeared, leaving no trace behind, after playing their part for many centuries on this narrow stage of being. We know something about the latest comers, but all is cloudland as regards any earlier tribes.

GEOLOGICAL CHANGES.

We have more records in the rocks, regarding the earlier changes through which this portion of the globe has passed, than of the evanescent human beings who first trod its surface.— Geology has much to tell us of vast transformations during the æons of the past; of the seas flowing over much that is now dry land; of the bottoms of old Cambrian and Silurian seas now elevated into hill-ranges; of vast denudations sweeping away later formations and spreading the wrecks over the floor of ocean; of volcanic operations that brought to the surface the mineral-bearing rocks, placing the precious ores within the reach of man. Above all, geology has much to say about an ice-age, (towards the close of the Tertian), when Newfoundland, in common with many neighbouring lands, was under a huge ice-cap many hundreds of feet thick, just as Greenland now is, and during which glaciers for hundreds of centuries were shaping its valleys and scooping out its bays and lakes and covering much of its surface with boulders of Archaean rocks. These glaciers have left their grooves on the rocks, by which their course can still be traced. This ice-covering at length began to shrink as the climate grew milder, and finally disappeared. Plants and animals, different from any now existing, lived and died. Species followed species, of which we can trace some faint outlines in the rocks. Whether any human eyes looked on them we know not; but, if so, they, too, passed away leaving no memorials of themselves. And when those daring voyagers crossed the stormy Atlantic and reached this sea-girt isle they found it inhabited by a race in all respects resembling the savage tribes of the neighbouring North American continent, and evidently belonging to the same stock. These early explorers from Europe for a long time believed that the country they had discovered was not a new continent, but the eastern shores of Asia, or India, as it was named, and hence they called the whole inhabitants, both in North and South America, "Indians." From their complexion the northern tribes were afterwards designated "Red Indians," and the whole tribes "American Indians."

THE BEOTHIKS.

The Indian race found in Newfoundland called themselves Beothiks. This was their tribal name. Their features resembled those of the continental Indians. They had high cheek bones, small black eyes, straight black hair, and were of a copper-color. Their weapons, canoes, tents or wigwams and domestic utensils resembled those of neighbouring tribes on the continent. Their habits of life were alike in many respects and they lived by hunting and fishing.

Among learned men who have studied carefully the few relics which have been preserved, and examined the meagre and uncertain vocabularies which contain all that remains of their language, there is a difference of opinion as to whether they were a branch of the wide-spread and warlike Algonkins who once occupied nearly the whole of Canada and a large portion of the United States, or whether they were a separate and older race of Red men, who had at an unknown date migrated to this island, where for many centuries they sustained themselves and increased in numbers. There is a certain amount of evidence in favour of the latter view, but no certainty can now be reached.

CONDITION OF THE BEOTHIKS.

When Cabot discovered the island, in 1497, the Beothiks were a numerous and powerful race, well-developed physically, ingenious and of quick intelligence, gentle in their manners, tractable, and not indisposed to friendly intercourse with the pale faces. They had lived for unknown ages unmolested. The island with its abundance of wild creatures of all kinds, its shores and countless lakes swarming with fish, was to them a very paradise. Countless herds of the finest reindeer wandered over the savannas of the interior, in their annual migrations. The ponds were abundantly stocked with beaver; the lordly salmon crowded the rivers; vast flocks of ptarmigan and other game birds were everywhere met with. Wild geese and ducks in the early spring arrived in myriads from the south. The Beothiks must have revelled in savage abundance, being "monarchs of all they surveyed." They practised no agriculture; but the wild berries, in their variety and luxuriant growth, supplied them with abundance of vegetable food. The skins and furs of the wild animals gave them abundant clothing. With their spears, clubs, bows and arrows, slings, and many ingenious devices for capturing their prey, they were rarely in want of food and clothing. Newfoundland is still a fine sporting country, but what must it have been in the time of the Beothiks!

SUFFERINGS OF THE BEOTHIKS.

The coming of the white men sealed their doom. For three hundred years afterwards they continued to exist but were gradually becoming weaker and weaker. For a short time friendly relations between them and the invaders existed, but soon quarrels arose. Deeds of violence led to acts of savage vengeance. The first rude trappers, hunters and fishermen, as they spread into the northern parts of the island, were outside the control of law, and but little disposed to try conciliation and kindness on a tribe of savages whose presence interfered with their pursuits. The poor Beothiks were treated with the most brutal cruelty and for a long period were regarded as vermin to be hunted down and destroyed. Such treatment led the Red Man to deeds of fierce retaliation and "war to the knife" became the practice between the two races. In such a contest the weak must go to the wall. Their weapons could avail little against the firearms of the white man. Gradually their numbers were reduced and they were driven from the best hunting and fishing grounds. Famine and disease thinned their ranks.

THE RACE EXTINCT.

When at length, in modern days, the spirit of humanity awoke and attempts were made in 1769, and renewed up till 1823, to conciliate the Red Men and save the poor remnant from destruction, it proved to be too late. Sad experience led them to distrust and hate the white men, and they could not be approached with kindness. In despair the forlorn band that remained retreated to their last refuge, at Red Indian Lake; and here they died, one by one, till not a living representative of a once vigorous and warlike race remained. There is no darker chapter in the history of the white man's progress in the New World than that which records the fate of the unhappy Beothiks.

A MELANCHOLY RECORD.

In 1828 a final effort was made to open communication with a remnant of them which were supposed to still survive. An expedition was organized which penetrated to their last retreat at Red Indian Lake. Only their graves and the mouldering remains of their wigwams were found, but no living Beothik. Silence deep as death reigned around. There were fragments of their canoes, their skin dresses, their storehouses, the repositories of their dead; but no human sounds were heard, no smoke from wigwams mounted into the air, their camp-fires were extinguished, and the sad record of an extinct race was closed for ever.

THEIR RELICS.

In the Museum at St. John's may be seen a collection of their relics and remains which have been carefully preserved. There are a few skulls, some bones, and the almost perfect skeleton of a boy, found in a grave on Pilley's Island, in a wonderful state of preservation. Their tools, arrow-heads, gouges, and other stone implements are to be seen, but they are gone –

"Like the cloud-rack of a tempest,
Like the withered leaves of Autumn."

DESCRIPTIVE ACCOUNTS.

A full account of all that is known about the Beothiks may be found in "Hatton and Harvey's Newfoundland," in Rev. Dr. Patterson's admirable paper read before the Royal Society of Canada on the "Beothiks, or Red Man of Newfoundland"; also, in "Cormack's Journey Across Newfoundland," and in Bonnycastle's and Pedley's Newfoundland. Dr. Patterson's is the most exhaustive account published.

THE NORTH MEN.

It is highly probable that the first white men who saw the shores of Newfoundland were the Northmen. Five hundred years before the time of Cabot these bold adventurers led by Lief, son of Eric the Red, sailed from Greenland in search of western lands. Newfoundland lay directly in their course, and according to their Sagas or books, on reaching it they gave it the name of "Helluland," or the land of naked rocks. The daring sailors passed on, however, and made no attempt at forming a settlement. Their adventurous voyage, in which they are said to have reached Rhode Island, took place in the year 1001.

COMING OF THE WHITE MEN—SIR HUMPHREY GILBERT.

Nearly five centuries passed. The year 1497 arrived, and on the 2nd day of May in that year a small caravel named *The Matthew* manned by 18 stout English sailors, left the port of Bristol. She was commanded by John Cabot, a Venetian by birth, who was in the service of Henry VII. of England. On the 24th of June following, hearty English cheers greeted the first sight of the Island of Newfoundland. Thus by right of discovery it belonged to England, but it was not till 1583 that it was formally taken possession of by Sir Humphrey Gilbert, in the name of Queen Elizabeth. This gallant English Knight had formed the purpose of colonizing the island, but misfortunes overtook him and when returning to England his little vessel the *Golden Hind* and all on board sank beneath the waves of the Atlantic.

THE FIRST FISHERMEN.

Nearly thirty years elapsed after the failure of Sir Humphrey Gilbert's expedition before any fresh attempt was made to found a Colony in Newfoundland. During that period, however, the island rose into increased importance in connection with its fisheries. Indeed long before, the news of the abundance of fish on the Banks and in the waters around the shores of the island had led the fishermen of various nationalities to visit these regions in pursuit of the finny tribes; and to use the harbours and coves for curing and drying them. The first to take advantage of this new sea-harvest were the fishermen of Brittany and Normandy. They were soon followed by the fishermen of the Basque Provinces in the North-west of Spain. The Portuguese speedily took part in the same fisheries. In 1577 there were 100 Spanish and 50 Portuguese vessels thus employed, but they soon began to diminish in numbers—the enterprise of both nations being drawn to the gold regions of South America. Ere long, hardly a Spanish or Portuguese fishing vessel was to be seen in these stormy seas.

FRENCH FISHERIES AND DISCOVERIES.

Not so with the French who followed up these fisheries with vigour and success. In 1577 the French had 150 vessels employed, while English fishing vessels numbered only 50. The great wealth which France was deriving from these seas led her to form new and extensive designs of colonizing North America. On the accession of Henry IV., the first Bourbon, the cod-fishery was placed under the protection of the government, and was regarded as being of great national importance, and such it has been ever since. Her great explorers pushed on their discoveries. Cartier discovered Canada and secured it for France, who held it for 225 years till Quebec fell before the conquering arms of Wolfe. Champlain, De Monts, Marquette, La Salle followed till the territories claimed by France extended to the mouth of the Mississippi.

ENGLISH FISHERMEN.

The same attraction, however, which brought the French to these western seas ere long became potent with Englishmen. Though later in commencing this fishery they soon gained rapidly on their rivals the French. During the ten years which followed the death of Gilbert, ending in 1593, the progress of the English fishery in Newfoundland waters was so great that Sir Walter Raleigh declared in the House of Commons " it was the stay and support of the west counties of England." In the year 1600, 200 English ships went to Newfoundland and they employed 10,000 men and boys as catchers on board and curers on land. Sir Humphrey Gilbert's attempt to form a settlement was therefore not fruitless, when Sir William Monson, an Englishman who wrote in 1610, declared that since the island was taken possession of, the fisheries had been worth £100,000 annually to British subjects—an immense sum in those days. He further said that these fisheries had greatly increased the number of England's ships and mariners. Beyond all doubt this was the beginning of England's maritime greatness.

NEWFOUNDLAND'S FISHERIES THE BEGINNING OF ENGLAND'S MARITIME SUPREMACY.

France and England had now between them the entire possession of these fisheries. Both nations drew enormous wealth from them year after year, and thus increased their national greatness; and both found them the best nurseries for bold and skilful sailors, and thus developed their maritime power. Colonies were planted by both originally with the view of protecting and carrying on the fisheries. In this way the Newfoundland fisheries really laid their foundation of the empire which England at length acquired in America when her supremacy was established after a long contest with France. The humble fishermen were the pioneers of the great host from the Old World, which in due time built up the United States and overspread Canada. In prosecuting these fisheries England first learned how to become mistress of the seas.

GUY'S COLONY.

Newfoundland at this time stood out prominently before the minds of Englishmen, so that it is not wonderful to find that other attempts at planting a colony on its shores should be made soon after Gilbert's failure. In 1609, John Guy, a merchant and afterwards Mayor of Bristol, drew attention in a pamphlet to the importance of colonizing the island. The enterprise which he started was shared in by Lord Bacon and other noblemen. Bacon declared that "the Newfoundland fisheries were more valuable than all the mines of Peru." Guy's plantation was, for some reason unsuccessful. Probably piracy then prevailing, was the cause of failure.

CAPTAIN WHITBOURNE'S ARRIVAL.

In 1615, Captain Richard Whitbourne, mariner, of Exmouth, Devonshire, was sent out by the Admiralty of England to establish order and correct abuses which had grown up among the fishermen in Newfoundland. He found 250 English vessels employed in the fisheries,—a sufficient proof of the flourishing condition of the cod-fishery at this early date. To Whitbourne we are indebted for the first book on Newfoundland—"A Discourse and Discovery of Newfoundland Trade"—in which he wrote enthusiastically of the country and its prospects. This book is now very rare and valuable.

SIR GEORGE CALVERT.

Next came another gallant knight—Sir George Calvert, afterwards Lord Baltimore—a gentleman of keen intelligence and high character. From James I. he obtained a patent conveying to him the lordship of the whole southern peninsula of Newfoundland which he named Avalon. He built a noble mansion at Ferryland, and brought out a number of emigrants of a superior type. His settlement, however, was so much harrassed by the French that he became disheartened and returned to England; but nearly all the colonists he brought with him remained to increase the resident population.

SIR DAVID KIRKE.

The brave sea-captain—Sir David Kirke—obtained the next charter from Charles I. in 1638, and it conveyed a grant of the whole island. He did much to promote the settlement of the country and governed wisely. He died at Ferryland in 1665, at the age of fifty-six.

THE FRENCH IN NEWFOUNDLAND.

All this time the French had been struggling to found an empire in the New World. In doing so they never lost sight of a project early formed for the conquest of Newfoundland. The possession of it they knew would enable them to control the fisheries, and also to command the narrow entrance to the St. Lawrence and their Canadian possessions. Hence they never ceased their efforts to obtain a footing in the island; and their presence and encroachments were a constant annoyance to the English settlers. As early as 1635 the French managed to obtain permission from England to dry fish on the shores of the island, on payment of a duty of five per cent. on the produce, which duty was afterwards remitted. In 1660 they founded Placentia on the southern coast, and erected a strong fortification for its protection. From this centre they succeeded in planting other settlements on the same shore. Desperate efforts were made by them again and again to effect the conquest of the island. Their successes, however, were short-lived; and though they captured St. John's more than once they were speedily driven out and their expeditions resulted in disappointment.

TREATIES OF UTRECHT AND PARIS.

The Treaty of Utrecht (1713) marked an important era in the history of the island. By one of its provisions the French agreed to surrender all their possessions in Newfoundland and the adjacent islands, and to retire from Placentia. Thus the sovereignty of the whole island was secured to England. But even after France had fought her last battle on the heights of Abraham, and her white flag no longer waved on the continent of North America, she clung pertinaciously to the idea of conquering and holding Newfoundland, well knowing its value in the prosecution of her fisheries, which she still regarded as the great training school for seamen. So late as 1762 they organized a final expedition for the conquest of the island. They succeeded in capturing St. John's which was weakly garrisoned; but it was soon wrested from them by a strong British force despatched from Halifax. Thus ended the last attempt of the French to gain possession of the island. The Treaty of Paris (1763) ended "the seven years war," and France renounced all claims to Canada, Acadia, Cape Breton and Newfoundland.

FRENCH TREATY RIGHTS.

Unfortunately, however, these treaties failed to deliver the Colony from the French troubles which had so long disturbed the settlers and retarded the prosperity of the country. Though the Treaty of Utrecht left the French no territorial rights, it gave them the right of fishing and curing fish on the western, northern and north-eastern shores of the island. This, which was conceded at first as a privilege, encouraged the French to push their claims to the sole right of fishing on the treaty-shore which the colonists strenuously repudiated. Bitter disputes have thus been engendered, which have gone on till the present hour and are still unsettled. The practical effect of this unfortunate concession has been that the people of Newfoundland have been virtually excluded from the fairest and most valuable portion of the island, and that they could neither prosecute the fisheries there, settle the lands, nor carry on mining or any other industry. The "French Shore Question" as it has been called, has been transmitted as a legacy from generation to generation. More than any other cause this has retarded the progress of the Colony. The French still hold on as pertinaciously as ever to their claims. This was the first of the long series of "historic misfortunes," as Lord Salisbury has named them, of which Newfoundland has been the victim. In vain has diplomacy wrestled with these antiquated treaties time after time. The Old Man of the Sea did not cling more firmly to the shoulders of Sinbad than the Frenchman to the shores of England's oldest Colony.

HISTORIC MISFORTUNES--UNJUST LAWS.

But even these unlucky treaties, formed by careless or incompetent statesmen, which deprived the colonists of the use of the best half of the island, were not the worst of its "historic misfortunes." For more than a century and a half, the settlement of the island and the cultivation of its soil were systematically thwarted and sternly prohibited by law; and continuous efforts were made to keep it as a fishing station to which English fishermen could resort in summer to catch and dry fish, and then return home at the end of the season with the products of their toil.

MIGRATORY FISHERY.

This strange policy, which was backed by English laws, requires some explanation. From the first the fisheries had been carried on by merchants, ship-owners and traders from the west of England. Each year they sent out ships and fishing-crews from England. The fish caught was salted and dried ashore. When winter approached the fishermen took their departure for England. These English "merchant-adventurers" as they were called, found that it was for their interest to discourage the settlement of the country, as they wished to retain its harbours and coves for the use of their own fishing captains and servants, and thus secure a very profitable monopoly of the whole fisheries.

This system went on for generations till these merchant-monopolists began to fancy that the whole island was their own, and that any one who settled there was an interloper whom they were warranted in driving away. Being wealthy and powerful they had great influence with successive English governments of those days. They were able to persuade the statesmen and people of England that the fisheries would be ruined if a resident population should be allowed to grow up in the island, and that they would no longer be a nursery of seamen for the Royal Navy. Further, they misled the English Government and people by representing the island as hopelessly barren, and in regard to its soil and climate, unfit for being a permanent residence for human beings, but a very convenient rock-mass for curing and drying codfish during the summer season.

SETTLEMENT PROHIBITED.

In this way it came about that unjust and injurious laws were enacted by the English Government to prevent the settlement of the island and to keep it forever in the degraded condition of a stage for drying fish. These laws forbade anyone to go to Newfoundland as a settler, and ordained that all fishermen should return to England at the close of each fishing season. Masters of vessels were compelled to give bonds of £100, binding them to bring back each year such persons as they took out. Settlement within six miles of the coast was prohibited under heavy penalties. No one could cultivate or enclose the smallest piece of ground, or even repair a house without license, which was rarely granted.

CONFLICT OF SETTLERS AND MERCHANT-ADVENTURERS.

Notwithstanding these hardships and discouragements the sturdy settlers held their ground and slowly but steadily increased in numbers. Between them and their oppressors a bitter antipathy sprang up, and it is not wonderful that it should have been so. There were among them men of a manly independent spirit, who carried on the contest bravely against the grasping fishing-capitalists, and at last conquered them and won their freedom. The conflict, however, was very trying and extended over one hundred and fifty years, entailing terrible sufferings on the settlers, who were kept outside the pale of law and without any civilizing influences. Perhaps the worst feature of the misrule of those days was the government by Fishing Admirals. It was enacted that the master of the first ship entering a harbour was to be Admiral for the season, and Magistrate of the district, with unlimited power to decide all questions regarding property and all other disputes. From their decisions there were no appeals. These rude and ignorant skippers were the servants of the merchant-adventurers and, therefore, personally interested in questions of property that arose. They were the enemies of the poor residents whom they wanted to trample out. They took possession of the best fishing-stations, and frequently drove out the inhabitants from their own houses and fishing grounds. They took bribes when determining cases and carried on for long years a system of robbery and oppression. How could the country make any progress under such conditions? The lot of the poor fisherman was very bitter. In their little wooden hamlets sprinkled around the sea-margin, they could hardly obtain the barest subsistence. They had no schools for their children and no ministers of religion among them. All around them were the dense woods extending to the sea-shore with a few paths cut through them. Before them the great ocean from which alone they were permitted to draw their means of subsistence.

DAWN OF BETTER DAYS.

They held on, however, and courageously resisted their selfish oppressors; and at last the day of deliverance dawned. The Government and people of England discovered at length that they had been misled and deceived both in regard to the country and its fisheries. Humane and intelligent men in England came forward to plead the cause of the poor fishermen. Restrictions on the settlement of the island were removed one after another. Obnoxious statutes were repealed, but so slowly that it was not till about eighty years ago that the last of these unjust laws was removed from the statute-book and the people were allowed to possess lands and build houses and take some steps towards self-government. In 1729 the British Government appointed a Governor, and for the first time Newfoundland was recognized as a British Colony.

IMPROVEMENTS--SETTLEMENT ALLOWED.

The resident population had then grown to be 6,000 strong. The Fishing Admirals, however, were not abolished till long afterwards, but they were brought under some sort of control; and as the population increased and intelligence spread, their claims to authority fell into well-merited contempt and passed into oblivion. Courts of Justice were established; the navigation laws were extended to the island and a collector and controller of customs appointed. Freedom of religion was proclaimed which ended a deplorable system of religious persecution which had grown up. Still so late as 1799 houses erected in St. John's without a license were pulled down by the order of the Governor and restrictions on building and enclosing and cultivating the ground were not entirely abolished till 1820. The year 1825 saw the first roads built by Governor Duckworth. A post-office and a newspaper had been established at an earlier date—1805 and 1806. In 1763 the resident population was 7,000; in 1785 it had increased to 10,244; in 1804 it was found to be 20,380 and in 1834 it was 75,000. The population of St. John's was then 15,000.

SUBSTANTIAL PROGRESS.

Since the removal of these noxious restrictions the Colony has made respectable progress, and of late years this progress has been greatly accelerated by the introduction of mining, lumbering and other industries. During the long European wars which followed the French Revolution, the fisheries became very prosperous and the price of fish trebled. The peace of 1815 terminated that artificial prosperity and brought on a commercial crisis. In 1832 the great boon of Representative Government was granted to the Colony, and the new era of self-government began. Provisions were annually made by the local legislature for building roads and bridges and for the establishment and maintenance of education. This concession was enlarged and completed in 1854 by the grant of Responsible Government. The discovery of valuable deposits of copper ore in Notre Dame Bay in 1857 and the opening of the first copper mine in 1864 gave a great impulse to the general prosperity of the country. A Geological Survey of the island was initiated in 1864, and its natural resources were found to be very great. The Atlantic Cable found a resting place on its shores, and connected it with England and America. Steam communication direct with Europe and America was established in 1873; and in 1880 the first decisive steps towards the construction of a railway were taken. In 1882 a splendid Dry Dock was constructed in the harbour of St. John's. In 1884 the population had increased to 197,589. The annual value of agricultural products is now about $750,000, and the value of land under cultivation, together with the cattle, sheep and horses, over $2,500,000.

DEVASTATION BY FIRES.

St. John's has grown into a city of 30,000 inhabitants. It has suffered terribly by fires which have recurred again and again. In February, 1816, a fire broke out which destroyed 120 houses and left 1,500 people homeless. On November 7th of the same year another fire destroyed 130 houses, and a third on the 21st November laid in ashes a considerable part of the business portion of the city which had escaped former fires. These, however, were small in comparison with the great conflagration of June 9th, 1846, which in a few hours left three-fourths of the city a smoking mass of ruins, and about 12,000 persons houseless. The loss was estimated at a million pounds sterling.

GREAT FIRE OF JULY 8th, 1892.

A still greater calamity, as far as loss of property was concerned, occurred on July 8th, 1892, when more than one-half of the city was consumed. Sixteen hundred houses were destroyed and some 10,000 people left without a home. The best part of the business portion of the city was destroyed, the Church of England Cathedral, several churches and many public buildings. The loss was estimated at three million pounds sterling.

SPIRIT OF THE PEOPLE.

The spirit and energy of the people may be estimated from the fact that they met these repeated calamities with courage and firmness, and in each instance the city rose from its ashes greatly improved and beautified. This is specially true of the last calamity of 1892. In two years, a large proportion of the houses destroyed by the fire, were rebuilt, many of them being of a greatly improved type, and in another year or two hardly a trace of the fire will be visible. The new portion is a great improvement on that which was destroyed.

VICTORY WON—VILLAGE HAMPDENS.

The enterprise and calm courage which have marked the people of St. John's in grappling with and overcoming their misfortune, have been in accord with the spirit displayed by the whole people during those long years when they carried on the struggle for freedom against such heavy odds. That was truly a battle, and was won, not through bloody strife, but by sore toil, and patient endurance amid sufferings and hardships. No colony of the British Empire ever received such harsh and unnatural treatment from the Imperial Mother. When Lord Salisbury described it in euphonious terms as having been " the sport of historic misfortunes," he would have been nearer the mark had he said " the victim of historic wrongs and cruelties." For a century and a half its people were forbidden under heavy penalties to cultivate the soil or build houses, or do anything to make a home for themselves in the wilderness. They were left to the tender mercies of Fishing Admirals and Surrogates, and every means used to drive them from their adopted country. That they held their ground and finally gained the victory, is proof sufficient that there were among them many " Village Hampdens" who with " dauntless breast" confronted tyranny and resisted the oppressor. Even when by Imperial Treaties the best half of their island home was torn from them and virtually given over to the

French, they did not despair, but made the best of circumstances and waited for the time when this wrong would be righted. Now that at last the colony is on the path of progress, is it not time that the great Mother of Colonies made some reparation for the wrongs of the past, by holding out a helping hand to the oldest of her children?

CHAPTER II.

PHYSIOGRAPHY AND TOPOGRAPHY OF NEW-FOUNDLAND.

GENERAL OUTLINE.

A brief account of the physical conditions of the island, its soil, climate, under-earth, configuration and relation to the neighbouring land-masses seems to be desirable at the outset of any attempt to present an intelligible picture of the country.

GEOGRAPHICAL POSITION.

Its geographical position is unique and singularly important and commanding. Anchored at no great distance off the North American Continent, and stretching right across the entrance of the Gulf of St. Lawrence, to which it affords access at both its northern and southern extremities, it might be regarded as a place of arms and defence; for the power which possesses it holds the key of the St. Lawrence. Its south-western extremity is within sixty miles of Cape Breton, which is substantially the eastern point of Nova Scotia; while its most eastern projection is but 1640 miles distant from Ireland. Thus it is adapted by nature to serve the peaceful interests of commerce, and to facilitate intercourse between the Old World and the New, being a stepping stone between them.

DEEP BAYS.

In another respect the hand of nature has marked the island as a centre of commercial activity. A glance at the map shows that its coasts are pierced by numerous magnificent bays, running in some instances eighty or ninety miles inland, and throwing out smaller arms in all directions. In these deep bays, whose entrances are sentinelled by jutting headlands, are some of the finest harbours in the world, as well as countless coves, creeks and minor inlets where the fishermen's craft find shelter. These great watery ravines, which in many instances expand into inland seas, bring with them the marvellous fish-wealth of the surrounding waters, and place it within reach of the fisherman's net and hook. At the same time they present unrivaled facilities for the transport of the products of the fisheries, as well as the riches of the mine and the forest, and the agricultural productions which human labour will yet develope. To such an extent are the shores indented that though the island is about a thousand miles round, measuring from headland to headland, its entire coast-line is double that extent of mileage. In fact it would be difficult to find anywhere an equal land-area presenting such an extent of frontage to the sea.

COMPARATIVE SIZE.

Size counts for a good deal, and in the long run must be a measure of power. In regard to size it counts tenth among the islands of the globe. Its greatest breadth is 216 miles, and its greatest length the same; its area is 42,000 square miles. We obtain the best idea of its extent by comparing it with other countries. It is almost equal to the Empire State of New York; it is twice the size of Nova Scotia, and one-third larger than New Brunswick. Ireland contains 32,500 square miles, so that Newfoundland is one-sixth larger. It is three times as large as Holland and twice as large as Denmark.

SHAPE—PENINSULAS.

In shape it is roughly triangular, having a wide southern base between Cape Race and Cape Ray and a long narrow apex towards the north. Three large peninsulas project from the main body of the island. The largest of these—the peninsula of Avalon—is almost severed from the principal portion of the island by the two large bays of Placentia and Trinity which are separated by a narrow isthmus, in one place but three miles in width. The Avalon peninsula is further divided by the two bays of St. Mary's and Conception. Owing to its extensive frontage on the Atlantic, its numerous harbours and its proximity to the best fishing grounds, Avalon is the most thickly populated and commercially important part of the island. The northern peninsula—called Petite Nord by the French—runs up long and narrow, almost to Labrador, like the arm of a huge frying pan. The smallest peninsula of the three projects southerly between the bays of Placentia and Fortune. The little peninsula of Port-au-Port, off the west coast, may also be named. It is joined to the mainland by the Gravels, an isthmus not more than a quarter of a mile in width.

COAST SCENERY.

The first sight of the coasts of Newfoundland impresses the traveller unfavourably. They are what is usually termed "ironbound." To say that they are rocky describes them tamely. They might rather be designated one great wall of rock, now shooting up into peaks, now breaking into wild fissures, now presenting dark frowning cliffs, bold promontories and headlands sculptured into grim fantastic forms by the blows of Atlantic billows. Then come miles on miles of rocky ramparts from two to four hundred feet high, grim, massive, awe-inspiring. Such is the aspect from the sea. But let the traveller enter one of the deep fiords which at intervals cleave the rocky walls, and, if the season be summer, he will ere long, find himself amid varied scenes of beauty such as are rarely surpassed in the world's most favoured lands. The fiords of Newfoundland strikingly resemble those of Norway, to which tourists resort from all countries, and when known and made accessible to travellers, will prove not less attractive. Verdant islands, of all shapes and sizes, stud the bosom of the larger estuaries. Dark-green forests often sweep down to the water's edge. Fishing hamlets line the shore with their rough stages and "flakes" for drying the cod. The little fishing boats are dancing in groups on the bright waters. The sky overhead is blue as that of Italy, and the air balmy and exhilerating.

THE ISLAND AS A FISHING-CENTRE.

The hand of nature has marked the island as one of the world's great fishing-centres. Not only do the arms of the Atlantic, penetrating far inland, carry the finny tribes almost to the doors of the fishermen, but at the distance of a degree from the shores is the greatest submarine island of the globe—the Grand Bank of Newfoundland,—which extends for a length of six hundred miles with a breadth of two hundred. This is the great capital of the cod-kingdoms, and its sub-marine valleys and hills are alive with countless colonies of this noble fish. Since the days of Cabot thousands of fishermen have been mining the silvery quarries of these inexhaustible seas. Then all around the shores of the island and of the great bays are countless smaller submarine elevations to which the cod-colonies resort, and which constitute the finest fishing grounds in the world. Vast shoals of the bait-fishes—caplin, squid, herring—follow each other in succession throughout the summer, furnishing food for the cod and drawing them shoreward. Winter and spring witness the migratory visits of enormous shoals of the finest herrings to their favourite resorts around the shores; and salmon crowd the estuaries preparatory to their ascent of the rivers to "repeat the story of their birth." This is not all. Labrador with its eleven hundred miles of coast fronting the Atlantic, is included in the jurisdiction of Newfoundland, and is the summer-resort of 20,000 of its fishermen. The climate of the island, with its cool winds and the absence of a burning sun in summer, is most favourable for the cure and drying of fish; while the land supplies abundant materials for ship and boat-building, cooperage and all other fishery purposes. The harbours of the Avalon peninsula present the most favourable points from which to carry on the seal fishery in spring, the value of which approaches at times a million dollars annually.

MOUNTAIN AND HILL RANGES.

Passing now from the rugged coast-line to the outer interior of the island, we find a country whose general character is hilly, but the eminences do not reach any great elevation. Further inland, the interior proper is found to be an elevated undulating plateau, traversed by ranges of low hills, the surface being diversified by valleys, woods, ponds and marshes. All the great hill-ranges have a N. N. E. and S. S. W. trend; and all the other great physical features of the country, such as the bays, larger lakes and rivers and valleys, have a similar direction. Probably this conformation has been shaped by glacial action during the Ice-Period. The most important range of mountains is the Long Range which commences at Cape Ray, and runs in a continuous chain in a north-easterly direction for 200 miles, terminating in the Petit Nord peninsula. Some of its summits reach a height of 2,000 feet. Outside the Long Range but parallel to it, and nearer the west coast, is the Anguille Range, running from Cape Anguille to the highlands of Bay St. George, with summits 1,900 feet high; and the Blomidons extending along the south coast of the Humber Arm, Bay of Islands, some of whose summits reach a height of 2,084 feet, being the highest in the island. The Middle Range stretches across the country from Fortune Bay to Notre Dame Bay. The Black River Range runs from Piper's Hole, Placentia Bay, to Clode Sound in Bonavista Bay. From one of its isolated peaks called Centre Hill, 1,081 feet high, may be seen in a clear day, the bays of Placentia, Fortune, Bonavista, Trinity and Conception, and 150 lakelets may be counted. The view is exceedingly fine. The Avalon Peninsula is traversed by an eastern and western range. The former commences at Renews, on the eastern coast, and extends for over twenty miles to Holyrood at the head of Conception Bay, having at each end a rounded hill named the "Butterpots," about 1,000 feet high. The western Avalon range begins at St. Mary's Bay and terminates at Chapel Arm, Trinity Bay. Its principal summits are North-East Mountain, 1,200 feet, from which 67 lakes are visible, Spread Eagle Peak, Trinity Bay, and the Monument. Over the interior are distributed a number of isolated sharply peaked summits which spring abruptly from the great central plateau, and are very serviceable as landmarks in guiding the Indian or the sportsman on their line of march. They bear the local name of Tolts. Some of the more conspicuous of these are Hodge's Hill, on the Exploits, (2,000 feet); Mount Peyton (1,670 feet), west end of Gander Lake; Lobster House, Hind's Pond; Mount Musgrave

There are other minor ranges and detached hills, such as that running along the south shore of Conception Bay by Portugal Cove to Cape St. Francis; Sawyer's Hills south of Placentia; South-side Hills running from Torbay to the Bay of Bulls, of which Signal Hill (520 feet) is a summit; Branscombe's Hill, near St. John's (870 feet); and Chisel Hill, St. Mary's Bay. These numerous mountain and hill ranges show that the country has undergone many disturbances and dislocations of strata, during the geological ages.

RIVERS.

It is a common mistake to suppose that the island contains no large rivers. It is true that, compared with its size, large rivers are few, but the want of these is amply compensated for by the numerous bays which pierce the land in all directions. One cause of the scarcity of large streams is the broken hilly character of many portions of the country. Down the small valleys flow the streams from the pond or set of ponds in their neighbourhood, forming numerous brooks which thus find the nearest course to the sea. Still there are three large and important rivers—the Gander, the Exploits and the Humber—and a number of others whose drainage and size fairly entitle them to be classed as rivers.

EXPLOITS RIVER.

The highest land is on the west coast; and the Long Range chain forms there the watershed, causing most of the rivers to flow north-easterly or easterly towards the east coast. The largest river is the Exploits which rises in the extreme south-western angle of the island near the southern extremity of the Long Range and after a course of more than 200 miles falls into Exploits Bay, in Notre Dame Bay. It drains an area of between 3,000 and 4,000 square miles. At its mouth it is a mile wide and gradually narrows to an average of half a mile which it maintains for ten miles. For this distance from its mouth it is studded with islands, the largest being Thwart Island, nine miles in length. Fourteen miles foom the mouth are Bishop's Falls, a succession of cascades, the total height being about twenty feet. Some twenty miles higher up the river the Grand Falls are met with, presenting one of the finest and most picturesque scenes in the island. Now that it is made accessible by the railway, it is sure to become a favourite resort of tourists. Seventy-two miles from the sea the river issues from Red Indian Lake which is itself 36 miles in length, its surface being 468 feet above the sea and its total area 69 square miles. This large river receives numerous tributaries. some of which from their size rank as rivers. It has long been famous for its salmon.

THE HUMBER.

The next largest river is the Humber, which falls into the Humber Arm of the Bay of Islands, after draining an area of 2000 square miles. Its main branch rises 20 miles inland from Bonne Bay, and after a circuitous course of some 70 miles, it falls into Deer Lake, which is fifteen miles in length, and from thence it flows majestically to the sea through magnificent scenery.

The Gander, the third of the large rivers, is 100 miles in length, and after flowing through Gander Lake, 36 miles long, it falls into Hamilton Sound. With its tributaries it drains an area of nearly 4,000 square miles.

GAMBO AND TERRA NOVA.

The Gambo is a small river flowing from Gambo Pond. Terra Nova is a considerable stream noted for its rapids, falling into Bonavista Bay. Rocky Rivar takes its rise in Hodge Water, a large lake in the peninsula of Avalon, and falls into the Colinet Arm of St. Mary's Bay. The scenery at Rocky River bridge and along the river's course from that point to the sea is unsurpassed. Colinet River falls into St. Mary's Bay.

Numerous rivers discharge their waters on the southern coast, but having short courses they rush in turbulent torrents to the sea. The principal of them are Bay-d'-Est River, Bay-de-North, White Bear and La Poile Rivers. Many of them make a fall of 1200 feet in a distance of 20 miles.

CODROY RIVERS.

On the west coast the principal rivers are the Codroy, which rises in the Long Range, and after flowing through a fertile valley of the same name, falls into the Gulf of St. Lawrence; the River St. George and Harry's Brook fall into Bay St. George.

LAKES AND PONDS.

One of the most remarkable of the physical features of the island is the immense number of its lakes and ponds. They are so numerous that were the island mapped out in detail, more than one-third of the whole surface would be represented by water. They are found in every possible position—in the mountain gorges; in the depressions between the low hills; in the valleys; and frequently in hollows near the tops of the highest eminences. They are of all sizes, from tiny pools and lakelets to sheets of water nearly sixty miles in length. In many districts they form a very beautiful feature of the landscape. From the tops of some of the highest hills, from fifty to one hundred and fifty lakes and ponds may be counted. These bright gems dotting the expanse of country, are generally over-hung with dense woods. It is generally believed among geologists that they are relics of the Ice Age, and were scooped out by glaciers when the island was loaded with its ice-mantle of two or three thousand feet in thickness.

GRAND LAKE.

The largest lake in the island is Grand Lake, fifty-six miles in length and five in breadth, with an area of nearly two thousand square miles. Its surface is but fifty feet above the sea-level, while at its deepest portion the bottom is more than three hundred feet below the level of the sea. Many brooks empty into it, but it has only one outlet—Junction Brook, which joins the Humber. Its south-western extremity bears about northeast from the head of St. George's Bay, from which it is distant about fifteen miles. It contains an island 22 miles long and four to five miles in breadth. Its shores are densely wooded, and its scenery at many points very beautiful.

RED INDIAN LAKE.

Red Indian Lake, through which the River Exploits flows, is 37 miles in length, with an area of 64 square miles. Around its shores are forests of fine timber indicative of a fertile soil. Gander Lake is 33 miles in length, and covers an area of 44 square miles. Its banks, and those of the Gander River which flows through it, present immense tracts of the finest agricultural and timber lands in the island. Deer Lake, through which the Humber flows, is 15 miles in length, and has an area of 24 square miles. The land around it is fertile in the highest degree. Sandy Lake, Victoria, Hind's, Terra Nova and George Fourth Lakes range next in size.

SOLITUDES INVADED.

The shores of these great lakes, and the valleys through which these large rivers flow, are still absolute solitudes, except where recently the lumbermen's camps have invaded them. Their pine forests have been left to rot or perish by fire, and the fertile soil, which might sustain thousands of people in comfort, is untouched by plough or spade. All is primitive wilderness. This is, to some extent, accounted for by the fact that, until a comparatively recent date, the very existence of fertile lands in the interior, or of forest-growths of any value or extent. or of metallic or non-metallic minerals in the rocks, was unknown, and by many was questioned or vehemently denied. Now that the great revolutionist, the railway, has obtained an entrance, all this will be gradually changed; the wastes will be occupied, and human industry will make them "blossom like the rose."

GEOLOGY OF NEWFOUNDLAND.

The Geological Survey of the island, which was commenced in 1864 under the late Alexander Murray, C. M. G., F. G. S., and is still continued by Mr. James Howley, F. G. S., constituted a new epoch in the history of the country. To it we are largely indebted for trustworthy information regarding the agricultural and mineral resources and the forest wealth of the island, which is slowly but surely revolutionizing people's views on these points and has led to the introduction of the railway system, and the application of capital and enterprise to a moderate extent, to the development of its great natural capabilities. While the survey has been conducted on strictly scientific principles in working out the distribution of the various rock formations and delineating these on maps, as the essential preliminary step, it aimed from the outset at the economic application of geological research and the realization of practical results.

TOPOGRAPHICAL SURVEY.

In such a country, much of which was unknown, a topographical survey was found to be indispensable, in order to construct a correct map upon which to delineate the boundaries of the geological formations, and otherwise represent the structural details. This topographical survey which was combined with the geological, led Mr. Murray and Mr. Howley to scale the principal water courses, keeping up a connected system of triangulation from all the most conspicuous heights, and thus on their map the whole of the great features of the island were accurately laid down. In carrying out this work, the officers of the survey were led to examine the surface of the country—the character and extent of its fertile belts—its forests and extent and position of its mineral bearing rocks and its coal beds. Their annual reports dwelt largely on these, and helped to disabuse men's minds of the erroneous ideas previously entertained, and to convince them that the natural resources of the country awaiting development were very great. An important impulse was thus given to mining, by the information furnished regarding the position, character and extent of the various mineral bearing formations. But above all, the discovery as the survey advanced of vast areas of excellent arable and grazing lands, especially in the valleys of the large rivers, and the existence of extensive forests of pine and other valuable timber, furnished abundant warrant for the construction of railways in various directions. Thus the geological survey proved to be of great and lasting benefit to the colony. It is not the province of the geologist to search for or discover mineral deposits or to engage in mining, but so to direct his study of the structure and composition of the rocks as to facilitate the extraction of useful minerals from the earth by those who are practically engaged in mining industry, and to be able to indicate where metallic and non-metallic minerals may be searched for with the greatest probability of success. This object has been steadily kept in view in connection with the geological survey.

COAL BEDS AND MINERALS.

In point of fact two things were especially aimed at. One of these was to determine whether a continuation of the rich coal deposits of Sydney, in the island of Cape Breton, might be searched for with a probability of success, in the carboniferous areas of Newfoundland, along the shores opposite the coal-bearing strata of Cape Breton. As there was a general analogy in the character of the measures on the opposite sides of the waters dividing them, it was for the geologists to determine whether the attitude of the strata in Newfoundland warranted the expectation of finding there coal beds that would be commercially valuable. The other important point to be kept in view was to determine to what extent the metalliferous zone of North America was developed in Newfoundland. This is called in Canadian geology the Quebec group, its middle division, the Lauzon group, being rich in metalliferous deposits all over North America. It was, therefore, of primary import to find whether there was a spread of this formation in the island and to what extent, as its importance as a mining region would depend on this. To what extent both these enquiries have been determined will be more fully seen when the mineral resources of the colony come to be described.

At present it is enough to say that all the ancient rock systems between the Lower Laurentian and the coal measures are more or less represented at one part or another of the island.

LAURENTIAN SYSTEM.

The Laurentian system has an immense spread in the island. It constitutes the principal mountain ranges, coming to the surface through the more recent deposits, or brought up by great dislocations. The Laurentian gneiss of the Long Range, on the western side of the island, extends in nearly a straight course from Cape Ray to the head waters of the Castor on the great northern peninsula, whose central portion is Laurentian. These rocks occupy the coast from Cape Ray to La Poile and spread over a wide expanse of country between Grand Lake, the Humber and Exploits rivers. In fact it may be safely affirmed that more than half the island is Laurentian.

HURONIAN ROCKS.

Three-fourths of the great Peninsula of Avalon are Huronian (equivalent to the Cambrian of English geologists). The Huronian consists mainly of a set of slates with conglomerate bands. The city of St. John's, and in fact nearly all the settlements between Fortune Bay on the south, and Bonavista Bay on the east, are built upon this formation.

SILURIAN ROCKS.

The Lower Silurian rocks have a large development and it is in these that the metallic ores occur which seem destined to render the island a great mining centre. The Lauzon division of the Quebec group, which is included in the Silurian, has an immense spread in the island. It consists of serpentine rocks, associated with dolomites, diorites, etc. As in other parts of North America, it gives evidence in Newfoundland of being more or less rich in metallic ores; and hence the strong probability that many portions of the island will become important mining centres.

The middle Silurian division of rocks is also widely spread; and the most fertile belts of land and the most valuable forests are nearly all situated on the portion of the country occupied by this formation. The valleys of the Exploits, Gander and several smaller tracts, which contain arable lands, belong to the middle Silurian formation.

CARBONIFEROUS.

The Carboniferous series, in which the coal-beds are to be found, occupies a large area on the western side of the island, in the neighbourhood of St. George's Bay and Grand Lake; and also along the valley of the Humber and around the shores of Deer Lake. The best land rests upon the rocks of this formation.

VERDICT OF GEOLOGY.

The verdict of geology then is that Newfoundland is a country adapted to sustain a large population engaged in a great variety of pursuits—farming, lumbering, shipbuilding, mining and manufacturing. When to this we add the fish-wealth of the surrounding seas, on which the present population of 200,000 are mainly dependent, we must form a high estimate of the natural capabilities of an island which has been so long unknown or rather mis-known. For the development of those yet dormant resources there is a robust race of people who have served a rough apprenticeship of toil and danger amid the billows— men of bone and muscle, whose lives are mainly passed in the open air in a wholesome bracing climate, and whose habits of life are simple. They need but some Moses to lead them, not out of, but into the wilderness to fell the giants of the forest, to drain the marsh and swamp, to drag up the treasures of the mine and to make the valleys wave with a golden harvest.

CLIMATE.

Erroneous ideas regarding the climate of Newfoundland are quite as prevalent as the delusions in reference to its soil and natural products. The bulk of outsiders still fancy that the island is enveloped in almost perpetual fogs in summer, and given over to intense cold and a succession of snow storms in winter. It is true that it partakes of the general character of the North American climate, and is therefore much colder than lands in the same latitude in the Old World. Its latitude corresponds to that of France, but its climate is very different. Still in the American sense of the word, it is by no means a cold country. Winter sets in, as a rule, in the beginning of December and lasts till the end of March or the middle of April. During this time a snow-mantle of greater or less depth, usually covers the ground, but the frost is occasionally broken by southerly winds and bright warm days, and much of the snow is melted. Then the wind changes, and fresh falls of snow are experienced. During the winter there are at times heavy gales of wind, and severe snow-storms. These, however, do not occur often or last long. Winter is the season of social enjoyments of all kinds, and is far from being unpleasant. Nothing can be more exhilerating than the bracing air of a fine winter's day, with the hard crisp snow under feet and a bright sun over head. The musical tinkle of the sleigh-bells when driving over the frozen snow, and the purity of the atmosphere add to the charms of the scene. The snow preserves the ground from the influence of the frosts, and in April when it melts, the fields soon become fit for the operations of the farmer. It is true the spring is late, owing to the chilling influence of the Arctic current which washes the eastern coast, and often

"Winter lingering chills the lap of May."

But once vegetation sets in it progresses with marvellous rapidity, and crops grow and ripen much quicker than in the eastern hemisphere. The frosts of winter too, aid the operations of the husbandman and help to pulverise the soil. The destructive tornados and cyclones which often spread havoc in certain portions of the North American continent are unknown in Newfoundland; "blizzards" are rare, and the American "cloud burst" is never experienced.

SILVER THAW.

There is one curious winter phenomenon which is often witnessed—called here "silver thaw." When rain falls with a low state of the thermometer near the earth, it is congealed as it descends, and thus a regular disposition of ice takes place on the branches and smallest twigs of trees and shrubs. The layer of ice goes on increasing till it attains a thickness of half an inch or more. A magical transformation is wrought. The trees are hung with glittering jewels, even the smallest twigs being loaded and the branches bent to the earth. When the sun shines a scene of dreamlike splendour is presented. Each tree has the appearance of a great chandelier of crystal, the play of the sunbeams on myriads of prisms producing a dazzling effect. The weight of the icy jewellry often breaks the thickest branches. Sometimes the wind rises suddenly and unloads the jewelled trees, and "like the baseless fabric of a vision" the whole vanishes.

AURORAS.

Another natural phenomenon witnessed often in perfection in winter is the aurora borealis. The play of these northern lights occasionally presents a magnificent sight. The whole heavens are lighted up with the brilliant display, and huge curtains of all hues seem to wave over the vast concave.

In winter the thermometer rarely sinks below zero, and then only for a few hours and but a few degrees. Once in thirty or forty years an exceptionally severe winter is experienced—such as that of 1893-'94—when the thermometer repeatedly reached ten or even fifteen below zero, and, in the more northern and exposed places, as low as thirty-four. This, however, is very rare and of short duration; usually, open fire-places are sufficient to heat the houses, only moderately heavy clothing is needed, and open-air exercise is throughout attainable.

NEWFOUNDLAND SUMMERS.

The summer temperature ranges from seventy to eighty degrees, not often exceeding the latter figure. The extreme heats and colds of Canada and the United States are unknown. A fine summer's day in Newfoundland is delightful. The heat is never oppressive; the nights are always cool, and the breezes are balmy and invigorating. From the middle of June till the middle of September is the true summer, and usually fine weather is experienced, though the changes are at times sudden; and, of course, there are, as in all countries, unfavourable summers. The robust and healthy appearance of the people, their fair complexions, and the numerous instances in which an extreme old age is reached, all testify that the climate is salubrious in the highest degree. Malaria is entirely unknown.

FOGS PARTIAL.

The fogs which have given the country such an undesirable reputation are confined to the south and south-eastern portion of the island. Enormous masses of vapour are generated on the Banks, which are at a considerable distance from the shores of the island, by the mixing there of the heated waters of the Gulf

CLIMATE.

Stream with the Arctic current. When southerly or south-westerly winds blow the fog is rolled in on the south-eastern and southern shores of the island, covering the bays and headlands with a thick curtain of vapour. It rarely penetrates far inland; so that while these coasts are shrouded in dense fog, the sun is shining brightly inland, and the atmosphere is dry and balmy. With southerly winds the great bays on the southern coast become receptacles of the sea-fog. It often fills Placentia Bay and drifts over the narrow isthmus into Trinity Bay, while Conception Bay is comparatively clear. Thus the fogs are partial in their influence. On the western shore, after passing Cape Ray, fogs are almost unknown. The same holds good of the northern and eastern coasts as far south as Bonavista. The summer months in the interior may often be spent without experiencing a genuine foggy day. However gloomy and disagreeable these sea-fogs may be, it must be remembered they are not prejudicial to health. The Gulf Stream which generates them modifies the cold, so that the climate is more temperate and wholesome than that of the neighbouring continent.

The mean annual temperature for eight years was 41.2 degs.; the average height of the barometer was 29.37 inches.

It is not difficult to account for the erroneous ideas prevalent regarding the climate of the Island. The climate of the Banks, which are over one hundred miles distant from the shores, and of the southern and south-eastern seaboard, which are affected by the sea-fogs, has been taken by voyagers and casual visitors as indicative of the climate of the whole Island. Hence, it has been concluded that the country is enveloped in almost perpetual fogs in summer; and, on the other hand, an impression has grown up that it is given over to intense cold and a succession of snow-storms in winter.

It may be desirable, therefore, to cite the opinions of a few intelligent persons who, from experience, have been enabled to form an estimate of the general character of the climate, in order to arrive at the truth. Sir Richard Bonnycastle, who spent some years in the country, in his excellent work on Newfoundland (1842), says: "We find that the extremes of temperature in Newfoundland are trifling compared with those of Canada. There the thermometer falls as low as twenty-seven degrees below zero, and even lower at times, in winter, and rises to ninety in summer. Here (in Newfoundland) the lowest temperature in winter scarcely exceeds zero, or eight or ten degrees below it, excepting upon rare occasions; and in the height of summer does not attain more, in common years, than seventy-nine degrees. Winter may really be said to commence here towards the latter end of November only, though fires are comfortable adjuncts during most of that month; and its severity begins after Christmas, runs through January and February, and becomes less and less stern until the middle of April, when it ceases altogether. In the winter of 1840 ploughing was going on after Christmas."

"It is generally supposed in England that Newfoundland is constantly enveloped in fog and wet mist; nothing, however, could be farther from the truth. The summers are frequently so hot and dry that for want of rain the grass perishes — the summer of 1840 was one of these — and the nights are unusually splendid; whilst in winter fog is very rarely seen."

He kept a register in regard to foggy days, from which it appeared that in 1841 there were only seventeen and a half days of thick fog in St. John's, "which is more exposed to the Bank weather, as it is called, than any other part of the Island"; and light fogs were prevalent only nineteen and a half days; giving thirty-seven days of foggy weather on the shore throughout the year. He remarks further on the light clothing with which the labouring classes went about in winter, and on their robust appearance, and pronounces the climate salubrious in the highest degree.

The Right Rev. Dr. Mullock, formerly Roman Catholic Bishop of the island, in one of his lectures, says: "We never have the thermometer down to zero, unless once or twice in the year, and then only for a few hours and for a few degrees, three, four or perhaps ten; while we hear of a temperature of ten and twenty below zero in Canada and New Brunswick; and this life-destroying cold continuing for days, perhaps weeks. Then see another effect of this—the Canadians and other North Americans of the same latitude are obliged to keep up hot stoves almost continually in their houses, while we have open fireplaces, or at most Franklins; our children, I may say, are lightly clad as in summer, spend a large portion of their time in the open air; and thus while our neighbours have the sallow hue of confinement tinging their cheeks, and their children look comparatively pale, our youngsters are blooming with the rosy hue of health, developing their energies by air and exercise, and preparing themselves for the battle of life hereafter, either as hardy mariners or healthy matrons—the blooming mothers of a powerful race." "The mean temperature of 1859 was 44 degrees."

Sir Stephen Hill, who was Governor of the island for six years, says: "The climate of Newfoundland is exceedingly healthy. The robust and healthy appearance of the people, and the advanced age to which many of them attain, testify to the purity and excellence of the air which they inhale and the invigorating qualities of the breezes of British North America."

Alexander Murray, C. M. G., Geological Surveyor, who spent eighteen years in the island, traversing it in all directions, says: "The climate of Newfoundland is, as compared with the neighbouring continent, a moderately temperate one. The heat is far less intense, on an average, during the summer, than in any part of Canada, and the extreme cold of winter is much less severe. The thermometer rarely indicates higher than seventy degrees Fah., in the former, or much below zero in the latter; although the cold is occasionally aggravated by storms and the humidity consequent on an insular position. The climate is undoubtedly a very healthy one, and the general physique of the natives, who are a powerfully-built, robust and hardy race, is a good example of its influence."

The climate of St. John's, it should be remembered, is not a fair standard by which to judge of the whole island. It is on the most eastern point in the peninsula of Avalon, and therefore most exposed to the chilling influence of the Arctic Current. At the heads of the great bays, in the interior of the island, especially in the sheltered valleys, and on the west coast, the climate is much warmer than at St. John's. In St. George's Bay the mean annual temperature for the year is 43·8 degrees ; that of Toronto is 44·3 degrees.

Mr. Howley, the present head of the Geological Survey, in one of his reports says : " I myself spent four months during the past season in the interior without experiencing a genuine foggy day, until reaching within twenty miles of the southern side of the island. During the entire months of July and August, the weather in the interior was delightful, while fogs prevailed at the same time along the southern shore."

The railway surveyors who have been engaged during the last two years in locating the new railway, all speak in glowing terms of the delightful climate of the interior in summer, and its freedom from fogs.

CHAPTER III.
ROADS AND RAILWAYS IN NEWFOUNDLAND.

In no other country has the material and social advancement of the people been so seriously retarded by the want of roads as in Newfoundland. The original settlement of the island took place entirely in connection with the fisheries. The gathering in of the sea-harvest was the only industry contemplated or attempted. Around the shores fishermen, chiefly from England and Ireland, collected at first in hamlets and small villages, situated in such localities as were found best adapted for catching, drying and shipping fish. These, as they multiplied and the population increased, were dotted around the shores of the great bays, or wherever there was a sheltered inlet where fish could be landed and the fisherman's stage and hut erected. Sprinkled thus along an extensive sea-board, they were generally widely apart from each other, and intercourse was maintained mainly or entirely by sea or by rude paths through the woods between neighbouring settlements.

BAD LAWS.

Had the clearing and cultivation of the soil been combined with fishing, the construction of roads would have become a necessity; but the unhappy policy adopted by the Imperial Government, at the prompting of the English capitalists who carried on the fisheries, effectually prevented colonization. The policy was to keep the island solely as a fishing station in order to train seamen for the British navy. All grants of land were prohibited, the cultivation of the soil made a penal offence, and a vigorous attempt was carried on for a long period to render the fishery migratory by carrying home the fishermen at the close of each season to return the following summer.

SLOW PROGRESS UNDER DIFFICULTIES.

In spite of these stupid, selfish laws the resident population in the fishing villages continued to increase and in many instances these grew into small towns. St. John's in particular made great strides. The laws, however, against the cultivation of the soil, and the erection of dwelling houses, were enforced up to the beginning of the present century. In 1790 one of the Governors publicly announced that he "was directed not to allow any possession as private property to be taken or any right of private property whatever, to be acknowledged in any land whatever which is not actually employed in the fishery in the terms of the Act, 10 and 11 William III." In 1799, Governor Waldegrave ordered fences which had been erected enclosing a piece of ground to be torn down, and prohibited chimneys even in the temporary sheds. The people were thus confined to the sea-margin, in small isolated settlements, the only inter-communication being by sea. Though the progress of the Colony was thus seriously retarded, still the hardy pioneers held their ground and increased in numbers, thus proving that there were among them men of the right stamp for building up a new community—men of moral worth and force of character, who saw in the midst of their rough surroundings that here was a spot which might one day be made into a desirable home for themselves and their children.

THE DAWN.

A better day at length dawned. The foolish and cruel laws were relaxed, and in 1813 grants of lands to settlers were for the first time permitted. Agriculture on a small scale immediately commenced around each settlement. Those who were interested in keeping the country unsettled had all along sedulously inculcated the belief that both in regard to climate and soil the island was wholly unsuited to agriculture. This view was speedily disproved when restrictions were removed, but to this day is not wholly eradicated.

A NEW ERA—ROAD MAKING.

It was soon found that no progress could be made in the cultivation of the soil till roads were constructed. The year 1825 was rendered memorable by the construction of the first road, nine miles in length, from St. John's to Portugal Cove, on the southern shore of Conception Bay. On the opposite shore of this bay were the thriving towns of Harbour Grace, Carbonear and Brigus, the centres of a considerable population. By establishing a regular system of boats to cross this bay, carrying mails and passengers, a route was established by which nearly half the population then living in the country were provided with a rough means of communication. To Sir Thomas Cochrane, Governor, belongs the honour of introducing this essential step in civilization. He also constructed a road to Torbay, a village north of St. John's; and a third along a beautiful valley through which flows a small stream falling into St. John's harbour, to a spot now called Waterford Bridge. This beginning of road-making took place only 69 years ago, but the progress made since has been remarkable. Year after year roads radiating from St. John's in several directions were built, along which farms and neat farm-houses soon became visible. One of these roads extended first to Topsail on Conception Bay, thence to Holyrood at the head of the bay, and onward to Salmonier, St. Mary's and Placentia. Efforts were made by the more distant settlements to connect themselves with each other by roads, though often of a very rough description, and to establish means of communication with the capital. When Representative Government was established in 1832, an annual grant was voted for making and repairing roads and bridges; and of late years over $150,000 per annum, have been devoted to this purpose. The Great Northern Mail road, for establishing communication with the people of the northern bays, was projected and commenced. At present there are about 1,000 miles of postal roads, and over 2,000 miles of district roads.

THOUGHT WIDENING.

Road-making, without which no country can advance or make progress in other arts or in social life, though of late introduction, has had a most important civilizing influence in this Colony. Still these roads only connected the fishing towns and settlements on the coast, and had little effect in opening up the good lands of the interior for colonization or in developing the natural resources of the Island. As the people increased in numbers and their views and aspirations began to widen, the question presented itself: Were they doomed to cling forever to the rocky shores and content themselves with a precarious subsistence derived from the stormy deep? Was it not possible to turn to some profitable account their huge territory of 42,000 square miles, and not leave it forever to the bears the wolves, and the deer? Must the interior remain forever an unpeopled solitude where so many of the population were finding the products of the fisheries inadequate to give them daily bread? If it be true, as so many have reported, that there are in the interior noble forests, rich mineral deposits and fertile lands, must these all remain as nature has placed them and be turned to no human use?

DOUBTERS AND SCOFFERS.

Still there were many who doubted or denied the existence of any such natural resources in the interior, and clung to the old belief that nothing was to be found but alternations of bogs, rocks and swamps, with little if any forest growths or lands fit for settlement. As to minerals, they scoffed at all reports of their existence as mere fables, propagated by wild enthusiasts or designing imposters.

ANOTHER GREAT STRIDE—GEOLOGICAL SURVEY.

Happily there was sufficient faith among men of intelligence in the resources of the country to secure the organization of a Geological Survey in 1864. Sir William Logan, the eminent Geologist of Canada, was applied to, and he nominated Mr. Alexander Murray, who had been his assistant for twenty years, to take charge of the work. He prosecuted the survey with commendable zeal and energy for over twenty years, and it has been continued by his able assistant, Mr. Jas. Howley, till the present time. Now, for the first time, the resources and capabilities of this neglected and misrepresented country were examined and reported on by competent scientific men whose statements were thoroughly reliable. The results exceeded the expectations of the most hopeful. Mr. Murray's reports, published year after year, showed that the interior contained extensive pine forests of excellent timber; fertile valleys, in which many thousands might find a home; a carboniferous region containing large coal-beds and mineral tracts, which the labours of many generations were not likely to exhaust. His survey showed that on the West Coast there were 1,320 square miles of fertile lands admirably adapted for settlement, and in the valleys of the Exploits, Gambo, Terra Nova and Gander, 3,320 square miles fitted for agricultural operations or cattle-raising—much of these regions being covered with valuable forests of pine, birch, and other trees—in all, nearly three million acres of land well fitted for settlement. He further found that the Island presented large developments of the "Quebec Group," which is the great metaliferous formation of North America, and therefore might be expected to be found rich in minerals—a prediction which has been amply verified. It could no longer be doubted that Newfoundland presented a promising field for mining enterprises or for extensive lumbering operations, or that its reclaimable land would sustain in comfort a very large population.

DISCOVERY OF MINERALS.

So far as the statements in the reports regarding the mineral resources were concerned they were speedily confirmed by actual discoveries. The first discovery of copper ore was made by Mr. Smith McKay, an enterprising explorer, at Tilt Cove, on the North-eastern shore of the Island, in 1857. It was not worked till 1864. At the close of 1879 this mine had yielded 50,000 tons of copper ore, valued at $1,572,154, and nickel ore worth $32,740. At the present time the working of this valuable mine continues and several hundred miners are employed.

PROGRESS OF MINING.

In 1875 Bett's Cove mine, a dozen miles further south, was opened, and up to 1879 had yielded ore to the value of $2,982,836. Little Bay mine followed in 1878, and proved to be still more productive, the workings being continued till about a year ago. At the close of 1879 it was found that the total value of the ore exported from the various mines had reached the amount of $4,629,889. The work has gone on up the present time with successful results. In 1892 the value of the ore exported according to the Customs' Returns was $1,006,592. It must further be considered that mining operations have hitherto been mainly confined to the shores of Notre Dame Bay. The interior, now to be opened up by railways, is still untouched, and may be expected to prove rich in minerals.

PROSPECTS OF MINING.

Thus science is pointing out Newfoundland as likely to become one of the copper-bearing regions of the world has been confirmed by actual experiment. It presents a wide development of that metaliferous zone which in other North American countries has yielded abundance of valuable minerals. The area of the serpentine rocks, in connection with which all the copper ore hitherto has been found, is estimated by Mr. J. Howley, Geologist, at 5,097 square miles. There is reason to believe that this serpentine formation runs across the island, and in the yet unexplored interior it may come to the light in many places.

A RAILWAY LOOMING DIMLY.

After being thus a mere fishing station for some 250 years, without farms or roads, the fringe around the coast began to be intersected with roads, and the cultivation of the soil made some progress. Then followed the revelations of the Geological Survey, which could not be disputed, and were confirmed in many points by the working of the copper mines, by which wealth began to be poured into the country; and also by the introduction of lumbering establishments along the larger rivers. Wider views regarding the destinies of the country began to be entertained among those who were at the head of affairs. The necessity of providing other means of sustaining the population than the fisheries had been felt for some time. The population was rapidly increasing, while their mainstay—the fisheries—showed unmistakable symptoms of decline, or, at best, were precarious. The idea of a railway began to float dimly before the minds of some of the more thoughtful, but was at first spoken of with bated breath lest its advocacy might expose the bold innovators to the suspicion of insanity. By the great mass of the people the project of building a railway was at first regarded as utterly beyond the means of the colony. Short-sighted people declared it would bring no returns and would speedily involve the country in bankruptcy. The opponents of progress and change regarded it with horror.

FLEMING'S PROJECT.

A proposal made by Mr. Sandford Fleming, who was then Engineer-in-chief of Canadian railways, helped to familiarize the public mind with the idea of a railway across Newfoundland. This eminent engineer published a paper in which he pointed out that the shortest and safest travel-route between America and England was across Newfoundland. He suggested a fast line of steamers from Valentia, Ireland, to St. John's, N.F., carrying only passengers, mails and light express matter. Thence he proposed to build a railway across the island to St. George's Bay, where another line of swift steamers would ply to Shippegan, in the Bay of Chaleur, where connection with American railways would be obtained. He calculated that by this route the ocean passage would not exceed four days, and that passengers from London would reach New York in seven days. It was a bold project, but founded on careful calculations. The Newfoundland Legislature voted a sum of money for a preliminary survey of the line, which was carried out in 1875 under Mr. Fleming's direction. It was found that there were no serious engineering difficulties in the way, and that the line could be constructed at a moderate cost.

THE FIRST RAILWAY PROJECTED.

Two years elapsed before any further steps were taken. At length, in 1878, Sir William Whiteway, Premier of the Colony, to whom belongs the high honour of not only introducing the railway system in the face of strong opposition, but of perseveringly carrying it out for more than fourteen years, as a prominent feature of his policy, undertook to grapple with the matter in earnest. His first proposal was, in following the lines laid down by Mr. Fleming, to offer an annual subsidy of £120,000 and liberal land grants along the line to any company that would construct and operate a line of railway across the island to be connected by steamers with England on the one side and on the Gulf of St. Lawrence, on the other, with Canadian railways. The Imperial Government, however, refused to sanction this project on the ground that it might be regarded by the French as an infringement of their fishing rights which were secured by treaty on the west coast where its terminus would be. The project, therefore, had to be abandoned.

THE HALL'S BAY LINE.

Two more years elapsed, and Sir William Whiteway, finding that the project of constructing a line across the island which would be a link in the chain of communication between the Old and the New Worlds, could not then be carried out, decided on building a narrow-guage railway suited to local requirements, and such as the Colony itself could undertake. The resolutions which he submitted to the House of Assembly proposed the construction of a railway from St. John's to Hall's Bay, the centre of the mining region, with branches to Harbour Grace and Brigus, the total length of which would be about 340 miles. Such a line would open up for settlement large areas of good lands and valuable and extensive timber districts in the valleys of the Gambo, Terra Nova, Gander and Exploits, and by connecting the mining region with the capital, would impart a great impetus to mining industry and give access to new mineral lands as yet unexplored.

REPORT OF PARLIAMENTARY COMMITTEE.

A joint-committee of both branches of the Legislature was appointed to consider the proposal. Their report was strongly in favour of such an enterprise. It pointed out the necessity of opening up new industries for the employment of the increasing population, for whose support the fisheries were now inadequate. It referred to the mineral wealth and the great extent of fertile lands which the Geological Survey of the island had made known; to the large importations of agricultural produce and live stock, almost all of which could be raised in the country; to the advantages the island possessed as a grazing country, and the facilities of exporting live stock to England; and to the benefits that would flow from the remunerative employment furnished to the people by the construction of a railway. It concluded by recommending the passing of an Act authorizing a loan of the amount required to construct the line within the limits of one million pounds sterling, and in sums not exceeding half a million of dollars in any one year. This report was adopted by the Legislature by an overwhelming majority of both branches. Railway Commissioners were appointed and Engineers were employed in the summer and autumn of 1880 in making a preliminary survey of the southern portion of the proposed line.

FIRST RAILWAY CONTRACT.

A new era was thus initiated. The Colony took a fresh departure in the direction of progress. The long-neglected natural resources of the island were now to be turned to profitable account. The horizon widened in the eyes of the people, and confidence in a great future for the country was developed. The funds necessary for the building of a railway were to be raised by a loan on the credit of the colony, and the Government was to direct and control the work. To this, however, grave objections of a political character were raised. It was considered by many that the construction of the line would be more economically carried out by a contract, and that the work would prove more satisfactory. When the Legislature met in February, 1881, the tender of an American Syndicate for building the railway was accepted. The leading features of the contract were as follows: A line of narrow-guage railway (3 feet 6 in.) to run from St. John's to Hall's Bay, with branches to Brigus and Harbor Grace;

the distance estimated at 340 miles. Steel rails of the best quality to be used. A money subsidy of $180,000, to be paid half-yearly by the Government for thirty-five years, conditional on the efficient maintenance and operation of the line, the proportions of this subsidy to attach while the railway is in course of construction; and as each five miles are completed and approved, land grants of five thousand acres per mile of good land to be secured to the company in alternate blocks along the line in quantities of one mile in width and eight miles in depth; and if not obtainable along the line, to be selected elsewhere. The company bind themselves to build a substantial and efficient road, subject to approval by a Government Inspector, and to complete it in five years.

FIRST SOD CUT.

The first sod of the railway was turned on the 9th of August, 1881. By September, 1882, thirty-five miles were completed and in running order; one hundred miles were located, and the remainder of the line northward was under survey. In November, 1884, the line was completed and opened for traffic between St. John's and Harbour Grace, a distance of $83\frac{1}{2}$ miles. The work of construction led to the distribution of large sums as wages among the labouring classes who were employed: while the trading classes also shared in the benefit. The enterprise was regarded with general approval throughout the community; and the passenger and goods traffic on the line developed at a satisfactory rate.

FINANCIAL TROUBLES.

Soon after, unfortunately, the "Newfoundland Railway Company" got into financial difficulties, and work on the line was discontinued. Legal proceedings followed: the company proved unable to fulfill their contract, and finally the portion of the line finished passed into the charge of a Receiver on behalf of certain bond-holders in England, who held a mortgage on it. Under this arrangement it has been most satisfactorily operated till the present time, and having a subsidy of $45,000 per annum a fair dividend is paid to the bond-holders.

RESULTS.

The financial collapse of the Newfoundland Railway Company was an unfortunate event, as the work of railway construction was thereby temporarily retarded, and more or less brought into discredit. Had the construction been undertaken by a financially strong and capable company the line would have been completed in 1886; whereas only 83½ miles, to Harbour Grace, were then in a working condition.

PLACENTIA RAILWAY.

In 1885 a change of Government took place and Sir Robert Thorburn became Premier. Nothing daunted by the previous break-down, he and his colleagues in 1886 commenced the construction of a branch line, 27 miles in length, from Whitbourne Junction to Placentia, the old French capital. It was completed and opened in 1888, and proved to be a well-built line in every respect. By this branch line not only was the large and thriving population of Placentia Bay brought into more easy and rapid communication with the capital, but for the people of the whole southern and western shores the travel-route was shortened and facilities of trade extended. By means of a steamer plying on Placentia Bay, the various settlements around its shores were enabled to participate in these advantages. Few would now be found to deny that the Placentia Railway is a highly beneficial public work, and well worth all it cost. Moreover, the first seven miles of the line from Whitbourne were available as a portion of the Northern extension towards Hall's Bay, should that work be resumed. The great innovator and civilizer had now got a firm footing in the island and the benefits were so apparent that the work of railway-building was sure to proceed, whatever government held the reins. The large sums distributed in the shape of wages among the labouring classes, in connection with railway-building, and the number of engineers and skilled mechanics and workmen employed, tended to advance the general prosperity of the people. The revenue advanced in proportion.

THE THORBURN RAILWAY POLICY.

In 1889 the Thorburn Government announced as part of their policy the extension of the railway northward from the Placentia Junction. Public opinion was strongly in favour of this as the only means of utilizing the agricultural, forest and mineral lands, and providing new outlets for the industry of the people. The successs of the Harbour Grace line and its rapidly increasing traffic furnished a sufficient warrant for further extension, and convinced all intelligent men that in this country the grand desideratum of progress is a railway to open up the interior and connect the extern districts with each other and with the capital. The Government wisely decided that the northern extension should be built under a contract. Accordingly they advertised for tenders in England, the United States and Canada, in order to obtain such information as to cost and other particulars as would enable them to formulate a plan to be submitted to the Legislature. In the Legislative Session of 1889 a Railway Extension Act of a comprehensive character was passed through both Chambers with little opposition. The Government were pledged to carry out a survey of the line to Hall's Bay that year, to immediately commence construction, pending a contract, and to provide for the completion of the whole line within ten years, the rate of construction to be at the rate of not less than 25 miles per annum. The work of construction was commenced in the fall of 1889 from Placentia Junction northward. Before winter set in some ten or fifteen miles were built.

SIR W. WHITEWAY AGAIN PREMIER.

The general elections took place in November, 1889, with the result that Sir William Whiteway was again called on to take the reins of government. He speedily showed that he had lost none of his former confidence in railway extension as a means of developing the resources of the colony. An Act was passed in the session of 1890 providing for the construction of a line of railway *towards* Hall's Bay, with a branch to Brigus or Clarke's Beach, authorizing a loan of $1,500,000, and empowering the government to accept a tender for construction. The tender of Mr. R. G. Reid, of Montreal, was accepted, and the work commenced, under contract, in October, 1890, to be completed in five years.

A CHANGE OF PROGRAMME.

Meantime a survey was made for a line of railway to the West Coast of the island from the Valley of the Exploits. This survey was made by way of the valleys of Deer Lake and Harry's Brook, in order to ascertain whether this route presented more favourable features than that already surveyed via Red Indian Lake. The result of the survey was as the report showed, that a most favourable line was found through large areas of a rich loamy soil, especially about Deer Lake, awaiting agricultural development. This line, too, would open up the fine Humber valley, famous for its pines, and reach the Bay of Islands with its grand scenery and lands. In every respect this route was found to be far preferable to that previously surveyed.

NORTHERN AND WESTERN RAILWAY.

The government now decided to carry the railway west from the Exploits. A new contract was entered into with Mr. R. G. Reid, by which he undertook to "construct and equip a line of railway commencing at the terminus of the road to be constructed under the Northern Railway contract, being a point two hundred miles distant from Placentia Junction, and running by the best, most desirable and most direct route to the north-east end of Grand Lake; thence to the north-east end of Deer Lake, and westerly along the north side (afterwards changed to south side) of Deer Lake and down the Humber River; thence by way of the north side of Harry's River; and thence to Port-aux-Basques." This contract was signed on the 16th May, 1893. On the same day another contract was signed, in which Mr. Reid undertook to operate the Placentia branch railway, and also the "Newfoundland Northern and Western Railway," as the new line from Placentia Junction to Port-aux-Basques was to be called, for a period of ten years, commencing Sept. 1st, 1893.

The whole length of the new line, from Placentia Junction to Port-aux-Basques, is estimated to be about five hundred miles.

THE CONTRACTS.

The main features of the contracts were as follows :—For constructing and equipping the railway "payments shall be made to the contractor upon the completion of each continuous and consecutive section of five miles, or a fraction of a section at the end of the work, at the rate of $15,600 per mile of main line, the said payments being in full for all the works and materials provided for under this contract and necessary for the thorough and complete construction and equipment of the line of railway herein provided for. All such payments shall be made by the government and accepted by the contractor in debentures of the Government of Newfoundland in sterling money of the United Kingdom of Great Britain and Ireland, maturing on the 1st day of January, 1947, with interest thereon at the rate of three and a half per cent. per annum, payable half-yearly ; principal and interest payable in London, England." "Payments will be made to the contractor on the written certificate of the engineer and the approval of the government that the works have been duly executed." The whole line is to be completed in three years from September 1st, 1893, and to be a narrow-guage of three feet six inches. The specifications are such as will secure a thoroughly safe and well-equipped line.

MAINTENANCE AND OPERATION.

The contract for maintenance and operation of the Placentia branch and of the Newfoundland Northern and Western Railway for a period of ten years from September 1st, 1893, provides that the contractor shall maintain these in a safe, efficient and satisfactory manner, and continuously and efficiently operate the same (the number of trains to be run being specified) ; also, shall erect telegraph lines along the whole line of railway for the purposes of its operation and work them at his own expense, and also shall, if required, work them as part of the government telegraph system on certain conditions. On the faithful performance of these engagements the government agreed "to grant in fee-simple to the contractor five thousand acres of land for each one mile of main line or branch railway throughout the entire length of the lines to be operated." Should the line, therefore, be five hundred miles in length, the land grant would be 2,500,000 acres. "The said fee-simple grants shall be made by the government to the said contractor as follows :—250,000 acres upon the completion of the northern line to Exploits ; 250,000 acres upon the completion of the western line to St. George's Bay ; 250,000 acres upon the completion of the line to Port-aux-Basques ; and the balance at the end of five years from the date of this contract, or as soon thereafter as practicable. "The land shall be located on each side of the railway in alternate sections of one or two miles in length with the railway, at the option of the contractor, on meridian or base lines, as the case may be, and eight miles in depth, the government retaining the alternate sections, and until the contractor has made his selection under this section, the government shall not dispose of any Crown lands, timber, or mineral rights within eight miles on either side of the line of railway." "Where such sections from any cause are not obtainable along the line, the said contractor may select Crown lands elsewhere to make up deficiencies, the last-mentioned selections to be made in sections or blocks of not less than one mile square and not more than ten miles square."

The contract contains stringent provisions for the due execution of the various agreements, so as to secure the construction of a first-class line of railway. One section stipulates that the wages of daily labourers shall not be less than one dollar per day, payable monthly.

THE WORK COMMENCED VIGOROUSLY.

Under the contract the work commenced in October, 1890, and was prosecuted with so much energy that at the close of 1891 sixty-five miles were completed and operated. The work of construction continued to advance vigorously, and early in the fall of 1893 two hundred miles were completed and trains were running twice each week between Exploits, Whitbourne and St. John's.

RESULTS.

The railway having now penetrated a region which was previously but little known, to a distance of two hundred miles, in little more than two years, we are enabled, to some extent, to form an estimate of the beneficial changes it has accomplished and is likely to accomplish in the future, and also to arrive at a conclusion in regard to the character and resources of the country which it opens up.

COMMON ROADS OPENED.

The first thing which strikes us is the wonderful extent of common roads already constructed or in course of construction, to connect the various settlements and towns on the sea coast with the railway. These have been mostly surveyed and built by the contractor, Mr. Reid, acting under the instructions of the Government. A good waggon road, forty miles in length, has been built from Trinity to Shoal Harbour, via Goose Bay. This opens up a large quantity of good land for settlement and secures access to the railway to a considerable population. Another road, ten miles in length, has been built to connect Indian Arm Bay with the railway; while a third, five miles in length, runs from Alexander Bay to the railway near Gambo. A road about forty-four miles in length, from Hall's Bay to the railway, joining the latter about four miles west of Badger Brook, has been surveyed and some work done upon it. It will doubtless be completed this season. Roads from Arnold's Cove and Come-by-chance have also been built. A line of road four miles long has been surveyed from Northern Bight to the railway; and another is projected from Exploits to Botwoodville and Gander Bay. It may be reasonably expected that wherever there is good land along these waggon roads it will be occupied by settlers and that farms will multiply. New life will be imparted to these lonely, isolated settlements thus placed in easy communication with the capital, and various industrial enterprises will be developed.

When so much has been accomplished in such a brief period in road-making, it may be safely predicted that hundreds of miles additional will soon be found necessary as feeders to the railway.

MAILS BY RAILWAY.

The railway now carries nearly all the northern mails, which in winter used to be conveyed by couriers on foot or with the aid of dogs over the surface of the snow. Small steamers ply from Shoal Harbour, Exploits and Clode Sound, around the bays conveying mails and passengers to and from the various settlements. A wonderful impetus has thus been given to civilizing influences in these districts, and both social and material progress has been initiated by the railway and its satellites the roads.

LUMBERING INDUSTRY.

The most marked feature, however, in the change already effected is the surprising development of lumbering industry which has followed railway extension. This far exceeds the most sanguine expectations and amply sustains the statements of those who have been proclaiming, too often in deaf ears, the value of the forest wealth of the island. Five large and well-equipped lumbering establishments have sprung up along the line of railway and are turning out large quantities of excellent lumber, mainly pine and spruce. These are the Campbell Lumbering Co., on the Terra Nova River; Murphy's Mill, at Gambo; Benton Mill, operated by Mr. R. G. Reid on Souli's Brook; Sterritt's Glenwood Lumber Co., Glenwood, on Gander River, and the Exploits' Wood Co., at Botwoodville, on Peter's Arm of Exploits Bay, and Phillips' fine Mill on Gander Arm. A large amount of capital is invested in these establishments, and hundreds of men are employed at good wages.

QUANTITIES AND QUALITY OF LUMBER.

In the winter of 1893-94 it is calculated that these various lumber mills will turn out nearly twenty million feet of lumber, most of which would have remained in its primeval condition but for the facilities afforded by the railway for conducting this new industry. A few of the lumber mills were in existence before the railway was built, but now these have greatly extended their operations. In winter everything required by the lumber-camps is brought by rail. If any doubt regarding the quality of this pine is still felt, the price which it brings in the English market furnishes a sufficient answer. Experts from other countries pronounce it excellent. It will require many years to exhaust the great forest growths along the Gander River and Lake, and the Terra Nova, Gambo and Exploits and Humber Valleys. Lumberers are at work already some sixty miles from the sea-board on behalf of the Botwoodville mills. Pine trees fifty to sixty feet high, and two to three feet in diameter, are commonly met with. Vast forest areas are still untouched.

FARMING FACILITIES.

The lumberer must precede the farmer in clearing the soil for cultivation. As the forest-growths are cut down settlers will occupy the land, and homesteads will take the place of the pine-forests. Facilities for colonizing these wildernesses are now furnished by the iron road.

A SPORTING COUNTRY.

The sportsman will reckon this country a paradise. Deer are there in abundance. It is reported that from 500 to 1,000 of these noble animals were slaughtered about Gander Lake when swimming across in November, 1893—a wanton and barbarous destruction. The North American hare is found in prodigious numbers and ptarmigan are plentiful. The beaver and other fur-bearing animals, bears and wolves are met with. Trout and salmon-fishing in the lakes and rivers is excellent. All the materials for attracting settlers and for furnishing openings for varied industries are to be found in this country to which the all-conquering locomotive has now given access.

CHARACTER OF THE RAILWAY.

Before giving an account of the various stations along the line and the physical features of the country whose solitudes are now for the first time invaded, it may be well to say something of the character of the railway under construction. Impartial and competent judges who have visited and examined the line are unanimous in pronouncing it one of the best new roads ever laid down. No flimsy work is to be found on it; all is solid and calculated to last. The road-bed is unsurpassed; the rails heavy and of excellent material and shape; the ties or sleepers most substantial; the bridges and culverts of granite and steel of superior quality. The passenger cars are of the same style as those used on the Canadian Pacific line. The trains run so smoothly that the traveller has some difficulty in realizing that he is passing over a road just carved out of "the forest primeval." An average speed of thirty miles an hour could be safely reached on such a road, so that the short-route problem between America and Europe may yet be solved here. It is difficult to fancy an express train with magnificent Pullman sleeping and dining cars, within two years from this date, rushing through the very heart of those Terra Nova solitudes, where the deer, the wolf, the bear and the fox were till recently the only dwellers; yet, by the close of 1895, these fancies will be translated into solid facts. Five hundred and fifty miles of railway from St. John's to Port-aux-Basque will be in active operation. A short run of one hundred miles across the Gulf of St. Lawrence, will place travellers in connection with the Continental railway-system; and Newfoundland will almost cease to be an island. Such are the magical effects of a railway in a new country. What the Canadian Pacific railway has done for the Dominion, the Newfoundland Northern and Western railway is destined to do for this island in coming years. Its dormant resources will be brought to light and its pathless wildernesses converted into "the happy homes of men."

ROUTE OF RAILWAY.

From Placentia Junction, seven miles from Whitbourne, the new line runs northerly, crossing the isthmus which connects the Peninsula of Avalon with the main body of the island, which at its narrowest part is but three miles wide. On either side of the isthmus are the heads of the great bays of Placentia and Trinity. Still following a northerly course, the railway traverses the Terra Nova, Gambo and Gander Valleys, and enters the great valley of the Exploits at Norris's Arm. From this point it turns westerly, following up the Exploits Valley and crossing the river at Bishop's Falls, ten miles from its mouth, on a fine steel bridge 630 feet in length with granite piers and abutments. From Bishop's Falls the railway crosses over into the valley of the Peter's Arm Brook, (the Grand Falls being about one and a half miles from the railway at the 222nd mile from Whitbourne), but returns to the Valley of the Exploits again near Rushy Pond at the 227th mile from Whitbourne. From thence it follows up the Exploit's Valley to Badger Brook where it finally leaves the river. From Badger Brook it takes a north-westerly route crossing the White Hill Plains, thence down the valley of Kitty's Brook to the north-eastern end of Grand Lake. The course is then along the southern side of Deer Lake to Bay of Islands, thence through the valley of Harry's Brook to Bay St. George. From this point the line passes back of the Anguille range of hills, down the valley of the Codroy Rivers to Cape Ray, about nine miles distant from Port-aux-Basque, which is the terminus of the line.

CHANGES TO BE EFFECTED.

From this outline of the route it will be seen that the new railway traverses and opens up the largest and most valuable areas of agricultural, forest and mineral lands in the island. In the course of years, branch lines and waggon roads will connect the outlying regions with this Grand Trunk Railway, and thus the various centres of population will be linked together and brought under civilizing influences, and new industries promoted. A closer glance at the country along the line will fully bear out these statements.

FIRST FIFTY MILES.

Tht first thirty or forty miles of the railway run through a wild rugged country, very rocky, especially across the isthmus, being interspersed with barrens and lakelets. Come-by-Chance valley, 50 miles from Whitbourne, is well wooded, and contains land which when cleared, will repay cultivation. It holds good, however, that the fertile belts are to be found in the valleys of the larger rivers and along the banks of the principal lakes. On the ridges and high lands are generally found marshes and "barrens," the latter of which can be utilized for sheep and cattle raising.

GRANITE QUARRIES.

At Random, sixty-one miles and at the one hundred and forty-third mile from Whitbourne, two fine granite quarries have been opened, the granite of which compares favorably with the best Scotch article. From these quarries the contractor obtains the stone used in building masonry, bridges, etc., on the railway.

TO PORT BLANDFORD, CLODE SOUND.

At Clarenville and Upper Shoal Harbour villages the line again reaches the salt water. A small steamer plies here for the conveyance of mails and passengers to and from the neighbouring settlements. To a limited extent the land here has been brought under cultivation. Opposite Clarenville on Random Island, Trinity Bay, is a brick-making establishment, where brick of a superior character are made. On Smith Sound, a short distance from Shoal Harbour, are slate deposits where slate of a superior quality is obtained. At Shoal Harbour is a small saw-mill, the logs for which are brought down the Shoal Harbour river along which the railway passes to Clode Sound, an arm of Bonavista Bay, ninety-seven miles from Whitbourne. Here the scenery is very fine. A growing settlement has sprung up and the land is being rapidly brought under cultivation. There is here a beautiful sandy beach where sea-bathing can be had in perfection. The salt water is also warmer owing to its distance inland. In the near future Port Blandford, Clode Sound, will be a favourite summer watering-place. The streams in the vicinity are well stocked with salmon and trout, affording to the angler excellent sport. There are also some fine mussel and clam-beds; and if the experiment were tried it is probable that oysters might here be successfully raised. At Port Blandford fogs are of rare occurrence, and from this point to Cape Ray are practically unknown.

At Terra Nova river, the next station, there is a fine saw-mill, owned by the Campbell Lumber Company, with the most approved machinery, in active operation. The country around is well stocked with game of various kinds; multitudes of wild geese visit this place each spring. The extent of the Sound is five miles in length by two miles in breadth.

GAMBO RIVER.

The fine Gambo River is crossed by a steel bridge eighty yards long, with piers of solid masonry. Both River and Lake are well filled with trout and salmon, and the surrounding country abounds in deer and other game. Some good land is found at Gambo, but as yet little is done in reclaiming it. A handsome hotel is in course of erection at this beautiful spot for the accommodation of visitors, tourists and sportsmen.

From Gambo to Benton, on Souli's Brook, a tributary of the Gander, the line passes through a country over which forest fires swept a number of years ago, burning vast quantities of splendid pine trees. At Benton another large saw-mill, having the best machinery, is in operation. Here, too, is another granite quarry, both being operated by Mr. Reid.

GANDER COUNTRY.

The railway crosses the Gander River at Glenwood about five miles below the point where it issues from the lake of the same name. The advent of the locomotive into this great valley will constitute an era in the colonization of the island. Here, when settled and cultivated, will be one of the finest agricultural regions of Newfoundland. Hardly anything was known of this region till 1874, when the Geological Survey was extended to the upper reaches of the river and was completed two years later. The total length of the main river is one hundred miles; and another branch of it, called the South-west River, also empties into the Great Gander Lake, and is eighty miles in length. The area drained is nearly three thousand square miles. Altogether, as shown in the reports of the Geological Survey, there are in this great expanse of country, including the whole of the Gander River and Lake and the neighbouring Gambo and Terra Nova valleys, no less than seventeen hundred square miles available for settlement. Gander River is approached from the sea at Sir Charles Hamilton's Sound by the great inlet of Gander Bay, the head of which is in latitude 49° 17' north, and longitude 54° 29' west. From this point to the lake the river is thirty-three miles in length. The lake is thirty-six miles long. The main branch of the river extends above the lake for a distance of sixty miles. For a small outlay this river could be made navigable for boats of good size, and down it timber could readily be floated were some present obstructions removed. The eastern portion of the lake stretches away in serpentine form towards Bonavista Bay, its extremity being separated from that bay by only nine miles of a level country, over which a road or tramway could easily be constructed. Thus, this great valley has two outlets to the sea, and is now by railway placed in communication with the rest of the island. The valley, drained by the South-west River, eighty miles in length, has excellent soil and luxuriant timber growths.

GEOLOGICAL REPORT OF GANDER VALLEY.

In the Reports of the Geological Survey of the Gander district it is spoken of in the following terms :—" The country lying above the great lake and forming the valleys of the two rivers presents everywhere a gently undulating surface, rising to a moderate height in its more elevated parts, and sloping gradually and with beautiful regularity down to the river's banks on either side. For a distance of thirty miles above the lake, and at least two miles on the western side of the main and eastern side of the south-west rivers, the country is of this character, giving a block of thirty miles long by ten wide, or an area of three hundred square miles, covered with a deep rich yellow

sandy loam. Nearly every acre of these three hundred square miles is well adapted for agricultural purposes, while magnificent pine, spruce, fir and white birch cover the whole. The islands or intervals in the rivers, especially near their outlets, are perfectly level, and covered with exceedingly deep and rich alluvial soil. . . . . . The soil here, over a very great area, is of excellent quality and capable of yielding rich harvests. Taking everything into account, there is no more promising country or one more easy of access in British America." . . . .
" In all my travels about the island I have no where seen anything like the quantity of pine timber to be met with here." . . . . "There is an area of not less than five hundred square miles worthy of being laid out as timber-limits where an immense trade might be carried on successfully." . .
"Were the tracts surrounding the head-quarters of the Gambo and the south-west branch to be taken into account, I have little doubt the area would be extended to a thousand square miles." Mr. Murray, the Chief of the Geological Survey, calculated that there was sufficient timber here " to yield 92,160,000 feet annually for one hundred years." The following is Mr. Howley's (then Assistant Geologist), estimate of the pine lands here :—

"Area of pine lands on the lower valley of the Gander River and north side of the lake .

	Sq.ms.
Area of pine lands on the lower valley of the Gander river and north side of the lake ...	200
Valleys of the main and south-west rivers ...	800
South side of lake and across to Freshwater Bay	200
Valley of the Gambo and Triton river and tributaries	150
Total	850

In addition to its agricultural and lumbering capabilities the Gander country gives abundant promise of being a mining district. The rocks of the serpentine group having all the characteristics of the copper-bearing formation in Notre Dame Bay are extensively developed in these areas.

SETTLEMENT.

Such is the Gander country which the railway has now tapped and rendered accessible. The rapid progress of the lumbering industry, already described, abundantly sustains the statements of the Geological Survey as to its forest wealth. Its fine scenery and capabilities as a sporting country will attract multitudes of tourists when once it is known. As the valley is gradually cleared of its forest-growths settlement will follow and one day it will be the seat of a large and thriving population.

Crossing the Gander River the railway runs to Norris's Arm on the Bay of Exploits and again reaches tide-water. This is destined to be an important place and here a village is sure to spring up soon. The scenery is reported to be very fine. A steamer plies from here on Notre Dame Bay for the conveyance of mails and passengers, and roads are projected to connect it with the neighbouring arms of the Bay. At Botwoodville, three and a-half miles across the bay, the Exploits Wood Company have a large mill at Peter's Arm and are carrying on an extensive trade in deals with the English market. They have extensive timber-grants in the Exploits and adjacent valleys.

At Burnt Bay, a short distance from Norris's Arm, there is a fine harbour having deep water and ample accommodation for the largest steamers. Passengers and mails landing here from England would shorten the distance greatly and get quick transference to Port-aux-Basque. A branch line, nine miles long, would connect Burnt Bay with the main line.

VALLEY OF EXPLOITS.

As already noted the line takes a westerly direction at Norris's Arm and enters the great valley of the Exploits, where the soil is superior to any yet reached. Timothy hay is seen growing here to a height of four feet on the lumber roads from seeds scattered by trains in hauling supplies to lumber camps. At Bishop's and at Grand Falls, further up the river, the scenery is exceedingly fine. The line now runs through a level country having an upward grade which continues till the water-shed between the Exploits and Grand Lake is reached at the 275th mile from Whitbourne. Situated on the water-shed are the White Hill Plains, "Great Barrens," where a splendid ranching country is reached equal, as a cattle and sheep-raising district, to the celebrated Foot Hills of the Rocky Mountains in Montana, or to Alberta in Canada. Game of all kinds abound here, and deer are especially numerous. Portions of the valley of Kitty's Brook are well adapted for farming and pasturage.

SOIL AND TIMBER OF EXPLOITS.

The great valley of the Exploits, now opened up by the railway, presents such manifold advantages for farming, lumbering and other industrial pursuits, that it must one day become the seat of a large population. With a splendid river, abundant timber and a fertile soil it will not long remain in its present wilderness condition. The Exploits, which is the largest river in Newfoundland, rises in the south-western angle of the island, and, after a course of 200 miles, falls into the bay of the same name. It drains an area of 4,000 square miles, of which it is calculated that nearly half are reclaimable and fit for settlement. It flows through Red Indian Lake thirty-seven miles in length and distant from the mouth of the river between seventy and eighty miles. The lower valley, between the Red Indian Lake and the sea, is capable of sustaining many thousand inhabitants. In the report of the Geological Survey it is said, " The soil is equal to the best parts of Lower Canada ; there is little swamp ; it is unencumbered with boulders, the hills wooded to their tops; the root-crops grown by the few settlers are excellent ; as a grazing and stock-raising country it can hardly be surpassed." " The timber is in many places still abundant, consisting of pine, white-birch, very large spruce and tamarack." . . . . " The river and its tributaries afford water-power to any extent." . . . . " The country south of Hodge's Hill and on the southern side of the Exploits presents an unbroken dense forest in a series of gentle undulations as far as the eye can reach. The country between the Victoria and the head of Red Indian Lake is well timbered throughout." . . . . . . " The quality of the spontaneous productions along the lower reaches of the river indicates a fertile soil."

CATTLE RAISING.

There can be little doubt that the facilities for cattle-raising will speedily attract attention to this region. Its proximity to English markets—only six or seven days' steaming—the excellent harbour for shipping cattle and the facilities for growing hay and root-crops—the abundant supply of nutritious wild grasses in summer—all combine to mark out many portions of the Exploits and other valleys as ranching districts of great promise. With the superior advantages for stock raising the island affords, it seems strange that we should still be importing large quantities of beef (97,600 lbs. in 1892), some of which is brought from Nevada, a distance of some 4,000 miles ; the cost of carriage alone being greater than it could be raised for here, besides, the grazing grounds are much inferior to our own.

GREAT HUMBER VALLEY.

After crossing the great Barrens the railway runs towards the north-eastern end of Grand Lake and enters the Humber Valley. This magnificent valley, in regard to its soil, timber and scenic beauty—its noble river and its fine lake surpasses anything yet described. The total area is estimated at 800 square miles. This includes the wide expanse of country around Deer Lake, the narrow valleys of the Lower Humber and Grand Lake, and also that above Sandy Lake, on the eastern branch. At the head of Deer Lake the valley widens and spreads out in all directions for miles. Its dimensions here are stated to be twenty-five miles in length and twenty in breadth—giving an area of five hundred square miles. In the last report of the Geological Survey it is said : "The wealth of timber resources still available on the magnificent Humber Valley, together with the superior quality of soil covering so large an area, and capable of being cultivated to advantage, far exceed anything on the eastern side of the island. It may be safely estimated that at least four hundred out of the eight hundred square miles that comprise the entire valley are of this favourable character ; while I have little hesitation in saying that half the remainder would compare favourably with most of the land cleared and cultivated on the eastern seaboard." "In point of scenic beauty, however, the views on the Lower Humber and along the Grand Lake are much to be preferred" (to the Deer Lake district) "especially those charming cascades, of which there are probably a hundred or more around the shores of Grand Lake and on the Great Island. The beauty and variety of the scenery alone is likely to attract many tourists to this region in the near future, so soon as better facilities for reaching it than those at present existing are afforded."

COURSE OF THE HUMBER.

The River Humber is about one hundred and fourteen miles in length, and falls into Humber Sound, an arm of the Bay of Islands. The bay is spacious and easy of access, its length being about fifteen miles. The scenery here is the most magnificent in the island. The arm known as the Humber Sound extends from the south-eastern part of the bay twenty-eight miles easterly into the country, with a width of more than two miles. The Blomidon Hills, from 1,000 to 2,000 feet high, rise to the south of the Sound. The Humber River, just before falling into the Sound, passes through a narrow gorge nearly three miles in length, having on each side lofty crags which in some places shoot up perpendicularly from the water's edge to the height of a thousand feet. In flowing through this gorge the river is in some places pent up to a chain in width, the current being deep and strong. Three miles from the mouth of the river a slight rapid is met, which is easily passed at high spring-tides. Above this rapid the Humber opens out wide, flowing through the beautiful picturesque valley till Deer Lake is reached, twenty miles from the mouth of the river. All round this lake is an expanse of fine country, extending in one direction for several miles.

A SOLITARY PIONEER.

A single settler is the sole occupant—Mr. Geo. Nicholls—who came here many years ago from Cape Breton. He has now a fine productive farm in which he grows crops of all kinds, including wheat. The soil is a deep sandy loam yielding root-crops which cannot be surpassed. Clover, buck-wheat and flax grow luxuriantly. Hay is cut from the natural grasses, and hops thrive luxuriantly. The nearest neighbour to this solitary pioneer is some thirty miles off. The want of roads and markets has hitherto prevented the settlement of this fine district, but the advent of the railway will change all this, and the value of land may be expected to advance rapidly.

BAY OF ISLANDS.

The railway reaches the Bay of Islands at Corner Brook, where there is every facility for the erection of good wharves for the exportation of farm-produce, lumber, minerals, etc. The fine herring fishery of this bay, which is carried on during the winter, will receive an impulse from the railway which, in all probability, will lead to a wonderful expansion of this industry. It is true that much of the pine along the river has been long since cut down, yet much good timber of other kinds is still to be found there in abundance, and there are still many portions which the lumber-man has not yet invaded. The shores of Grand Lake are densely timbered with every variety of forest-growth, white pine being abundant. The country between Grand and Sandy Lakes and the banks of Goose Brook, are regions yet almost untouched, and contain a large proportion of pine. In all these there is ample space for a large lumbering industry for years to come, which will be developed by the railway.

MARBLE BEDS.

All these, however, do not exhaust the natural resources of the Humber Valley. It has long been famous for its marble deposits, which are of enormous extent, but yet untested. Specimens have been found of white marble of a very fine grain which appears adapted for statuary purposes should it exist in sufficiently massive beds, which is yet undetermined. "The variety of colours displayed in other specimens is very considerable and often very beautiful." Marble quarries are among the possibilities of the future, and a large export of this valuable article at no distant date.

THE NEW COAL FIELD.

Still more important is the discovery of a new coal field in the vicinity of the Grand Lake, which is now being tested under the orders of Government by Mr. Howley, head of the Geological Survey. While the indications are exceedingly hopeful, it would be premature to say that workable coal-seams of any great extent have been found. What is certain, however, is that the carboniferous series of formations occupy a large area of the Humber Valley, indeed, the entire plateau of the valley is almost exclusively composed of these rocks. Borings were made in 1879-'80 along the side of Sandy Lake, which revealed the existence of at least a portion of the upper or true coal-bearing measures, with a few small coal-seams. On the southern side of Grand Lake the coal-measures form a deep narrow trough, the best and most extensive exposures of coal-measures being at Aldrey and Coal Brooks. Here borings were made in 1891-'92 with the following results as detailed in Mr. Howley's report :—
"Altogether eleven actual outcrops were seen on Coal Brook ; indications of at least six on a small brook west of it, and twenty-eight on Aldery Brook. Of course, most of these represented but thin unworkable seams of coal, often of an inferior character. Nos. 4 and 7 of Coal Brook, 6, 7, 15 and 16 of Aldery Brook, are about the largest and best seams. Of these, four average over three feet of coal each, while the fifth and sixth contain about two feet each of a very superior quality. But, though most of the seams are of smaller dimensions, yet, I take it, that their peculiar position and attitude in the sections greatly enhances their value as a whole. For instance, in the sections on Aldery Brook, in a horizontal distance of 335 feet across the centre of the trough, which in reality represents only 167.7 feet vertical thickness, nine distinct coal-seams are recognized on one side, only two of which have as yet been clearly seen and measured on the other side. The remaining seven are also there beyond question, though not uncovered, yet sufficient

coal detritus was met with in costeaning to indicate their presence. Hence, we have at least eighteen layers of coal succeeding each other in nearly vertical attitude within a total horizontal distance of 335 feet, leaving an average of less than nineteen feet of strata between each layer. Such being the case, it appears to me all these seams could be worked from one opening, especially as they approach each other nearer and nearer as they descend."

PROSPECTS.

The foregoing report indicates, at least, a strong probability that a workable coal-field in this locality, close to the new line of railway, will be developed. It would be difficult to over-rate the importance of such a discovery should it turn out in accordance with expectations. It would promote the settlement and industrial development of this fine region to an extent which is now hardly conceivable, especially when the railway is so close to the coal-field.

IRON ORE FOUND.

Even this is not all. Iron ore is found here in abundance associated with coal. The following is an extract from Mr. Howley's report :—" The clay iron-stone bands interstratified with the coal-measures on Aldery and Coal Brooks are to all appearances similar to those found in most other coal fields. In England, this ore has been the principal source of the iron of commerce for which that country has been so far-famed. It has been said that England's greatness was chiefly due to her coal and iron. Judging from external appearance, the ore here is of a fairly good quality, and there can be no question that the deposits are very extensive. It occurs as usual in the form of irregular nodules, nodular bands and compact solid bands, intimately associated with the principal coal seams. Its prospective value on that account to the future development of large industries in this section of the island can hardly be realized now."

SCENERY—BAY OF ISLANDS.

At Corner Brook, where the railway station will be built, Fisher's saw-mill is in operation, the water-power being obtained from the brook by a wooden sluice a quarter of a mile in length. The quantity of cultivable land here though limited in quantity owing to the steep hills around, is of excellent quality. Garden produce of all kinds grow well ; fruits, such as greengages, plums, apples, all kinds of berries, thrive luxuriantly. To reach the wide farming lands the narrow gorge through which the river flows into the Sound must be passed. At " The Devil's Dancing Point," where the river is narrowed to about one hundred feet, the scenery is most impressive. Great marble and limestone cliffs rise almost perpendicularly to the height of a thousand feet. The rushing current has cut a succession of caves in these great marble walls, presenting a most picturesque appearance. The over-hanging rocks and trees, the mountains towering on each hand, the swiftly-flowing but silent river, all combine to form a scene which could hardly be surpassed in any other country. Every year witnesses the arrival of tourists from England, the United States and Canada, in larger numbers, to view the fine scenery of the Bay of Islands and the Humber Valley, and to enjoy the trout and salmon fishing, while the more adventurous stalk the deer around the shores of Grand Lake. The splendid climate in summer, the air of the plateau being intoxicating, the unrivalled opportunities for sport, the scenic beauty for the artist, must render this region, once the railway is complete, the favorite resort for summer visitors.

FROM BAY OF ISLANDS TO ST. GEORGE'S.

From Corner Brook, the railway ascends the hill and passes behind Birchy and Petrie's Cove, the principal settlements on the bay. Between these two places are the Court House, the English, Presbyterian and Methodist Churches, with school-houses belonging to several denominations. Leaving Bay of Islands, the line now turns southward towards the St. George's Bay, passing through a somewhat broken country. Some of the lands on Cook's Brook, Spruce Brook and Harry's Brook, will be found fit for farming and pasturage. At Spruce Brook the line comes within four miles of the fine Asbestos mine, leased a short time ago to American capitalists, which is likely to be very productive. It is also the nearest point on the railway to the Port-au-Port Asbestos mines. The great drawback hitherto in working this and other asbestos mines has been the want of roads for the conveyance of supplies for the workers and the transmission of the mineral to the place of shipment. The railway meets all such difficulties.

THE GARDEN OF NEWFOUNDLAND.

At St. George's Bay the railway enters the finest region in the whole island, all its natural capabilities being taken into account. Here are numerous valleys of fertile land opening on the bay, well wooded with pine, juniper or tamarack, fine yellow and white birch, spruce and balsams, the soil capable when cleared of yielding excellent crops. It is found to be especially productive of the richest grasses of various kinds, while the climate is very fine. Gypsum of the best quality is abundant. Asbestos has been recently discovered at several points, and mines are opened at Port-au-Port and elsewhere. Clay fit for brick-making has also been found. As a farming, lumbering and mining region its capabilities are very great. Above all, here is the great coal-field of Newfoundland, which the eminent geologist Jukes estimated to be twenty-five miles wide and ten in length. Coal seams three and four feet in thickness at the out-crop have been found here. It is yet untouched but will not long remain so after the railway has reached it. At St. George's Bay, opposite Sandy Point, the principal settlement, there is a fine site at the Seal Rocks for a town to grow up and to become an important industrial centre. At the neighbouring Port-au-Port there are large deposits of lead containing a proportion of silver ore. Iron ore is also reported to be found in the neighbourhood of the coal seams.

CULTIVABLE LAND.

According to the reports of the Geological survey there are around the shores of St. George's Bay and the valleys which open into the interior, and are traversed by rivers flowing from the highlands, 164,506 square acres of reclaimable land fit for settlement, a large portion of it containing excellent soil.

CODROY VALLEYS.

From St. George's Bay the line passes within a mile of the villages on the coast, and, at Crabb's Brook, runs behind the Anguille range of mountains down the Codroy Valleys to Cape Ray, and thence a distance of nine miles, to Port-au-Basque. The Anguille hills are too high and steep for ordinary tillage, but contain the finest sheep and cattle runs, where immense flocks and herds might be fed. The Codroy Valleys have long been celebrated for their fertility and are partially settled. They contain at least seventy thousand acres, much of it fit for settlement. They are well wooded with spruce, balsam, fir, yellow and white birch, and tamarack. The islands and flats of the lower part of Great Codroy River yield a luxuriant growth of wild grass, affording an ample supply of good fodder for cattle. The cattle and sheep reared on the small farms here produce excellent beef and mutton, and the grass, grain and root-crops testify to the excellence of the soil on which they are grown. The dairy produce is of the best description.

WESTERN NEWFOUNDLAND.

If we take the whole tract of country from the Humber Valley (inclusive) to Cape Ray, through which the line passes, we have what will undoubtedly be one day the garden of Western Newfoundland. Apart from its mineral treasures and forest wealth, the agricultural capabilities of this region are such that it should supply all the markets of the island and also be able to export largely to other countries.

PORT-AUX-BASQUE.

From Cape Ray to Port-aux-Basque the line passes over nine miles of rocky barrens, but the valleys cutting the barrens contain good farming and pasture land and are partly taken up and settled. Sheep ranching could be carried on here with advantage. This port, which forms the terminus, is large, safe and commodious, the largest steamers being able to enter at all periods of the tide. It is the nearest winter port to the Dominion of Canada. Once the railway is completed connections will be formed by a line of swift steamers, and the transmission of daily mails will soon follow. It is not difficult to conceive that at no distant date this may become the shortest route between the two hemispheres. By it the ocean passage proper may be reduced to a little over three days—a weighty consideration with the majority of travellers.

ASBESTOS MINING.

There is a new industry springing up along the western coast, which is likely to prove important and remunerative. The very valuable mineral substance called asbestos has been discovered in so many different places that there can no longer be a doubt that Newfoundland will become one of the very few sources of supply which at present exist. Asbestos, as is well known, is one of the scarcest minerals, while its use is extending so rapidly that the demand is constantly increasing. The Province of Quebec is at present the chief source whence manufacturers on this side of the Atlantic derive their supplies. It is there found in the magnesian rocks known as the Quebec Group. There are immense areas in this island covered by the same magnesian rocks; and in recent years the efforts of prospectors have been rewarded by the discovery of an excellent quality of this mineral in several localities. So far these discoveries have been chiefly confined to the neighbourhood of Port-au-Port. Here Mr. Jones, an English gentleman, author of an excellent work on asbestos, has been at work for two seasons with very encouraging results. Two other deposits have been found in the same locality, and a still more important one between Bay of Islands and Bay St. George near the line of railway, to which reference has already been made. The total absence of roads has greatly retarded progress at these mines. When supplies of food, tools and all equipments have to be carried on men's backs for miles through the woods in order to reach these mines the cost of working becomes enormous and capitalists are discouraged. Roads in many directions to connect with the railway will soon be found necessary. As the rocks holding this mineral are widely developed, both along the sea coast and in the interior, it is highly probable that asbestos mining will form a valuable industry of the future, especially as facilities for its prosecution are now secured by the new railway. On Sandy Bay, on the west coast, near the Straits of Belle Isle, discoveries have recently been made of crude petroleum, and if found in any quantity it will prove a valuable addition to the resources of the island. A company has recently been formed to work this claim.

In conclusion, it is difficult to over-rate the beneficial results likely to flow to the country from the new railway which has been thus described in outline. The employment furnished during its construction and afterwards in its maintenance and operation, the large sums distributed as wages among the working classes, will improve the condition of a large number. Many of those working on the line will probably take up land and become permanent settlers in the interior. All around the shores are many hundreds of families living in unfavourable localities, often in the depth of poverty from the failure of the fisheries, which along the coasts are becoming more and more precarious. These poverty-stricken people will not continue to cling to the naked rocks and starve when they can find work, good wages, land for settlement, fuel for the gathering along the newly-opened line of railway. In fact, there should be no poverty among the able-bodied. As their material condition improves higher wants will be experienced and civilizing influences will extend. Education will exert its benign influence.

There is another aspect in which this great work may be regarded. America is rapidly filling up. The good lands of the United States are pretty well all taken up. Restrictions on immigration are increasing each year. The tide of emigration which has hitherto flowed past these shores may now send some rills that will help to people these solitudes in the interior of this island which is now opened up, and whose natural resources are so abundant. Its proximity to Europe will prove an attraction to emigrants when contrasted with the thousands of miles to be travelled in order to reach the far west of the United States and Canada. The healthful climate, in which neither the scorch-

ROADS AND RAILWAYS.

ing heat of American summers nor the blighting cold of their winters have to be encountered, will be a weighty consideration with those who are changing their homes.

It is also a matter of certainty that a constantly increasing influx of tourists, sportsmen and travellers, will find their way to Newfoundland during the summer months now that its noble scenery and attractions for the sportsman are made known and rendered accessible. The island is really the Norway of the New World, and compares favourably with Ireland or Scotland as regards scenery and natural resources; and were facilities for travel matching those in Norway, provided, hosts of visitors would every year be seeking its shores. All those developments will come in due time now that the grand essential, a trunk railway has been constructed.

NEWFOUNDLAND RAILWAY COMPANY.

Under the careful and skilful management of the Receiver, the Newfoundland Railway, from St. John's to Harbour Grace, (83½ miles) has made most satisfactory progress in the development of passenger and goods traffic. The road-bed, track and rolling stock are maintained in excellent condition, and the road is efficiently and continuously operated. The trains run with remarkable regularity, winter and summer; and up to the present time, there have been no serious accidents and very few injuries to passengers or employees.

In order to show the advance which has been made, we shall take for comparison the year 1886, when the line was first operated under the present arrangement, and 1893.

1886.

In 1886 the gross earnings of the railway were $46,772. There were carried over the line during that year 37,649 passengers, the average distance travelled by each being 30 1-5 miles, at an average rate of fare, including all classes, of two five hundred and twenty-two—one thousand cents per mile. The total passenger earnings amounted to $29,010.

During the same year there were carried over the line 4,996 tons of freight, being an average haul per ton of 51 8-10 miles, at an average rate of three ninety-two-one hundred cents per ton per mile. The total freight earnings were $10,156.

1893.

In 1893 the gross earnings of the railway from all sources were $79,884, being an increase, as compared with those of 1886, of $33,162, or over 70 per cent.

In the same year there were carried over the line 58,791 passengers, for which service the sum of $48,815 was received. The earnings per passenger per mile, including both 1st and 2nd classes, were 2.37 cents, and the average distance travelled by each passenger was thirty-five miles.

There were, in 1893, 10,181 tons of freight carried, for which was received the sum of $22,294 ; the earnings per ton per mile were 4.18 cents ; and the average distance hauled each ton was 52.40 miles. This shows an advance in the freight traffic of 104 per cent. as compared with 1886, and an increase in passenger traffic of over fifty per cent. The receipts for mail service between St. John's and Harbour Grace are $7,200 per annum.

Considerable improvements on the line were carried out in 1892-'93, including the substitution of six iron bridges on granite abutments, for trestle bridges, and improvements at the St. John's and Whitbourne stations—the erection of snow fences, etc. The engines and all other rolling stock were maintained in excellent condition. In September, 1893, a reduction of 20 to 25 per cent. on the freight tariff was made.

All this shows a steady and satisfactory advance, and proves that in Newfoundland, as elsewhere, railways will create a growing traffic for themselves, and when judiciously managed, will give fair returns. The Government subsidy of $45,000 per annum, added to the earnings, gives a fair dividend per annum to the bond-holders after the expenses of operation and maintenance are met.

NOTES.

A REMINISCENCE OF 1878.

The first public utterances in favour of a railway, of which a record has been preserved, occurred in a lecture on "This Newfoundland of Ours," delivered by the Rev. M. Harvey before the St. John's Athenaeum on February 11th, 1878, and afterwards published. The following are a few sentences from this lecture : "What we want is a grand trunk railway with branches radiating to all the principal districts. My firm conviction is that Newfoundland has reached that stage in which a railway has become an absolute necessity if she is to make further progress ; and that we ought to strain every nerve and submit to almost any sacrifice in order to obtain this grand necessity of modern civilization. . . . . . . Look at our internal condition as suggesting the necessity of a railway. What are we going to do with this huge territory of forty-two thousand square miles? Are we going to leave the interior forever to the wolves and the deer? Are the fine agricultural districts to remain solitudes when our own people and the people of other countries, who are in need of bread, would occupy them if they were made accessible, and transform them into smiling farms? Must our noble forests be left to rot or burn? Our coal beds and mineral deposits to sleep forever where bountiful nature has stored them? Shall our people cling forever to the rocky shores, and content themselves with a precarious existence derived from the stormy deep? Shame on us if we do not rise to a nobler conception of our destiny as a people, and utilize the gifts of a bountiful Providence.

"To me it seems that the present generation are brought face to face with the task of constructing a railway across the island, and that they will prove untrue to their duty if they do not lay aside all party considerations and unitedly and valiantly gird themselves for the work. Think for a moment what the construction of such a railway means! It means the opening up of this great island—the union of its eastern and western shores—the working of its lands, forests and minerals; its connection, by a rapid means of communication, with the neighboring continent. It means the increase of its population; the conversion of the country into a hive of industry; the commencement of a material and social advance to which at present no limits can be set. It means employment and good wages for the people, many of whom, alas! are now very scantily supplied with the poorest necessaries of life—'too little to live on and too much to die on.' To St. John's itself a railway means a vast increase of business of all kinds, and an advance in the value of real estate. It means openings of all kinds for the talents and energies of the young generation. But wanting a railway, none of these benefits will come, and we shall be simply at a stand-still, and all the natural resources of the island must remain undeveloped.

"But then it is asked how is a poor colony like this to build a railway? We can't afford it. I reply we can't afford to do without it. Our poverty is our strongest argument for undertaking it, in order to transform that poverty into wealth. To me it seems that a railway is perfectly within our reach, if rightly gone about. It is really one of the easiest countries in the world to pierce with a railway. What is wanted is that the people should arouse themselves to the necessity of getting a railway and tell their representatives that it must be done, and that if there are difficulties they are sent to the halls of legislation to overcome difficulties and to lead the way in the path of progress. If I were Premier of this colony, I would, in Yankee phrase, 'freeze to this railway.' I would plot and scheme, and scrape and pare, and revise the tariff, and do everything short of stealing, till I got money enough to build the railway. Once it is built, all things are possible. Hail! to the great Hereafter, when Newfoundlanders will be making excursions by rail, on their public holidays, to Gander Lake, and holding picnics at the Grand Falls on Exploits River, or dancing parties in the great international hotel in the Humber

Valley; while return tickets for Japan and China *via* the Canada Pacific Railway at cheap rates, will be sold at the Saint John's Railway Depôt. Not able to construct a railway of three or four hundred miles, with a revenue of nearly a million dollars!! Well might we ask—

> "Is our civilization a failure,
> Or is the Caucasian played out?"

The foregoing dreams of a lecturer are now (1894) seemingly to be soon realized in some fashion; but sixteen years ago, when believers in railways were few and far between, it required some nerve and moral courage to give utterance to such heretical opinions. Now, however, they are shared by almost everyone, and the opponents of railways are difficult to discover. It is the history of all new ideas. They are held at first by a minority of two or three; then they gradually spread till the whole mass is leavened.

In the same lecture occurs the following paragraph on roads: "Roads are types of civilization. Where there are no roads the people are savages. Where roads are few and bad, law is weak and society semi-barbarous. If you want to know whether a people is stagnant or progressive, look at their roads. Wherever there are mental activity, enterprise and a liberalizing spirit of any kind, you will see their manifestations in the building of roads for travel and intercourse. All the great epochs of civilization in the world's history were ages of roads. Nothing marked the splendid era of the Roman Empire so strikingly as the magnificent system of roads which radiated from the Forum of Rome to the furthest extremities of the most distant provinces. This is, emphatically, the age of roads, not only of stone but of iron, along which rushes the iron horse with heart of fire, muscles of steel and breath of steam. Then, we make roads over the ocean by our steamships, and roads for thought by the telegraph wire; and the day is not far distant when the world will be one vast sensorium, with nerves of communication to the very ends of the earth."

ASBESTOS.—MR. R. H. JONES.

As the new line of railway opens up that portion of the island in which asbestos has been found, and where there is every reason for believing it will become a valuable branch of our mining industry, the following extracts from a letter which appeared in the *Harbour Grace Standard* of May 16th, 1893, from the pen of Mr. R. H. Jones, will be found interesting. Mr. Jones, who is an Englishman, has been two years in this country, and has opened an asbestos mine near Port-au-Port. He is an able mineralogist and an expert in asbestos, having written one of the best books on that mineral :

"Asbestos is serpentine, simply serpentine in a fibrous form; but when you ask me how it comes to be in that peculiar form, you go a step or two beyond me. No one knows how or why this should be so. Asbestos is by no means the only mineral which assumes this strange form; we cannot tell you why. In the present state of our knowledge, we simply know that it is so. It is found in this state in every part of the world, but, strange to say, it is not found in any two places alike. It varies not only in colour, but in strangely different forms of crystallization, just according to the place in which it is found. It is most usually found in Canada of a light or dark green colour, sometimes amber, at other times it takes a fine golden tint, although really the colour has little to do with its value for commercial purposes; because, as a matter of fact, when the fine silky fibre is teased out, it is mostly white, whatever shade it may assume in its rock-like form. In that state it takes the colour of the mother rock, and that varies very much according to local surroundings. In Australia it is frequently of a bluish green, taking exactly the peculiar colour of the foliage of the eucalyptus, that wonderful Australian tree which has such manifold uses; and in South Africa, near the Orange River, it is found of a dark Prussian blue colour. In many other places, in the Pyrenees and the Savoy, for instance, it is of a pure white. The most valuable quality is found in the Quebec province of Lower Canada. Here it takes a singularly beautiful form, but little differing in appearance from the product of the silkworm; whilst in America it usually appears in a woody state, very often exactly like a brown stick.

"No, there is no asbestos of any value in America; that is, according to our present ideas. It is strange that, in all that great country, none has yet been found of that beautiful silky texture we are accustomed to in the product of the Canadian mines. Much valuable asbestos, judging from surface indications, is to be found here in Newfoundland, not only on the West Coast, but in many other parts of the island. I fully believe that I shall find it as pure, as silky and as generally valuable as any that has yet been found in Canada. The great difficulty is, that this is a roadless country. It is the business of its rulers to open it up by means of roads and bridges, and until that is done, but little can be undertaken by private individuals to utilize Newfoundland's great mineral wealth. We may know where her treasures lie, but the difficulty of reaching them, or of utilizing them when found, in the absence of such means of communication as are to be found in every other civilized part of the world, is far too great.

"When did I first come to take an interest in the mineralogy of Newfoundland? Well, it is very easy to tell you that. On geological grounds I had long been of opinion that the peculiar formation in which asbestos in its purest form is found in Canada was also to be found in Newfoundland. If you will look at a geological map, you will see that the great belt of serpentine which runs through so large a part of Quebec, appears and disappears frequently, sometimes dipping under or being overlaid by other rocks, until it finally crops out again and is largely displayed in the Peninsula of Gaspe. There it is lost, that is to say, it dips under the sea, but only to reappear again on the western coast of your island. Now, although you may have many hundreds of miles of serpentine, it is only here and there and in extremely few places, that any tendency to the fibrous form is found. But still, if the formation is the same in that part of Newfoundland where the serpentine is found, then it is only fair to assume that the same minerals which occur in the Canadian part of the belt will also be found in that part of it which lies in Newfoundland. This I was determined to investigate; but year after year slipped by without my being able to undertake the journey. In the spring of last year, however, being in Canada, I went to Ottawa to consult my friend, Dr. Selwyn, the Director of the Geological Survey there; and to him I mentioned my ideas. 'Well,' said he, 'I am convinced of it. I have long been of opinion that good asbestos would be found in Newfoundland. Indeed, for years past, whenever any one has come to consult me regarding asbestos, I have always said, 'Go to Newfoundland, that is where you will find it.' That practically decided me, and I determined to go. A little later on in the year I came over here, and the result of my investigation was such that I determined to pay your island another visit, to continue the investigation, and if possible to give effect to the discovery. Yes, I intend to set to work at once, and shall leave by the next coastal steamer for the West Coast, with men and material; and if my efforts meet with success, I believe that it will be a good thing for Newfoundland, by amongst other things giving employment to her increasing population, which cannot, under present conditions, be kept at home, but has to go abroad in quest of that which its own land is powerless to afford it. The staple trade of the country is fish, of course, fish before anything; but a country is generally prosperous, in proportion as she has some alternative business to fall back upon. The fishery may be a bad one some seasons, and the whole island suffers; but, if any part of the population is engaged in some other business in addition to the staple trade, the difficulty and consequent distress are certainly in some measure ameliorated. But to give effect to any of these things, the country wants opening up, so as to welcome the introduction of capital. At present it is not so. Look, for instance, at my own case. I have found asbestos on the West Coast, and wish to give effect to the discovery by opening a mine there: but, to do this I have to encounter extraordinary difficulties. If we had only a cattle track to pass over it would be something; but unless men of energy and perseverance can be found to follow up any discovery of this kind, the great mineral wealth of Newfoundland might just as well, for all the benefit the island can derive from it, be in Alaska or Timbuctoo. When I reach the Gravels, at Port-au-Port, I have about twelve miles to go; but the country there is in a primeval state—there is no road or path, or even cattle track, consequently we must go by water. All our goods, too, must go by water, and the products of the mines must also go the same way. The coast line here is rugged in the extreme, and by water, I believe, the distance is about 15 miles. Now, so great is the difficulty of this passage occasioned by the cross currents and sudden squalls passing over the crest of the hills, that I have frequently been kept out for twelve hours during the trip; and the landing on the rocks is, from the state of the surf on that rocky coast, always more or less in the nature of a shipwreck. Twice I have had my dory smashed up, and twice the men were wrecked, and on one occasion I was detained on this inhospitable coast for three mortal days before we could launch a boat to get off. Such a state of things is discreditable to the country, and nothing I believe can be found like it in any other part of the civilized world. Oh, yes! I readily admit that you have got good roads here, so they have in St. John's. You ought to give all honor to Sir Thomas Cochrane for teaching you how to make them and how to utilize them when made.

"Well, Mr. Editor, I am afraid I have occupied a great deal of your time without telling you about asbestos after all. I should like to have spoken about its many valuable and totally dissimilar uses. It is strange that a mineral substance which can be utilized for the manufacture of clothing and even of lace-curtains, is the only substance that will effectually close the breaches of the big guns—the 100 or 110 pounders for instance—so as to prevent the escape of gas when the gun is fired. It can also be used as a covering for balloons for use in warfare, in the manufacture of incombustible paper and ink, and for protecting the sides of our ironclads. The number of uses to which it can be applied is simply incredible."

Writing from London to a friend in Newfoundland, under date January 13th, 1894, Mr. Jones says :—" I am glad you are interested with the Corsican fibre" (asbestos). " You are quite right in regard to its brittleness ; but, all the same, it would be made use of if the islanders were not so pig-headed about their lands. I had a sample of it over two feet long. I enclose a sample of Italian 'siltry' (asbestos). This is a lovely fibre, but has the same fault as the Corsican. There is nothing to touch *Canadian Chrysotile*" (asbestos), " *and, as I wish to show, Newfoundland also*, for genuine, good, all-round qualities." " I will send you, soon, a specimen of *African blue fibre.*"

CHAPTER IV.

AGRICULTURAL RESOURCES AND FOREST WEALTH.

The previous chapter furnishes some general idea of the agricultural lands of the island which the new line of railway will open for settlement. These, we have seen, are of considerable extent and value, and capable of sustaining a very large population when reclaimed, while at present their forest wealth is very great and can now be turned to account. A more detailed account, however, is necessary for the information of those who are disposed to invest capital in lands suited for settlement, and also to aid those who are desirous of settling on the unoccupied lands in finding such locations as may repay their industrious efforts.

EXTENT OF ARABLE LANDS.

To many it will be a surprise to find Newfoundland spoken of as an agricultural country. The prevailing idea, still to some extent prevalent regarding it, is that it is a dismal, fog-enveloped country, whose savage climate and poor soil preclude all attempts at agriculture. This is very far from being in accordance with facts. It is quite true that there are wide tracts in the island irreclaimably barren; others unfit for arable purposes, though excellent for grazing; and others covered with marshes and what the people call "barrens." Lakes and ponds occupy a third of the surface of the whole island. But the same holds good of much of the United States and Canada, where vast areas are hopelessly barren and would never repay cultivation. The agricultural lands of the island lie in belts, and mainly along the valleys through which the principal rivers run, or around the heads of the great bays or the margins of the smaller streams. In the aggregate these comprise a very fair proportion of the whole land area of the island. If we take the whole area to be 42,000 square miles, and deduct from this one-third for lakes or ponds, we have 28,000 square miles, of which fully a fourth, or 7,000 square miles, or 4,480,000 acres, are available for settlement, either as arable land or for grazing purposes, and are capable of sustaining in comfort a very large number of people. To this must be added the lumbering and mineral resources which are capable of furnishing employment to many thousands. These are not the random assertions of enthusiastic optimists; they are sustained by solid facts which cannot be set aside. The evidence in support of these conclusions is derived mainly from the reports of the Geological Survey, conducted by scientific men who are thoroughly trustworthy; also from reports of the government surveyors who have been for years engaged in mapping the Crown lands; as well as from the accounts given by residents, by intelligent travellers, and others who have visited various sections of the island. All these, when combined, utterly disprove the views regarding the barrenness of the soil once entertained and will revolutionize men's ideas regarding this neglected and misrepresented island. No doubt some writers have erred in the other extreme, and presented accounts too highly coloured. No lasting good can result from exaggerations on such a subject, and great injury may be done by awakening unwarrantable expectations. The aim of the present writer is to be guided by facts and to affirm only what is warranted by these, in the views which he presents regarding the present condition and prospects of the country.

WESTERN NEWFOUNDLAND.

The western portion of the island, in an agricultural point of view, is by far the most important, having, in addition to a large extent of fertile soil, valuable forests, coal-fields, marble, gypsum and lime-stone beds and mineral deposits. It is the carboniferous section of the country, the rocks of this formation always underlying good soil. Its climate, too, is by many degrees superior to that of the eastern or southern shores, being entirely out of the range of fogs, while the cold easterly winds blowing over the Atlantic are modified before reaching the west coast. Now, that it is opened up by the railway, it seems destined in the near future to become the seat of a large agricultural industry. To this will be added cattle and sheep-raising on an extensive scale, as well as mining and lumbering, to say nothing of fishing. The coal beds will not remain much longer unworked when the railway touches them. This grand desideratum is at length secured, and western Newfoundland becomes accessible from both east and west, and presents a wide field for enterprise. It is of importance, therefore, to ascertain what is the character of its soil and what are its general capabilities.

THE CODROY VALLEYS—THEIR CONFIGURATION.

Western Newfoundland, beginning at Port-aux-Basque, comprises the Codroy Valleys, St. George's Bay, Port-a-Port, Bay of Islands, Bonne Bay, and the coast of the great northern peninsula to the Straits of Belle Isle,—some four hundred miles in extent. The Great and Little Codroy Rivers, which have but short courses, fall into the sea about sixteen miles north of Cape Ray and six miles south-easterly from Cape Anguille. Their mouths are but a few miles apart. The valley which they drain, though of no great extent comparatively, is one of the finest agricultural districts in the island. It is bounded on the north-east by the Cape Ray mountains, rising, rugged and barren, to a height of 2,000 feet. The Cape Anguille range forms its northern boundary; "these," says the Geological report, "present a soft and gentle outline, while the higher elevations attain an altitude of 1,000 to 1,200 feet, richly covered by forest trees nearly to the summits." The lower part of this valley, between the two ranges of hills, gives an expanse of low flat land, the breadth of the valley being about twelve miles. In the upper part of the valley the hill-ranges converge towards each other, and "the valley gradually becomes more and more contracted in width until shut in nearly altogether where the main stream at the end of the survey becomes split up among the mountains of the Long Range into a succession of small turbulent mountain brooks."

EXTENT OF GOOD LAND.

These Codroy valleys are about forty miles in length, with a width of from ten to twelve miles. There are some marshes and some portions covered with boulders, but for the most part the soil is excellent, and there is nothing to impede farming operations on an extensive scale. The following extract from the Geological report will convey some idea of the character of thi region :—" The area occupied by level or gently undulating land in the valley amounts, by rough measurement on the plan, about seventy-five square miles, or 48,000 square acres, a very large proportion of which is available for settlement. For th most part the country is well wooded with stout mixed timber consisting chiefly of spruce, balsam firs, yellow birch, frequently of large size, white birch and tamarack. The islands and flats of the lower part of the Great Codroy River yield a luxuriant growth of wild grass, affording an ample supply of admirable fodder for cattle. Along the sea-coast, between Tranvain Brook and the little village of Codroy, the country is partially settled all the way, the attention of the settlers being about equally divided between the cultivation of the land and fishing operations; but up the Great Codroy River, which is more or less occupied on either side of the estuary, the calling of the inhabitants appears to be more purely agricultural, and it may be fairly stated that, notwithstanding the very rude process by which the land is cultivated, the crops produced—of grass, grain and roots—highly testify to the excellence of the soil in which they are grown. Cattle and sheep are raised upon most of these small farms, producing most excellent beef and mutton, besides dairy produce of the very best description. The greater part of the Anguille Range and some of the lower slopes of the Cape Range are also capable of improvement, and, if cleared of timber and sown in grass, would afford grazing land not easily surpassed in any country."

THE LATEST SURVEY.

A later and more complete topographical survey states that the number of farm lots in actual possession on the coast line and shores of the estuary of Grand River, located and laid off, was 93 in all, having an average of over 163 acres, or a total of 15,204 acres; and that a further amount of 2,121 acres had been applied for. On the Little Codroy River about 8,860 acres were occupied or held in possession. About 13,421 acres were available in the upper and unoccupied portion of the Codroy Valley. The total area of cultivable land in the valleys was 56,862 acres.

A SURVEYOR'S REPORT.

The report of a Government Surveyor General, made many years ago, states that the soil in these valleys consists of a "rich loam capable of the highest degree of cultivation, and fit for the production of any description of crop." . . . "Lying to the northward of the valuable tract of land referred to is found a range of hilly ground admirably adapted for grazing, its natural productions consisting of herbage, which early in the summer attains a height of between two and three feet." . . . "It would be difficult to imagine a more beautiful or picturesque scene than the whole presents; and whether with reference to the soil around it, to its fisheries or to its geographical situation, forming as it does part of the Northern Head, and therefore commanding the entrance to the Gulf of St. Lawrence, a more desirable or important place for a settlement could scarcely be found."

A TRAVELLER'S OBSERVATIONS.

A traveller from Cape Breton, who visited this region, wrote of it in the following terms: "The land is hardly surpassed by any in the Lower Provinces of Canada for its fertility. We travelled about 24 miles along this beautiful and romantic river. There is a range of good upland extending some nine miles above the settlement. This is studded with birch, spruce and fir. Then commences what is called the "Big Interval." This great tract of rich land I travelled for about 15 miles either side of the river, some places extending over a mile in width. The extent and appearance of this splendid "interval" struck me so forcibly that I stopped to examine carefully the nature of the soil. I could see along the banks that the soil was exceedingly good and four feet in depth ; while the grass, balsam, and balm of gilead trees and tall alders gave proof of its surpassing fertility."

ECONOMIC MATERIALS.

The Geological Report further states that "the coal rocks were perceived to be distributed along the base of the Cape Ray mountains." "Gypsum too is largely developed on the coast near Codroy and in Bay St. George. The vast masses which come out in the cliffs between Codroy Island and the great Codroy River can hardly fail to prove some day of great value and importance. Admirable building stone is found on Codroy Island and on the great Codroy River." Limestone too is abundant.

Such then is this fine region whose valleys, by the close of next year, will be traversed in their entire length by the new railway in its route to Port-aux-Basque. The value of all its natural resources will be vastly enhanced by the railway which will furnish an outlet for its various products, and stimulate a variety of industries now undreamt of. The great drawback to its progress—the want of roads and a market for its agricultural and mineral productions,—will now be removed. Although the dimensions of these valleys are limited, their natural capabilities are comparatively great, and these will now be turned to account. Having a favourable climate, fertile soil, enormous development of gypsum and limestone, abundance of timber and indications of coal and minerals, it is evident that the valley is rich in all that can minister to man's comfort and material progress. At least ten or twelve thousand people might find a comfortable home here. The census of 1891 gives the population as 508.

ST. GEORGE'S BAY—ITS PROSPECTS.

About 35 miles to the north of Codroy is the fine Bay of St. George. More properly it might be called a gulf, being 40 miles wide at its entrance and 50 miles in length. It is long and tapering, and receives at its head and along its southern shore

AGRICULTURAL RESOURCES.

numerous streams and rivers. A long low tongue of land runs out at the south side of the head of the bay, forming an excellent harbour. Now that it is rendered accessible by a railway, there can be no doubt that the region around this bay is destined, in the near future, to become the seat of a large agricultural, mining and lumbering population. When we take into account the extensive tracts of fertile lands around the shores, the quantity and excellence of the timber, the minerals and coal-beds, indications of which are abundant, and add to this the superior climate it enjoys, it seems every way likely it will yet become the garden of Newfoundland. Towns and villages will yet dot its shores, and a prosperous population will occupy its valleys and hills. These are not the visions of an enthusiast, but views which rest on an array of sober facts.

After repeated surveys, the Geological Reports state the extent of land available for settlement at 560 square miles. The south side of St. George's Bay was, in 1885, laid out in ten townships containing 340 square miles, of which it was calculated 220 were capable of a high degree of cultivation. The geological formation is chiefly carboniferous, which really means that the soil is of the best in the country. The same formation in Canada affords the most valuable agricultural land. The soil is so good, says the report, that the settlers have, in some cases, worked the same ground for twenty years in succession without the use of manure. The district is well watered. The rivers Crabb, Fishel's, Barachois, Robinson's, and Flat Bay all flow west from the Long Range Mountains into St. George's Bay. Though shallow they are smooth-flowing except at the heads, and are well stocked with fish. They all run through excellent land which is covered with large timber, principally birch, spruce, fir and poplar. Crabb's River region is especially good. It is the northern boundary of a settlement of Cape Breton Scotchmen who have emigrated to the coast between it and the Anguille Range of mountains during the last 25 years. These Scotch people are very thrifty, and have here carved out comfortable homes for themselves. They have looms, and weave from wool of their own growing all the clothing they need or use. North of them, and extending to th Barachois, is a large settlement of Englishmen who came chiefly from the south coast of the island.

GEOLOGICAL SURVEY REPORT.

Here are a few extracts from the Geological Survey Reports which present this region in a very favorable light : " North-eastward from the terminating point of the Cape Anguille mountains, the whole country between the coast and the Long Range is of a flat or undulatory character, densely covered with forest trees, except in such parts as have been swept by fire, or occasional tracts of marsh. The trees of this forest consist of white and yellow birch, spruce and balsam, fir, poplar, tamarack or larch. Much of the timber of this great plateau is very large. Trees of yellow and white birch are frequently met with, and particularly on the river flats, having a diameter of three feet, and even more, many of which are tall and straight, resembling the hardwood forests of Canada. Spruce, balsam, poplars and tamaracks also reach a maximum size and seem to be of excellent quality." . . . "These valleys and much of the higher lands, now primeval wilderness, appear to be nearly in every respect well adapted for agricultural settlement. By deducting the tract occupied by the Anguille Range of hills, amounting to 256 square miles, which is too high and too steep for ordinary tillage, although well-suited as runs for sheep or cattle, the remainder of the block, viz., 560 square miles, is certainly to a large extent reclaimable ; and there can be but little doubt that the construction of roads, which must necessarily be the consequence of occupation, together with the clearing of the forest, will lead to mineral discoveries of vast importance to the Colony. . . . Tracts of considerable extent upon the coast, and nearly all the valleys of the principal streams, bear a soil of the most fertile description, which is even already shown by the few and rudely cultivated spots here and there where the produce in grass, green crops, and even cereals are all first class both in quantity and quality. The richness of the soil at this part of the coast is probably due to the calcareous material derived from the adjacent mountains, together with the disintegration of the trappean rocks of which the sub-soil is composed.'

RIVIERE BLANCHE.

Of Riviere Blanche a river falling into St. George's Bay near Indian Head, the Report says:—"This river was measured about six miles up its course. A block of rich flat land, supported on members of the carboniferous series, is shut in, as it were, by the Silurian mountains on the north and west, and by the Indian Head Range on the east, which is chiefly drained by the Riviere Blanche and Romain's or Kippen's brook. The area of the block is between 30 and 40 square miles or about 22,400 acres. The whole of this area (excepting the small clearings at the mouths of the streams) is densely covered with forests of large and vigorous growth, with abundance of yellow birch, spruce, fir and other trees, but scarcely any pine."

HARRY'S BROOK VALLEY.

"The valley of Harry's Brook, above the western fork, is rugged and barren for the greater part, and much of it is hilly and mountainous. Below the junction of Spruce Brook patches of good land begin to appear, chiefly on the right bank; and back from the lower reaches, on the same side, there is a broad tract of very good country. The islands and low banks near the outlet are of the best soil for grass meadows. To the south-east of Spruce Brook nearly the whole country is spread over by vast marshes which extend up to the flanks of the hills on the southwest side of the Grand Lake."

PENINSULA OF PORT-A-PORT.

North of St. George's Bay extends the small peninsula of Port-a-Port, between it and the Bay of Islands. The mineral indications are of the most promising character and warrant the expectation that it will one day be a mining centre. A lead mine was opened here many years ago, but owing to the jealousies of the French, who have fishing rights on this coast, the Imperial Authorities ordered operations to be suspended. Such orders, however, would not be issued now. Copper and asbestos have also been found here. Its agricultural capabilities, however, are far from despicable. The Geological Report states that there are nearly 100 square miles in the peninsula available for agricultural purposes. A luxuriant grass grows in certain places; while the timber in some portions is of good quality consisting of white spruce, balsam, fir, and yellow birch (commonly known as witch-hazel). The valley of Benoit's Brook contains an area of 60 square miles, at least one-half of which could be reclaimed. The whole area of the valley of Serpentine River is about 58 square miles, much of the lower lands being of good soil. Here too, are found pine and tamarack trees of large size. The recent discovery of asbestos here is most promising.

ST. GEORGE'S COAL FIELD.

In addition to the resources of this region already enumerated it should be remembered that St. George's Bay contains a large coal-field, not less than twenty miles in width and ten in length, awaiting development. The discovered seams are four feet, three and a half and one and a half feet thick respectively. Competent authorities have calculated that if shipments of 250,000 tons per year were made the coal-beds of St. George's Bay would not be exhausted in a century. Further account is reserved for the chapter on the mineral wealth of the island.

OTHER ECONOMIC RESOURCES.

The Report already quoted contains the following:—"The immense gypsum deposits, so frequently met with throughout this region cannot fail to become of considerable economic importance in the future, especially as much of it partakes of the character known as alabaster. Its value as a fertilizer when the country becomes settled with an agricultural population, can hardly be over-estimated. Many substances of minor importance, such as building stones, limestones, brick-clays, grindstones, whetstones, etc., occur in abundance. The Laurentian hills in the rear give promise of considerable deposits of iron ores, boulders and fragments of which are found plentifully distributed along the beds of the principal streams. These and other less known resources, combined with the greatly superior character of the soil, must in time render the district of St. George's Bay one of the most flourishing and prosperous in the island of Newfoundland."

MONSIGNOR SEARS' OPINION.

The late Very Rev. Monsignor Sears, who spent many years in St. George's Bay, wrote of it as follows:—"As the soil here is surpassingly productive, especially in the growth of various grasses, I believe there is no country in our latitude to surpass it for grazing sheep or cattle. Wherever the trees are removed by fire, wind or other causes, a spontaneous growth of grass springs up." He tells of meadows which he has known giving hay for the last nineteen years, and "the nineteenth crop better than the first." "The wood is abundant and of excellent quality, especially the birch for fuel and shipbuilding.

DR. JOHN BELL ON ST. GEORGE'S.

So far back as 1870, Dr. John Bell, M. A., M. D., of Montreal, spent part of a summer on the West Coast, and afterwards published an account of his visit in the Canadian *Naturalist*. The following is an extract from one of his papers:—"Along the river flats, in the valleys and on the 'barrens' when these are drained and the country is a little more cleared, there will be room for thousands of farms, and the hills will afford walks for immense flocks of sheep, and pasture for countless herds of cattle, the surplus of which will find a ready market at the ports and fishing stations, at the lumbering, manufacturing and mining establishments, which ere long will make this old and neglected colony one vast scene of active and profitable industry. The climate of the island is favourable to the developments of its agricultural resources of every kind. Instead of the cold foggy atmosphere which is generally supposed to hang over the island, quite the reverse is the case. The air is clear and warm, and the temperature during the year remarkably equable, the mercury in winter seldom falling below zero of Fahrenheit's scale, or in summer rising above 80 degrees. I never saw finer weather than during the two months I was on the island. It is only on the south-west corner that fogs prevail to any extent, from the proximity of that part to the Gulf Stream."

All this natural wealth has hitherto remained dormant and undeveloped from the want of a railway to open up the country. The advent of this great agent of civilization will create a new era in the history of this region. Its fisheries, too, will receive a new impulse from the same cause. St. George's Bay is one of the great seats of the herring fishery. The finest herrings are taken here in abundance ; but hitherto this fishery has been prosecuted with little energy or success. Cod, salmon and smelts are also abundant.

BAY OF ISLANDS.

About 50 miles from the north head of St. George's Bay the Bay of Islands opens, famous for its magnificent scenery. Its entrance, which is fifteen miles in width, is studded with lofty islands. This fine region, only second to St. George's Bay in regard to its lands, timber and mineral wealth, contains as yet but a small population. There are several arms extending from its eastern side, but the most important is that known as the Humber Sound, 28 miles in length, which receives at its head the Humber River, the second largest in the island. To the south of this Sound rises the fine Blomidon hill-range, some of whose summits are from 1,000 to 1,500 feet in height. On approaching the Humber their height and abruptness gradually level down until on the banks they do not rise higher than three hundred feet, while they present to the eye a rich clothing of the most varied foliage, which goes down to the water's edge. This, however, does not hold good on the first or lower course of the river, which passes through a narrow gorge nearly three miles in length, shut in by precipitous rocks which shoot up several hundred feet perpendicularly and present a scene of marvellous grandeur. At the termination of this gorge the Humber river widens, the hills recede, and the stream flows through a fine valley from three to seven miles wide till the lower end of Deer Lake is reached, twelve miles from the Sound. In the report of the Geological Survey it is stated that the rise from the sea to the level of Deer Lake is only ten feet. Deer Lake through which the Humber flows is fifteen miles in length and three in breadth. Around it, especially to the eastward and northward, is a fine expanse of flat rolling country, reaching away in the former direction towards Grand Lake.

The reader is referred to the previous chapter, on the new line of railway, for an account of the agricultural, lumbering and mineral resources of the Great Humber Valley and the Bay of Islands. There it is shown that the area of the Humber Valley is 800 square miles, of which fully one-half contains soil of a superior character, capable of being cultivated to advantage. The forest wealth is also great; while half of the remaining 400 square miles compare favourably with most of the land cleared and cultivated on the eastern sea-board. One striking feature of this region is the new coal field recently discovered in the vicinity of Grand Lake, and which is now being tested. The splendid herring fishery of Bay of Islands will be greatly benefited by the opening of the railway and will speedily develope into very large proportions.

COMPARATIVE REPORT.

The Report of the Geological Survey remarks:—" Thousands of square miles have been laid out in townships, and already settled, in Canada, either for the purpose of lumbering or farming, on the northern shores of Lake Huron and many parts of the Lower Provinces, far inferior in most respects to this region of Newfoundland, which there can scarcely be a doubt is capable of supporting a very large population." In this valley of the Humber many thousands might find employment in agriculture, while those living on the lower reaches of the river and on the banks of the Sound could combine fishing, lumbering and ship-building with farming.

BONNE BAY.

North of the Bay of Islands another fine bay opens named Bonne Bay, the scenery of which is very fine. It has not yet been surveyed and is but partially known. Judging by the reports of those who reside in this bay, there is around its shores a very considerable extent of good land, giving excellent crops when cultivated, and a still larger area suitable for grazing purposes. The herring fishery of Bonne Bay has long been celebrated, the quality of the herring taken here, as well as in the Bay of Islands, being equal to the best Labrador article.

NORTHERN PENINSULA.

In regard to the bays further north little is known; but casual visitors concur in declaring that at the heads of nearly all these north-western and northern bays there are large stretches of good land; so that farming could be combined with fishing, by settlers, with great advantage.

GREAT PLAIN ACROSS THE ISLAND—HUMBER VALLEY TO HALL'S BAY.

From the Humber district to Hall's Bay, an arm of Notre Dame Bay, on the northeastern coast, a level plain extends across the island, the greatest height of land between these two points not exceeding 200 feet. From Humber Sound to Hall's Bay the distance is 100 miles. In this plain the land is in many places excellent and of considerable extent, the timber abundant and of large size, and the mineral indications at several points of a very promising character. At one time it was designed to construct a common road along this plain, and a survey was made in 1878, but the project was not carried out. The surveyor's report furnished full information regarding the soil, timber, minerals and other features of this great plain, from which it appeared that from 5,000 to 8,000 people could settle here with every prospect of making comfortable homes for themselves, as farmers, lumbermen or miners. Ere long, it may be safely affirmed, a branch line of railway will connect this region with the grand trunk line, and so open up the great plain for settlement. A chain of small lakes with rivers flowing from them, extends from Hall's Bay to the shores of Grand Lake, with only one portage a mile in width. From Grand Lake the route lies across a portage nine miles wide, and the Humber river is reached. The scenery along this plain, especially at the Birchy Ponds, is very beautiful, and several places compare not unfavourably with the lake scenery of the British Isles. Game of various kinds is abundant, and deer are met with in large numbers. The surveyor said in his report that the Indian Brook Valley, which opens into Hall's Bay, contains 50 square miles or 32,000 acres of land available for farming purposes which would give 80 acres each to 400 families; and that the area of timber-bearing land is not less than 100 square miles. The timber is principally white pine, white and black spruce, white birch and fir. The pines vary from one foot to three and a half feet in diameter at the butt. Unfortunately, the timber in Indian Brook Valley has been swept over by fire, and although left standing, it gives the country a desolate appearance. "The soil is of a rich, sandy loam, easily worked." "There is still a considerable quantity of timber available for lumberers, and a very large quantity suitable for farmers and builders."

MINERALS.

"There is a probability that copper may be found in the eastern section of the plain. The chloritic slates, which are so rich in copper on the sea-coast, are found in several localities on this route, and traces of copper and iron pyrites are observable at a point about two miles in from the south-west arm of Notre Dame Bay; also about four miles in, and at the east and west extremities of Indian Pond." "There are several marshes which are not deep, having a solid bottom at the depth of two or three feet, and these if drained would make very good meadow land. On both sides of Shoal Pond the soil is of a rich sandy loam."

THE GREAT VALLEY OF THE EXPLOITS.

Reference has been made in the preceding chapter to the Valley of the Exploits, through a portion of which the new line of railway runs. The bay of Exploits forms a deep bight on the south coast of the great bay of Notre Dame. It has numerous arms, the greatest being the inlet which leads to the entrance of the Exploits River. There are several islands in this arm, the principal being Thwart Island on the eastern side. The water is deep, and there is no impediment to navigation for vessels of any size until reaching Peter's Arm, where there is good anchorage. The entrance to the Exploits River is at Wigwam Point, in lat. 49° 5' N., long. 55° 19' W. Immediately opposite this entrance is Norris's Arm, stretching for about six miles a little north of east, with an average width rarely exceeding half a mile, at the head of which another considerable stream falls in from the eastward. The Exploits River takes its rise near the south-western angle of the island, within a moderate distance of St. George's Bay. With its numerous tributaries it drains an area of 4000 square miles, and reaches the sea after a course of 200 miles.

The valley may be divided into two sections—the lower extending from Red Indian Lake to the sea, a distance of seventy to eighty miles; and the upper from this lake to the sources of the river.

LOWER EXPLOITS VALLEY.

In its course from Red Indian Lake downwards the Exploits receives the waters of eight tributaries, the largest being Great Rattling Brook, Chute, Sandy and Badger Brooks, while four large streams discharge into the lake itself. The smaller tributaries are very numerous.

The following extract from the Geological report will give some idea of the soil and timber:—"The main river valley, from Red Indian Lake downwards, is nearly for the whole distance a level or gently undulating country, broken only by occasional abrupt hills or rocky eminences, and densely wooded for many miles back from either bank of the stream. . . . . The forests of the Exploits Valley consist of pine, spruce, balsam, fir, tamarack, white birch and poplar. The quality of the spontaneous productions may fairly be taken as indicative of a fertile soil. The width of this fertile belt of land varies at different parts of the river; but taking its average about two miles on either side (and it probably is much more), there would be an area of reclaimable country of 280 square miles, or 179,200 acres." The report adds : "At the mouth of the river the reclaimable land extends to the northward for about five miles, terminating with the northern arm ; and there are large tracts about Norris's Arm and in the valley of the Great Rattling Brook which are capable of cultivation. The fertility of the soil at this part of the region is amply testified wherever cultivation has been attempted, producing roots, potatoes, grass and other crops of the finest description ; while as a grazing or stock-raising country it can hardly be surpassed. The surface soil is generally of sand or sandy loam, which at the upper end of the valley is underlaid by a drift of clay and gravel, while at the lower parts the subsoil is tenacious, bluish, or drab-coloured clay which is occasionally slightly calcareous." . . . "No observant person visiting the valley of the Exploits could fail to be impressed with the manifold advantages it presents for the prosecution of industrial pursuits, such as lumbering and agriculture. With a splendid river, abundant timber and a fertile soil, the region that is now a wilderness might, by energy and enterprise, be soon converted into a thriving settlement, maintaining a large population."

UPPER EXPLOITS' VALLEY.

Above Red Indian Lake the river is divided into two branches—the main river, or Exploits proper, and the Victoria branch. The former rises not more than twelve miles from the sea-coast, flows through George IV. Lake and several smaller ponds. From this lake the course of the river is remarkably straight, in a north-easterly direction, till it joins the Red Indian Lake at the end of upwards of forty miles. The Red Indian Lake is four hundred and sixty-eight feet above the level of the sea. The Victoria branch of the Exploits takes its origin between the White Bear and Grandy's Brook waters, which interlock each other, and the eastern branch of the La Poile, and it flows generally nearly parallel with the main river to its junction with the Red Indian Lake, about four miles above the inlet. South-west from that junction, at the end of forty-seven miles, the river expands into a magnificent sheet of water called Victoria Lake, which is sixteen miles long by an average breadth of three-quarters of a mile. The character of the country through which these streams flow is varied. South of King George IV. Lake "the country is one vast desolation of bare rock with marshes interspersed." On the left bank of the Victoria there are areas of well-timbered land, averaging five miles in width, and rich "interval lands" between Lloyd's Pond and Red Indian Lake. "Sixteen miles up the Victoria River the country greatly improves, and a large tract, well wooded, generally level and covered by a good soil, prevails nearly up to Victoria Lake. This level and reclaimable land seems to extend eastward, with a few interruptions, to the Great Rattling Brook."

HALF A MILLION ACRES FIT FOR SETTLEMENT.

The conclusion of the Geological Surveyor is that there are, upon the Exploits alone, 800 square miles, or 512,000 square acres, more or less capable of supporting settlement, including arable and pasture lands. "The pine timber, spruce, tamarack and birch over extensive areas, are of excellent quality and vigorous growth."

THE VALLEY OF THE GANDER.

The next great agricultural area is the Gander Valley, which surpasses even that of the Exploits. Including the neighbouring Gambo and Terra Nova valleys, there is here an area of 1,700 square miles, or 1,088,000 square acres, available for settlement according to the estimate of the Geological Survey. The topography of this region has been already outlined in the preceding chapter, as well as the character of its soil and timber. Here we have the finest lumbering section in the island. In addition to the extracts from the Geological reports already given, the following will be found of interest :—"Of this great expanse of country a very large proportion, particularly eastward from the main river, is of rich and fertile soil, as amply testified to by its indigenous produce, which to a great extent consist of pine and spruce of a superior size and description * * With the almost unrivaled capabilities the country possesses for grass growing, breeding and rearing of stock can hardly fail to become one of the great future industries of the province. * * * Nowhere else in the island is there seen anything like the quantity of pine timber, to be met with here ; and although the soil on the western side of the island is richer in some places, this country, taking all its advantages into consideration, offers more immediate inducement to settlers." (This was written before the railway reached western Newfoundland.)

THE GAMBO COUNTRY.

The Report states as follows :— "The timber on the Gambo, especially in the valley of the Triton River, is very fine. Pine is abundant, and though not so large as that of the Gander, is of excellent quality. The white birch, spruce and fir, along the banks of the river, are remarkably fine ; indeed I have seldom seen finer in any part of the island. The land available for general agriculture in the valley of the Gambo is not extensive, being chiefly confined to the alluvial flats on either side of the river. These, however, are frequently richly luxuriant, as testified by the indigenous vegetation, especially in the valley of the Triton River where they are generally upwards of a mile in width."

TOPOGRAPHY OF THE GAMBO.

"The Gambo River is approached from the sea by a long, narrow arm of the great bay of Bonavista, which stretches inland some twenty miles from the open water of the latter, bearing generally south-west by west, and north-east by east. The river enters at its extreme head, its mouth being situated in lat. 48° 46′ 5″ and long. 54° 12′ 32″. Two miles and three-quarters from its outlet, it expands into a long narrow lake, known to the lumber-men as the First or Lower Gambo Pond. It then contracts at a place called the Straits for a little over a mile, and expands again into the Second or Upper Gambo Pond, nearly equal in length to the first, but somewhat wider."

SMALLER AGRICULTURAL SECTIONS.

We have now gone over the great agricultural regions on the western and eastern divisions of the islands, and shown the extent and character of the lands suited for settlement in those regions, as well as their chief topographical features. The smaller tracts of land fitted for agricultural operations are too numerous to admit of a detailed account. They are found along the banks of the smaller streams and around the heads of all the great bays. In many places they are in small and detached patches, with large stretches of swampy, rocky, or boulder-covered land between ; but united, they constitute a large area of valuable land. The principal of these minor farming districts are in Bonavista Bay, around the shores and arms of which there is much fertile soil ; the north side of Smith's Sound, Trinity Bay, Placentia Bay, St. Mary's Peninsula, and especially the Salmonier Arm of that bay. Though much of the great Peninsula of Avalon consist of a poor, rocky, swampy or absolutely barren soil ; yet there are, here and there, wide areas of soil which admit of profitable cultivation, and which when duly treated with manure, yield excellent root-crops of all kinds, as well as oats, barley and luxuriant grass-crops. The gardens and cultivated areas in the neighbourhood of nearly all the settlements in Avalon bear witness to this ; and the neat and comfortable farmsteads along the various roads testify to the industry of the people. Avalon, however, is specially adapted to become a cattle and sheep-raising region. Its rather thin soil furnishes admirable grazing ground, and extensive areas of it might be thus turned to profitable account.

A TOWNSHIP SURVEY.

That part of Avalon, which lies between Conception and Trinity Bays, and through which the railway from St. John's to Harbour Grace runs, has been laid out in townships, in order to promote settlement, and with satisfactory results. The townships are each six miles square, and thus contain thirty-six square miles. They are sub-divided into square mile blocks, each having its own number, the numbers ranging from one to thirty-six, and are arranged on a map. Each square mile again is sub-divided into four equal parts, each containing one hundred and sixty acres, which constitute a farm. This township survey has made known many valuable tracts of land where previously none was supposed to exist. The proximity of the railway has greatly enhanced their value. The land reclaimed and cultivated in the neighbourhood of Whitbourne, where a pretty village is growing up, is an illustration of the revolution wrought by the introduction of a railway. A large quantity of good timber has been cut along portions of this locality, and more remains to be utilized. The total area of reclaimable land even in this unpromising section of the country is far greater than might be supposed, so that numbers of farms might be located here at no great distance from the railway. The eight townships laid out here contain seventy square miles, or 48,800 acres, of fairly good land. This would give four hundred and forty-eight farms of one hundred acres each.

TESTIMONY OF COMPETENT MEN.

In corroboration of the reports of professional and scientific men, it may not be amiss to cite the opinions of some other competent judges in regard to the agricultural capabilities of the island. Sir John Harvey was appointed Governor of Newfoundland in 1842. He was a man of much intelligence and energy, and was well acquainted with Canada and the Lower Provinces. In one of his speeches at the opening of the Legislature, he used the following words:—" And here I will not deny myself the satisfaction of recording this public declaration of my conviction, derived from such observation and information as a residence in the island for upwards of a year has enabled me to acquire, that, both as regards climate and agricultural capabilities, Newfoundland in many respects need not shrink from a comparison with the most favoured provinces of North America. Its summers, though short, enjoy an extraordinary degree of vegetative power, which only requires to be duly taken advantage of; its winters are neither unusually long nor severe;

and its autumnal seasons are as open and fine as those of any of the neighbouring colonies. In point of rich natural grasses, no part of British North America produces greater abundance.— Newfoundland, in fact, appears to me calculated to become essentially a rich grazing country, and its varied agricultural resources appear only to require roads and settlements to force them into highly remunerative development." It should be remembered that he spoke in these terms of the island, being acquainted only with the poorest portions around a portion of the eastern coast and bays. The very existence of the fine valleys described in the preceding pages was unknown in his day.

SIR R. BONNYCASTLE.

Sir Richard Bonnycastle, a military officer of distinction who spent some years in the island, and has written one of the best books on the country, was strongly impressed with its agricultural resources. His work bears the date of 1842, and in it he earnestly advocates colonization and agricultural development. He speaks of Newfoundland as "possessing a climate of extraordinary salubrity," and predicted that if opened up for settlement it would "take its rank amongst the more flourishing colonies of the neighbouring continent." He enumerated among the vegetable productions which he saw growing and thriving admirably, cucumbers, melons, cabbages, cauliflowers, broccoli, parsnips, carrots, peas, potatoes. "The garden strawberry and raspberry of every variety thrive without more than the usual care. Potatoes, oats, turnips and all the necessary vegetables can readily be reared, even on the very worst portions of such a wilderness as that of the littoral." . . . "The very worst portion of the soil is that in the neighbourhood of St. John's, and yet here, in all directions, the plough speeds and the ancient forest has vanished."

Bonnycastle's reference to the soil in the neighbourhood of St. John's is correct. It is amongst the poorest in the island. Moreover, as this is the most easterly projection of the coast, it is that on which the effects of the Arctic current are most felt and the

AGRICULTURAL RESOURCES.

harsh easterly winds are most chilly, and yet in every direction for miles around the city are well-cultivated, productive farms, and a considerable farming population. Oats and barley of the best quality are grown, and even wheat has been tried with success, as an experiment. "The district of St. John's," says Bonnycastle, "is especially well adapted for a grazing country, and the imported and home-raised cattle look as plump and as sleek as those of any other part of the world : and I have seen cows at some of the farms which would not discredit the dairies of Devon."

AGRICULTURAL SHOW.

Since Bonnycastle's day farming around St. John's has made great advances, and a superior stock of cattle and sheep has been introduced. The annual agricultural shows held in the city would not discredit any country. The exhibits of root crops and grain, the products of the dairy, the cattle and sheep, all bear witness to the industry of the people and the productiveness of the soil when duly cultivated. What then may we not anticipate when the deep soil of the sheltered valleys in the warmer interior and the more favoured west coast are brought under cultivation.

SIR STEPHEN HILL.

Sir Stephen Hill, who was Governor in 1873, says in one of his despatches that "the agricultural capabilities of the island are far greater than are usually assigned to it, and that large portions of it are capable of a high cultivation. The area of the fertile portions, added together, amount to many millions of acres. With respect to the products of the colony, potatoes, turnips, cabbages, peas, beans and indeed all vegetables which grow in England, arrive at the highest state of perfection in Newfoundland. Of cereals, its barley and oats will not suffer by comparison with the produce of Nova Scotia ; and even wheat can be ripened in spots, though as a rule not as a profitable crop. As regards fruit, currants, strawberries, gooseberries and cherries, with other fruit, grow in the gardens ; and countless species of berries are found in great profusion throughout the country."

REPORT OF THE JOINT COMMITTEE.

In 1880 a Joint Committee of the Council and House of Assembly, appointed to consider the question of constructing a railway in the island, presented a report of which the following are extracts :—" Our agricultural industry, though prosecuted to a valuable extent, is yet susceptible of very enlarged development. Vast stretches of agricultural land, extending from Trinity Bay north, along the heads of Bonavista Bay, Gander Bay, and Exploits River, as well as on the west coast, need only the employment of well-directed labour to convert them into means of independent support for thousands of the population."
. . . " The inquiry is further suggested whether this colony should not become an exporter of live stock ; and we have little difficulty in affirming this position. For grazing purposes we have large tracts that we believe cannot be surpassed in British North America ; and when we regard our proximity to England, and the all-important consideration of a short voyage for live stock, the advantages which we possess in this connection are too manifest to be the subject of question or argument."

SIR HENRY BLAKE'S OPINION.

Sir Henry Blake, now Governor of Jamaica, was Governor of Newfoundland in 1887, and was one of the ablest and most energetic rulers the island has seen. In opening the annual agricultural exhibition at St. John's, in that year, he said :—" That a society of between 40 and 50 members should get up such an agricultural show as this, in which prizes to the amount of $500 and $600 are offered, besides the two handsome silver cups, presented for competition, is highly creditable to the members of the society. As I went around the show-yard, if I had not already formed an opinion as to the capabilities of the soil from what I have seen since my advent to the Colony, I should have been surprised, as I am gratified, to see such exhibits in every branch of the farmer's industry. You have demonstrated that even in this Peninsula of Avalon, which is quoted by all authorities as the least productive portion of the island, you can produce live-stock, root-crops and even cereals worthy of a place in exhibitions of far greater pretensions." His Excellency then referred to a visit he had recently paid to Placentia, and gave it as his opinion that "the encouragement of agriculture was of cardinal importance," and dwelt on " the facilities presented here for stock-raising, and general cultivation of the soil and the vast additions to the prosperity of the country that were thus possible." At this exhibition were 656 entries for produce and 304 for stock. In addition to fine specimens of horses, cattle, sheep, dairy cows, poultry, geese, turkeys, etc., specimens of root-crops were exhibited which would compare favourably with those of any other country. There were cabbages weighing each from 30 to 40 lbs.; turnips—20 of which filled a barrel, and splendid beet, carrots and parsnips. The butter, cheese and cream exhibited were specially good. The potatoes could not be surpassed.

PRODUCTS OF CULTIVATED LAND.

Perhaps the best answer to those who are incredulous regarding the agricultural capabilities of Newfoundland, is to show what has been accomplished already in the cultivation of the soil, and the rearing of farm-stock. Owing to the causes already enumerated—the early prohibition of settlement, the want of roads and railways to a comparatively recent date, so that the larger tracts of good land were inaccessible; and the almost exclusive employment of the people in the fishing industry,—the progress of agriculture has been very slow. Still, with all these drawbacks, it is marvellous to find how great are the results of the limited industry as yet devoted to farming. The cultivation of land is confined to the neighbourhood of the settlements and towns, and the portions opened up by the roads which connect them. There are but few farms more than three or four miles from the sea-coast; so that only the poorest portions of the soil have yet been brought under culture, and in the regions least favoured in regard to climate, the eastern shore.

CENSUS OF 1891—AGRICULTURAL PRODUCTS.

The Census for 1891 enables us to form a correct estimate of the condition of agriculture at the present time. According to the returns of the census, there are 179,215 acres of land occupied; 64,494 acres of improved land; 20,524 acres in pasture; 21,813 acres in gardens; and 6,244 acres of improved land unused. At the low estimate of $50 per acre, the land under culture is therefore worth $3,224,700. The Census of 1884 gave the quantity of improved land as 46,498 acres; so that in seven years the increase has been 17,498 acres—a proof that a favourable impulse has been given to farming by various legal enactments, the extension of roads and the formation of agricultural societies. Wherever farming is combined with fishing the people are prosperous and the cases of want very few.

The following table shows approximately the value of the animals, and also of the annual farm produce for the year 1891:—

6,138 Horses, valued at $40 each	$245,520
10,863 Milch Cows, valued at $30 each	325,890
12,959 Other Horned Cattle, valued at $20 each	259,180
60,840 Sheep, valued at $4 each	243,360
32,011 Swine, valued at $3 each	96,033
8,715 Goats, valued at $2 each	17,430
Total	$1,189,413

FARM PRODUCE.

The farm produce for 1891 amounted to

491 Bushels of Wheat and Barley, at $1 per bush.	$491
12,900 Bushels of Oats, at 50 cents per bush.	6,450
36,032 Tons of Hay, at $20 per ton	720,640
481,024 Barrels of Potatoes, at $1 per brl.	481,024
60,235 Barrels of Turnips, at $1 per brl.	60,235
86,411 Barrels of other roots, at $1 per brl.	86,411
401,716 Lbs. Butter, at 20 cents per lb.	80,343
Milk and Green Vegetables, estimated at	96,000
154,021 Lbs. Wool, at 20 cents per lb.	30,804
Total	$1,562,398

AGRICULTURAL RESOURCES.

The following table shows by comparison with the preceding table the advance in the leading products enumerated above, in seven years—from 1884 till 1891:—

CENSUS 1884.

462 Bushels of Wheat and Barley.
5,393 Bushels of Oats.
28,312 Tons of Hay.
302,649 Barrels of Potatoes.
24,006 Barrels of Turnips.
21,144 Barrels of other root crops.
5,534 Horses.
8,040 Milch Cows.
11,844 Other Horned Cattle.
40,326 Sheep.
21,555 Swine.
7,934 Goats.
247,064 Lbs. Butter.

ANNUAL INCOME FROM CATTLE, ETC.

There is an addition to be made to the value of the farm products in 1891 in order to arrive at the real annual value of the cultivated land. It will be seen that the Census does not note the annual income derived from cattle, sheep, swine and goats, which must reach a large amount. Only an approximate calculation can be made; but if we take the number of calves and lambs produced during the year 1891, and the products of 21,555 swine, the value of the whole could not be less than $520,000. When we add to this the annual products of 6,138 horses; of 8,715 goats; of 127,420 fowl; together with fruits (including wild berries), vegetables, etc., $212,000 would not be an excessive estimate of their value; so that we arrive at a total of $732,000 derivable from these sources, which being added to the value of the growing crops as already stated ($1,562,398) gives a total of $2,295,398 as the agricultural products of the island in 1891.

Let us now look at the amount of agricultural products and animals imported into Newfoundland, all, or nearly all, of which could be raised in the country, if our agriculture were conducted on a more extensive scale and with greater skill. The following table shows the imports of such products in the year 1891 :—

2,512 Oxen and Cows, valued at	$101,486
118 Pigs and Calves, valued at	590
3,485 Sheep, valued at	10,455
230 Horses, valued at	16,100
2,071 Cwts. Bacon and Hams, valued at	26,923
13,971 Brls. Beef and Pigs Heads, valued at	167,652
14,510 Cwts. Butter and Oleomargarine, valued at	217,650
1,384 Cwst. Cheese, valued at	19,376
39,288 Lbs. Feathers, valued at	3,829
367,978 Lbs. Fresh Meat and Poultry, valued at	36,787
7,459 Brls. Indian Meal, valued at	22,377
Indian Corn, valued at	5,050
20,867 Bushels Oats, valued at	8,346
3,009 Brls. Oatmeal, valued at	12,036
6,642 Brls. Pease, valued at	26,568
19,982 Brls. Pork, valued at	259,766
88,542 Cabbages, valued at	4,427
54,531 Bushels Potatoes, valued at	10,906
6,758 Bushels Turnips, valued at	1,351
Eggs, valued at	1,748
Tallow, valued at	3,608
Onions, valued at	5,530
Yarn, valued at	19,530
Barley, valued at	2,642
Hay and Straw, valued at	16,530
Beans, valued at	4,189
Lard, valued at	3,376
Meat (canned), valued at	16,179
Total	$924,940

FARMING IN THE FUTURE.

If we suppose this amount of produce raised in the country, which, in the near future, may be the case, now that a railway has opened up the fertile lands, then nearly a million dollars which are annually sent out of the country to pay the agriculturists of other lands, would be retained to benefit Newfoundland farmers and furnish increased employment to the people. If home manufactures are worthy of encouragement, still more so are food factories in the shape of farms. It is evident from the foregoing returns that, for some time to come, the produce of the farm and the dairy, and the raising of stock will find a remunerative market in the island itself, apart altogether from exportation. Much can be done to promote agriculture by the establishment of model farms; the increase of agricultural societies; the introduction of improved breeding stock; the impartation to the young of a knowledge of the elements of agriculture by means of a good text-book to be used in the schools and colleges. Now that the old traditions about the barrenness of the soil are largely dissipated, and that we begin to have confidence in the capabilities of the country it becomes evident that the progress and prosperity of the colony depend very largely on the employment of the people in agricultural pursuits. There is room for thousands of emigrants from other countries; but meantime our surplus population, who cannot find subsistence from sea-farming, should be drafted to the land and along the lines of railway. Ere long a minister of Agriculture will become a necessity, and his department will become the most useful in connection with the public service.

PROBABLE INCREASE OF PRICES OF FARM PRODUCTS.

There is another consideration—the proximity of this island to the Old World from which the stream of emigration chiefly flows. Six days' steaming lands the emigrant here, at a trifling cost and without incurring the danger and fatigue of a long journey to the far West of the United States or the North-west of Canada. In the United States the good wheat-growing lands are nearly all occupied; there are no more fertile regions to conquer. The big farms, where most of the labour is done by machinery and horses, are no longer found to be bonanzas owing to the low price of wheat, and the tendency now is to small farms. In the United States a million a year are added to the population; so that, ere long, consumption will overtake production, and the prices of farm produce will rise, and small farms of one hundred acres will give a comfortable living to a family. As population increases here the value of farm products will be increased and farm-life will become more attractive. The small-farm system, for which Newfoundland is admirably adapted, is now superseding the large food-factories of the west, where the aim is to eliminate the hand of man by machinery, to the destruction of social life in the country. Better times for our people are not far off. Newfoundland has at last a chance for turning to account her long-neglected fertile lands.

CATTLE AND SHEEP RAISING.

With small farms the raising of cattle and sheep on a large scale, as has been already stated, could be carried on over many thousands of acres which are admirably adapted for ranching purposes. Cattle thus raised could be transported in six or seven days to England, and would arrive in excellent condition, and would compete, at a great advantage, in the market over animals that after a railway journey of hundreds of miles have to undergo a sea-voyage of twelve or fourteen days, arriving in a deteriorated condition after many losses.

FREEZING PROCESSES FOR MEAT.

Science has made great strides, in recent years, in the different methods of preserving meats in a fresh state, so that the superfluity of one country can be transported to another, where it is scarce and costly. Millions of tins of canned meats are now sent to all the great markets of Europe, and the increase in this trade every year is enormous. The freezing process for the preservation of meat of all kinds, game, poultry and fish, has now reached such a state of perfection that it is no longer necessary to preserve them with salt, in order that they may "cross the line" when sent from Australia or India to England. In cold countries, such as Russia or Canada, when the season of uninterrupted cold arrives, animals are slaughtered and frozen by the icy hand of nature, and are thus preserved fresh for long periods. If frozen on ice, or kept in contact with ice, the flavour will be greatly damaged; but, if dry-frozen and kept in an icy atmosphere, the flavour and appearance do not suffer, and the meat is found very easy of digestion. Once frozen, however, it should never be allowed to thaw until it is about to be cooked, otherwise it will spoil with great rapidity. The reason of this is that as water expands in freezing, the watery fluid, combined with the muscular fibre, bursts the surrounding membraneous tubes, and when thawed it is in a condition to undergo rapid chemical changes.

TRANSPORT OF FROZEN MEAT, ETC.

Should Newfoundland become a cattle and sheep raising country, not only does its geographical position furnish important facilities for the transportation of live stock, but the coldness of its climate in winter would be favourable for a frozen meat trade. Once the steady winter's cold sets in meats of all kinds, venison, game—such as ptarmigan—could be frozen, and in refrigerating apartments on board transported to other countries.

FOREST WEALTH OF THE ISLAND.

The old tradition which represented the island as incapable of producing trees, except of very small size, and declared that only a wretched stunted growth was to be met with, is not yet quite extinct. How entirely contrary to fact are such reports has been already shown in the foregoing chapters. It is quite true that, from time to time, forest-fires have destroyed some sections of the heavily-timbered districts; but the standing trees are not seriously injured in these burnt districts, and most of them could still be turned to profitable account, though the appearance presented by their bleached trunks and leafless arms is sufficiently ghastly. The forest wealth, however, still remaining unutilized is immense. As already stated, these forests are found chiefly in the valleys of the great rivers and along the banks of their tributaries; also in the country around St. George's Bay. The principal varieties of the indigenous forest growths are white pine, white and black spruce, tamarack or larch, fir, yellow and white birch. The yellow birch, which abounds largely in St. George's Bay, is said to be equal in durability to English oak, and, with the spruces and larches, is admirably adapted for ship-building purposes.

The lumber trade already developed by the portion of the new railway which has been completed and operated as far as Exploits, furnishes ample proof of the forest resources of the country, and gives good promise for the future. (*See chap. III.*)

TIMBER OF THE GANDER DISTRICT.

The great valley of the Gander is destined to be the most important lumbering region in the island. Its topography, soil and forest growths have been already touched on in Chapter III, on Roads and Railways. The Geological report contains the following:—"Except where partially denuded by fire, the whole valley of the river, the shores of the lake and the banks of the tributaries are all densely clad by forest, among the most conspicuous trees of which are pines, to all appearance of the finest description. Upon the south-west arm, and at various parts of the lake, groves of pine may be seen where the average girth of the trees is not much, if anything, less than nine feet. On about one acre of surface I measured 15 or 20 trees, the diameter of which varied from two and a-half to four and a-half feet; and these, moreover, were straight, tall and sound, with stems running up symmetrically for upwards of fifty feet without a branch or knot." The report estimated the available pine limits here at 850 square miles, including the valley of the Gambo and Triton river and the country along the south side of the lake and across to Freshwater Bay. "Most, if not all, the pine here referred to is of the white variety, -*Pinus strobus*,- probably the most valuable species for the manufacture of lumber. Fires swept over many portions of this district, but the pine, though scorched, does not appear to be much injured so long as it remains standing."

THE FORESTS OF THE EXPLOITS.

Next in order as a lumbering country is the Exploits Valley, which contains a very large quantity of pine and other valuable timber, to which reference has already been made. The report already quoted says: "Between the Grand Falls and Badger Brook, at many parts on both sides of the main river, pine flourishes luxuriantly, much of which appears to be of excellent quality, being often of fair diameter, straight and tall. These reaches also display a fine growth of other varieties of timber; and at some parts, especially above the forks of Sandy Brook, white birch often attains a very large size. About Red Indian Lake there is a superb growth of pine, and spruce of large size, straight and tall. . . . "The southern side of the Exploits presents an unbroken dense forest, in a series of gentle undulations, far as the eye can reach. From the Victoria River to the head of the Red Indian Lake, the country is well-timbered throughout." . . . " With a splendid river, abundant timber and a fertile soil, this region is marked out for a prosperous settlement."

THE HUMBER FORESTS.

The valley of the Humber is another district richly wooded, where lumbering operations have been carried on for many years on an extensive scale. "Tamarack or juniper is not rare; yellow birch of large dimensions are abundant; white pine and spruce grow in the greatest profusion, frequently of a size and quality not greatly inferior, if not equal to the best that is now brought to market into Gaspe and other parts of the Lower Province of Canada."

Mr. McLeod, a Canadian civil engineer, said in his Report of 1875:—" To give a rough estimate of the extent of fine timbered land from the mouth of the Humber to the Grand Lake Brook, I should say that in all there is not less than 20 square miles, which would on the average yield five trees of from 1,000 to 2,500 superficial feet each to the acre. This would give 3,200 trees to the square mile, which at an average board measurement of say 1,500 feet, gives per square mile 4,800,000 square feet.

This multiplied by 20 gives 96,000,000 feet as the quantity of standing pine on the Humber." The quality of the pine he pronounced "above the ordinary market run."

ST. GEORGE'S BAY LUMBER.

These are the principal lumbering regions; but, as already stated, the valleys around St. George's Bay and the Codroy Valleys contain a fine growth of mixed forest timber—spruce, pine, birch and fir. On most of the smaller streams there are also groves of pine and various other trees, while the same holds good regarding the heads of many of the bays. From all this it is evident that "in regard to forest wealth and lumbering capabilities, Newfoundland holds a very important place."

CHAPTER V.

MINERAL RESOURCES.

THE FIRST MINES.

It was not till a comparatively recent date that Newfoundland was known to contain mineral treasures of immense value. The late Mr. C. F. Bennett was the pioneer of mining enterprise. Mr. Smith McKay was the first discoverer of copper ore at a small fishing-hamlet called Tilt Cove, in the year 1857. Here a mine was opened in 1864 under the joint management of Messrs. Bennett and McKay. During the following fifteen years Tilt Cove mine yielded about 50,000 tons of copper ore, valued at $1,572,154; and nickel ore worth $32,740. It continues to be worked till the present date and now gives employment to some 500 miners, and the village contains over a thousand inhabitants. In 1875 another copper mine was opened at Bett's Cove, about a dozen miles south of Tilt Cove. In four years the quantity of ore exported from it amounted to 122,556 tons, valued at $2,982,836. In 1878 a still richer deposit of copper ore was opened at Little Bay, at no great distance from Bett's Cove. Up to 1879 the total quantity of ores exported from all the mines reached in value $4,629,889 or nearly a million pounds sterling. This placed Newfoundland sixth among the copper-producing countries of the world.

VALUE OF MINERAL EXPORTS AT PRESENT.

That it still maintains its character as a mining country appears from the Customs Returns for 1891 and 1892. In the former year the value of all the ores exported was $624,750; in 1892 the value rose to $1,006,592. Thus, at the present time, mining constitutes one of the leading industries of the country; though it may be safely affirmed that it is yet in its infancy, and the near future will witness great advances when the railway has opened the country.

METALLIFEROUS ZONE.

The verdict of science warrants such an expectation. The large development of the serpentine rocks in the island is a fact of primary importance. These serpentines belong to what in Canadian Geology is termed the Quebec Group of the Lower Silurian Series, and to the middle or Lauzon division of that series. "The Lauzon division," says Sir William Logan, "is the metalliferous zone of the Lower Silurian in North America. It is rich in copper ores, chiefly as interstratified cupriferous slates, and is accompanied by silver, gold, nickel and chromium ores." This Lauzon division is the one which is developed in Newfoundland, and in which all the copper mines are situated. It is of importance therefore to ascertain what is the extent of these serpentine mineral-bearing rocks in the island. The Geological Survey's Report gives the following trustworthy estimate of the serpentines :—

Between Hare and Pistolet Bays	230 Sq. ms.
North from Bonne Bay	350 "
South from Hare Bay	175 "
South from Bonne Bay	150 "
South from Bay of Islands	182 "
Surrounding Notre Dame Bay	1,400 "
Gander Lake and River country	2,310 "
Bay d'Est River	300 "
Total	5,097 "

EXTENT OF DEPOSITS.

The whole shores of the Great Bay of Notre Dame, where copper was first found, are of the serpentine formation, and so are its numerous clusters of islands. On the opposite shores, on the West Coast, at Bonne Bay and Bay of Islands, there are large developments of the serpentine; and there are strong reasons for believing that the serpentine formation runs across the island, between these two points, and probably comes to the surface at many places far inland. The new line of railway will greatly facilitate the exploration of this region with the view of turning to account its mineral deposits. It must be remembered too, that these remarks apply to copper mining alone; but, as has been already shown, other ores, such as asbestos, nickel, iron pyrites, lead and iron, are found, and give promise of profitable developments. The coal-beds too, await examination and working. All these considerations seem to mark out the island as one of the world's mining centres, in the near future. While the great beds of serpentine hold the copper treasures, present indications warrant the belief that the Huronian and Lower Silurian rocks contain lead in workable quantities, in many localities, having a percentage of silver, while indications of gold are not wanting. The whole island, therefore, may be fairly regarded as more or less metalliferous, while coal-areas on the western coast increase the value of the whole mineral resources. Quite recently too, petroleum has been discovered on the western coast, but whether it is present in workable quantities has yet to be determined. A company has been formed to turn it to account, and an analysis shows that the quality of the oil is excellent.

OPINIONS OF PROFESSOR STEWART.

Professor Stewart, an eminent American mining expert, visited the island a few years ago, and made a careful examination of the mining region. In his report he said, among other things, "the copper ore of Newfoundland is a beautiful yellow sulphuret, free from arsenic or any undesirable ingredient, with a little iron, and containing from eight to twelve per cent. of pure copper. Finer copper ore is no where found. The character of the rocks in which it occurred gives an absolute assurance of perpetuity in the working. The rocks are metamorphosed and laminated; and the extent of mineral indications over extensive areas renders exhaustion in the working a practical impossibility."

LEAD ORE:

Lead ore was first discovered at La Manche, near the north-eastern extremity of Placentia Bay, where for several years workings were carried on. The quality of the ore found here is very fine. It produces 82 per cent. of metallic lead, and also contains a percentage of silver. In Port-au-Port, on the western shore, a rich deposit of lead ore was discovered in 1875, and was worked for a short time with very promising results; but on the protest of the French, who alleged that the working of a mine here was an infringement of their treaty-rights, the Imperial authorities ordered the work to be stopped.

Magnetic iron ore has been found in large quantities in St. George's Bay, and the Laurentian hills contain indications of it.

GYPSUM AND MARBLES.

The Geological Survey's report states that "gypsum is distributed more profusely and in greater volume in the carboniferous districts than in any part of the American Continent of the same extent." In St. George's Bay and Codroy the developments of gypsum are immense. Marbles, too, of almost every shade of colour, have been produced from various parts of the coast, on both the eastern and western shores. The development at Bay of Islands is extensive. Granite of the finest quality, building stones, whet-stones and lime-stones are in ample profusion.— Roofing-slate can also be supplied in abundance.

Before passing from the mineral resources of the island it may be well to make special reference to the Iron Pyrites' Mine in Pilley's Island, Notre Dame Bay. This mine has been worked for eight or ten years, and is at present one of the most valuable and profitable mines in the country. The quality of the pyrites which it yields is said to be the finest in the world, containing fifty-two per cent. of sulphur, and giving a residuum of iron, after the sulphur is extracted, which is manufactured into the finest steel. The pyrites is shipped at the rate of from 30,000 to 40,000 tons annually to the United States, where it is used for the manufacture of sulphuric acid, copperas, etc. A visit to this now celebrated mine will be found most interesting. The workings are extensive and are carried on with the most improved machinery and under scientific direction. Adjoining it is another deposit of iron pyrites of the same quality, which is reported to be very extensive and will probably be shortly worked, as the tests applied to it, under the direction of mining experts, are said to be very satisfactory. The facilities for working it are all that could be desired. The application of capital and enterprise is alone needed to convert it into a productive mine. There is an excellent harbour close to the deposit, having deep water within a few feet of the shore. The demand for this mineral is steadily increasing.

PILLEY'S ISLAND—IRON PYRITES—TOTAL EXPORTS OF ORE.

Returns of the quantities of iron pyrites shipped in 1893, compiled by T. N. Molloy, Esq., American Consul, appeared in *The Trade Review* of March 10th, 1894. These returns show that in that year there were exported to the United States 38,214 tons of iron pyrites from the Pilley's Island mine, the aggregate value of which was $195,780. The mine shows no signs of exhaustion; and the adjoining deposit, above referred to, is reported to contain a much larger quantity of the same mineral. A few years ago the mine which is now worked was sold for $300,000, and would now probably bring a much higher price. Copper ore is also shipped to the United States from Tilt Cove in considerable quantities.

In 1893, according to Mr. Molloy's returns, 23,097 tons of copper ore were thus shipped, the value of which was $68,604; so that the shipments of ore from Pilley's Island and Tilt Cove, that year, aggregated 58,311 tons, the value of which was $264,384.

In a valuable little pamphlet on "The Mineral Resources of Newfoundland," by J. P. Howley, F.G.S., head of the Geological Survey, published in 1892, statistics are given, compiled from the Customs' Returns, showing the exports of the various ores since the mines were first opened. According to these Returns the value of copper ore, regulus and ingots exported from 1864 to the end of 1891, was no less than $9,193,790. The value of iron pyrites exported from 1886 to the end of 1891 was $247,087. To this must be added the value of pyrites exported in 1892, (Customs' Returns), $316,584; and that of 1893, $195,780 — making a total of $759,451, as the value of the exports of pyrites since 1886. All the exports of other minerals, such as lead, nickel, etc., according to Mr. Howley's table, when added to the value of the copper and pyrites exports, show an aggregate value of $9,594,714 for the total exports of ore till the end of 1891. Adding to this amount the value of copper ore and pyrites exported 1892, ($1,006,592,) and the value of pyrites exported 1893, we get an aggregate of $10,777,086 as the value of all the minerals exported from 1864 to the end of 1893.

ECONOMIC SUBSTANCES.

In addition to the ores already named, Mr. Howley enumerates molybdenite, antimonite, iron ores, manganese, lead, asbestos, silver, gold, as occurring in various places, and sometimes in promising quantities. Building and ornamental materials, such as granites, syenites, sandstones, limestones, marbles, serpentines, slates, as well as a variety of mineral substances applicable to the fine arts and ornamental purposes, are also mentioned. Mr. Howley very justly remarks that "The possession of so many useful minerals and economic substances in this island (the oldest and nearest British-American possession to Europe) should point to Newfoundland as a country most favourably situated for mining and manufacturing industries, second indeed to none of the other British-American possessions. The construction of main lines of railway through the island, now being vigorously pushed forward, must in the near future result in bringing about a greater activity in this direction. Already, although the immediate coast-line only is accessible to mining capitalists, Newfoundland ranks as one of the chief copper-producing countries of the globe. Yet even this industry may be said to be merely in its infancy."

PROSPECTS OF MINING ASBESTOS.

Mr. Howley, in the pamphlet referred to, speaks of the recently discovered asbestos deposits in the following terms:— "Asbestos, or chrysotile, deserves special mention, as it is likely to prove of very considerable economic importance ere long. This mineral has been recognized amongst the serpentine deposits of the island in many localities. It occurs in strings and threads of fine silky texture, traversing the masses of serpentine in all directions. Not until quite recently, however, was the attention of capitalists called to its existence here, and fairly enlisted in its development. The comparative scarcity of good material in America, and the not distant prospect of the Canadian deposits of this valuable mineral giving out, led to the large manufacturing firms of Chalmers, Spence & Co., of Boston, and the John's Co., of New York, sending persons to prospect in this country. Certain properties known to contain asbestos, in the vicinity of Port-au-Port and Bay of Islands, were leased by them and operations commenced by costeaning the surface, laying bare the deposits, and running open cuts into the side of the serpentine ridges. A good deal of excellent fibre was obtained thereby, though the deposit is exceedingly irregular. The fibre varies from less than half to about five inches in length, averaging about two inches. So far as quality goes, it is, I believe, all that is requisite for ordinary use. Other parties opened up deposits of serpentine nearer the shore, showing abundance of short fibre, in numerous small veins. Some of this is two to two and a half inches long, and is of a beautiful fine and silky texture, approaching amianthus in purity. Its greatly enhanced value of late years, and its comparative scarcity in the market, render it an object much sought after. Serpentines and their associated rocks, identical in character with those holding the material in Canada, occur abundantly in many parts of Newfoundland, which is already regarded in Canada as, in all probability, ' Quebec's greatest rival,' in the near future, in the production of this valuable commodity."

MR. WILLIS'S PAPER ON ASBESTOS.

A paper was read before the Mining Society of Nova Scotia December 3rd, 1893, on "The Asbestos Fields of Port-au-Port, Newfoundland," by Mr. C. E. Willis, a high authority on the subject. A few extracts are subjoined : " The metamorphic rocks and serpentines of the Eastern Townships of Quebec and the

Gaspé Peninsula, in which the Canadian asbestos, or more properly speaking chrysotile, is found, dip under the Gulf of St. Lawrence, appear again on the west coast of Newfoundland and extend many miles inland, probably entirely across the island, though in places, specially the great elevated central plateau, they are capped with granite rocks, and seemingly have disappeared. This entire area, extending about 100 miles north and south, and the entire width of the island east and west, can be safely called a serpentine country, and contains, according to Mr. James P. Howley's estimate, 5,097 square miles of serpentine rocks.

"The serpentines, with the granulite dykes which everywhere intersect them, contain vast deposits of minerals, and are to-day nearly virgin fields, except on the immediate coast line, for the prospector or miner, and certain to become, in the immediate future, the seat of great mining operations.

"That the country has not long ere this taken a first rank as a mineral producer, is due to its former isolated position, difficulty of access, except in small sailing vessels, and other ulterior causes; but now, with regular and frequent steam communication, the prospector and engineer are forcing their way into the country, and soon it will be the scene of prosperous mining camps and a large mining industry.

"The minerals met with are copper, which is found everywhere, magnetic, hematite, chromic and specular iron ores, coal and petroleum, gold, silver and lead, nickel, iron pyrites, antimony, marbles, gypsum, mica and asbestos.

"The existence of asbestos in this great belt of serpentine has long been known or supposed, and several well-known geologists, in their writings, as far back as ten and fifteen years ago, have predicted that it would be discovered in quantities sufficiently large to be of economic value; but it is only within the past three years that the attention of the miner has been turned in this direction, and is now attracting much interest in the island.

"On the eastern coast of Port-au-Port, rising out of the sea to a nearly vertical height of 1,800 feet, is a mountain known as

Bluff Head. This mountain determines the southern boundary of the serpentines.

"It was here the asbestos first attracted much notice. Bluff Head was long known to the fishermen of the neighbourhood as 'Cotton Rock;' and it came to the knowledge of the Hon. Philip Cleary, of St. John's, who, some three years ago, equipped a small expedition to do some prospecting work in the neighbourhood. The success met with was so immediate and marked that other claims were immediately secured, till in a short time thirty square miles were taken up by prospectors and speculators, and the past summer has witnessed a large amount of development work. Much of this work has been of the most satisfactory nature to the owners, and proves the field to be a large and valuable one."

The paper then goes on to describe the operations of the "Halifax Asbestos Co." in this region, which appear to be of a very promising character, also those of the "Newfoundland Mineral Syndicate"— an English Co.,—and the Cleary claims, all of which show satisfactory results. The writer closes in the following terms: "Labour is both abundant and cheap, and supplies can be readily obtained and landed from a vessel within a short distance of the mines. With water transportation at hand for the product, cheap labour, and being much nearer the European markets than the other sources of supply will enable the operators to compete successfully with mines in other countries."

COAL AREAS.

Reference has already been made in the 3rd chapter to the coal beds of St. George's Bay, which is the principal caboniferous region in the island. Fifty years have elapsed since the discovery of coal there by the subsequently distinguished geologist, Mr. J. B. Jukes, who was for many years Director of the Irish Geological Survey. When a young man he spent twelve months in the island and afterwards published a most interesting book on the results of his survey. He found a coal seam, three feet in thickness, containing cannel coal of excellent quality cropping out on the right bank of the Middle Barachois Brook, on the south side of St. George's Bay. In his report Mr. Jukes says:— "There is no doubt of there being more beds in this vicinity, and of the probability of all the centre of this low district being occupied by a productive coal-field." From fair data Mr. Jukes calculated the extent of this small portion of the coal-basin of Newfoundland at about 25 miles wide by 10 miles in length.

Mr. Murray, formerly Director of the Geological Survey, after a careful exploration of this region, mapped it out, and calculated that the plan of one seam there drawn as three feet in thickness, and occupying an area of 38 square miles, contains 54,720,000 chaldrons of coal, a very considerable portion of which he believed may be found within workable depths.

MR. HOWLEY'S COAL SEAMS.

In 1873, another seam of coal was discovered by Mr. J. P. Howley, F. G. S., at present Director of the Geological Survey, on Robinson's Brook, about nine miles from its mouth, its thickness being four feet. It is a very bituminous caking coal, emitting much gas under combustion, and burning freely. A second seam occurs in the same section, one foot five inches in thickness. The three seams give a thickness of eight feet of coal. None of these seams has yet been worked; but the advent of the railway will pioneer the way for their development. In 1891 the importation of coal, mainly from Cape Breton, amounted to 97,327 tons, value $243,316. Were the coal mines in St. George's Bay worked, there is no reason why the whole of this large consumption should not be supplied from these local deposits. Its transportation by the railway or by sea would be easy, and the price to consumers would no doubt be lowered. The money now sent out of the country would be employed in paying the wages of miners, and carrying on the mining operations; and thus a great impulse would be given to trade in all its branches. The coal required for working the mines and operating the railway could be supplied from this source at a reduced cost.

LATEST SURVEY.

In 1889, a more thorough examination of this coal district was carried out by the staff of the Geological Survey. The result is thus described by Mr. Howley: "Several seams of good coal were found which were uncovered at their outcrops, and traced for some distance, so as to obtain accurate and reliable measurements, and good average specimens of the quality of the mineral. Referring to the report of that year it shows that altogether fourteen seams of coal, of a varying thickness, from a few inches up to six feet were uncovered on one small brook; three seams on another, two miles distant, and four small seams on a third brook, still farther eastward some two and a half miles. . . . "These with some smaller ones aggregate a thickness of 27 feet of coal in the section which is repeated by being brought again to the surface on the other side of the synclinal trough. There is reason to believe that these do not represent all the seams in this section.

"In the central carboniferous trough which was the object of special investigation last season, several seams of coal were found in the region of the Grand Lake, occupying another long, narrow synclinal trough. Two sections cross this trough, and at two miles distant from each other on the strike, were measured with the result that, in the first one, sixteen outcrops of coal were observed, and in the second, twenty-eight outcrops. These are not separate and distinct seams, but the same seams repeated by the doubling up of the strata. None of the seams are large; only a few averaging three feet of coal each. Many of the smaller seams of good coal are so close together, being divided only by five or six feet of loose shaly strata, and all in vertical position,— that I believe several of these could be worked as one seam by a single drift along the strike. All the coal as yet discovered in this island is of the soft bituminous variety; some of it approaches cannel coal."

CHAPTER VI.

THE CROWN LANDS' ACTS.

CONSOLIDATED 1891.

THE law which regulates the sale or leasing of Crown Lands, for agricultural, lumbering or mining purposes, is of the most liberal character, and well calculated to promote the settlement of the country and the development of its natural resources.

The Crown Lands Acts, Consolidated 1891, (a copy of which may be obtained by application at the office of the Surveyor General) amend all former Land Acts, and consolidate all former statements relating to Crown Lands into one elaborate and compendious enactment.

TOWNSHIP SURVEYS.

These Acts first provide for the laying off of Crown Lands as far as practicable, in quadrilateral townships, containing thirty-six sections of one mile square each. Each section is to be divided into quarter sections of 160 acres. Provision is also made for grants of a half-quarter section, or eighty acres, and of a quarter-quarter section, or forty acres.

ORDINARY PURCHASE AND SALE OF LAND.

Section 12th provides that unappropriated Crown Lands, the surveys of which have been duly made, shall be open for purchase, in entire sub-division of sections, or in lots, at an upset price to be fixed by the Governor in Council, according to the location and value of such lands, the upset price in no case to be less than thirty cents per acre. Every such grant to be upon the condition that the grantee shall, within five years from the date of the grant, *bona fide* clear and cultivate ten acres for every one hundred acres comprised in the grant, and in the same proportion for any less quantity.

LICENSES OF OCCUPATION OF CROWN LAND.

The 15th Section provides for the issue of licenses of occupation of unappropriated Crown Land, on payment of a fee of five dollars for each one hundred and sixty acres, and for not more than 6,400 acres, subject to the condition that the licensee shall, within two years, settle upon the land one family for each 160 acres, and for a period of five years cause to be cleared at least two acres per year for every 100 acres so licensed, and continue the same under cultivation, and continue the same families thereon, or others in lieu thereof, for a period of ten years from the expiration of the said five years; upon the performance of which conditions the licensee shall be entitled to a grant in fee of the said land.

LICENSES ENTITLING TO GRANTS.

The 16th section provides for the issue of licenses of occupation of areas of 5,000 acres, which licenses shall entitle the holder to grants in fee on performance of the following terms and conditions: that the holder of the license shall, within two years from the date of the license, clear and have ready for crop at least one per cent. of the area comprised in the license; within three years two per cent.; within four years, four per cent.; within five years, seven per cent.; within six years, ten per cent.; within seven years, thirteen per cent.; within eight years, sixteen per cent.; within nine years, twenty per cent.; within ten years, twenty-five per cent.; and shall settle upon the land at least one family for every 320 acres.

FIFTY ACRES' LICENSES.

The 17th section provides for the issue of licenses of occupation for quantities not exceeding fifty acres, entitling to a grant in fee persons who shall continuously occupy for five years and shall have cultivated within that period two acres of the said land.

WATER POWER LEASES.

The 18th section provides for leasing the water power of lakes and rivers, guarded with conditions for preventing the water being reduced below certain levels or being rendered noxious or deleterious.

LICENSE FOR FISH-BREEDING.

The 19th section provides for leasing for a term of years the use of any pond or river, and such quantity of land adjoining as may be necessary for such purposes, subject to such terms and conditions as may be deemed necessary.

HOMESTEAD LAW—(36th VICTORIA.)

Sections 24 to 48, inclusive, provide for Homestead Estates and Homestead rights. Any person who shall settle on any of the wilderness lands of the colony and cultivate and improve the same, and erect a dwelling-house thereon, shall be entitled to an estate of homestead therein not exceeing twenty acres, and such homestead, and all right and title therein, shall be exempt from attachment, levy, or execution, sale for the payment of his debts or other purposes, and from the laws of conveyance, distribution, and devise or bequest, except as further provided in the Act.

GRANT IN FEE FOR HOMESTEAD.

Any head of a family, or male of the age of eighteen, may, by paying a fee of $10, obtain a location ticket for any quantity not exceeding one hundred and sixty acres for the purpose of securing a homestead right. To secure a grant in fee of such homestead, the holder of the location ticket must commence clearing within six months after its date ; must build a house fit for habitation of not less dimensions than twenty feet by sixteen, and clear and cultivate not less than three acres within two years, six acres within three years, and continuously cultivate all the land cleared during such three years, and reside continuously upon such land for the term of three years next succeeding such date, and thence up to the issue of the grant.

A person holding a location ticket for a homestead right shall be entitled, on payment of a fee of ten dollars, to receive a license to occupy an adjoining one hundred and sixty acres, or less, quantity of Crown land then unreclaimed ; and, at the expiration of the period of three years, he shall be entitled to a grant of the said land so licensed at the Government price of thirty cents an acre.

IMMIGRANTS IN COMMUNITIES.

The 40th section makes provision for the settlement of immigrants in communities, and of homestead settlers in groups of not less than twenty families, should such desire to settle together in hamlets or villages. In such cases the Governor in Council may, at discretion, vary the requirements as to residence, but not as to cultivation of each separate quarter section as a homestead.

TIMBER AND TIMBER LANDS.

Sections 54 to 65, inclusive, regulate the leasing of timber lands, subject to such reservations as are necessary for the purposes of the fisheries.

LICENSES TO CUT TIMBER.

After one month's notice in the *Royal Gazette* the Governor in Council may grant licenses to cut timber on the ungranted Crown lands for a period not exceeding twenty-one years; the lessee to erect a saw-mill or mills of a certain capacity, and commence work within two years from the date of said license; also to pay, in addition to the bonus, an annual ground-rent of two dollars per square mile, and further, a royalty at the rate of fifty cents per 1,000 feet, board measure, on the trees cut down. For the other conditions attached to timber licenses the Act itself must be consulted.

PAPER PULP ACT.

The Governor in Council may, after one month's notice in the *Royal Gazette*, grant licenses to cut timber on ungranted Crown lands, in extent not less than five or more than one hundred and fifty square miles, which shall be in one parcel or block, for the purpose of manufacturing paper or paper pulp, for a period not exceeding ninety-nine years, and containing the following conditions: The licensee, on the issue of his license, to pay at the rate of twenty dollars for each square mile of land included in his license; and, at the end of twenty-five years of the said term, a further sum at the rate of twenty dollars for each square mile; and, at the end of fifty years a similar sum, and at the end of seventy-five years a further sum of the same amount for each square mile. Also, the licensee shall, within five years after the date of his license, expend a sum of not less than $1,000 for each square mile on the erection of buildings and machinery for said manufacture, said expenditure to commence within two years of the date of license. See the Act itself for other conditions.

MINERAL LAND.

When any person shall discover a vein, lode or deposit of mineral, and desires to obtain a lease, he shall mark the land by four boundary posts or cairns, the extent of enclosed land not to exceed one square mile, and shall, as soon as possible, apply to the Surveyor General for a license, and deposit a fee of twenty dollars ; the first notice filed to give priority of claim. The first license shall be for a year ; a payment of thirty dollars shall entitle to a license for another year ; and a further sum of fifty dollars to an extension for another year. During the second year the licensee must expend the sum of two hundred dollars, or its equivalent in labour, in exploring and developing the minerals in the said mining location ; during the third year four hundred dollars must be spent in further development. At any time during the continuance of said license, or renewals thereof, the licensee may apply for a lease of the location, depositing with the Surveyor General the sum of fifty dollars, when the Governor in Council may issue a mining lease and a lease of fifty acres of unoccupied surface land within such mining location, for the term of five years from the date of application therefor. But such lease shall be subject to the condition that the lessee shall expend in and about the working of such mines and minerals, during each of the first four years from the date of the lease, the sum of eight hundred dollars, and during the fifth year two thousand eight hundred dollars.

GOLD.

Sub-sections of Section 71st provide that licenses of search for gold over an area not exceeding one-half square mile, may be issued for a period of one year on payment of a fee of $25 ; renewable for another year on payment of a fee of $50. Leases to mine and work gold, over an area not exceeding one-quarter of a square mile may be issued for a period of 21 years, subject to a Royalty of 3 per cent. on the gold mined.

AGRICULTURAL ACT - 52 VICTORIA.

This Act provides for the appointment, biennially, of a Board of Agriculture of nine persons, nominated by the Governor in Council, of whom the Surveyor General is to be one. This Board is to promote the formation of agricultural societies throughout the Colony ; to acquire and diffuse information about the requirements of agriculture; to introduce improved breeds of animals, new varieties of grain seeds, plants, etc.; to supervise and conduct a Stock or Model Farm ; to hold exhibitions of agricultural products, animals and domestic manufactures, etc. The sum of $5,000 per annum is appropriated for the use of this Board. An Agricultural Society may be formed in any locality when 25 persons become members, each paying not less than $1 annually to the funds thereof ; each society is entitled to draw from the grant to the Central Board an amount equal to double the amount of the subscriptions of the members so raised and paid.

SHEEP FARMING.

The 104th section provides for granting licenses of occupation upon ungranted Crown Lands for the purpose of sheep-farming to the extent of three square miles for each license (such licenses not to exceed ten in number), for a period of ten years, subject to such terms and conditions as the Governor in Council may determine. The lessee will become entitled to a grant in fee of the land so licensed, provided he maintains on the land so licensed a flock of at least 500 sheep for a period of ten consecutive years. An offer is made of a bounty of $400 to be paid to the first two persons or companies, or to any one of them, who shall actually establish, stock with 500 sheep, and work sheep farms in the island, in accordance with the terms of the Act.

CHAPTER VII.

THE FISHERIES.

The fisheries of Newfoundland constitute the grand staple industry of the country. The gathering in of the sea-harvest has been and will long continue to be the chief employment of its people. On the export of the products of the fisheries the trade of the colony mainly depends. Other industries are developing as years roll on; but as yet these do not compare with the fishing interests. This appears very clearly from the census returns of 1891 which show that out of a population of 202,000 there are 54,775 engaged in catching and curing fish; while 825 are engaged in lumbering; 1,258 in mining and 1,058 in factories and workshops, and 8,668 in other employments. The products of the fisheries constitute about four-fifths of the entire exports.

AVERAGE EXPORT OF FISHERY PRODUCTS.

The following table compiled from the Customs' Returns for the year 1891, the latest reliable returns which are available, shows the value of the exports of fishery products for that year:

Codfish, (dried)	$4,032,201
" (boneless)	20,000
" (green)	7,240
Oil, (cod)	227,392
" (cod-liver)	3,798
" (Herring)	360
" (Seal)	414,584
" (Whale)	3,600
Salmon (Pickled)	78,553
" (Preserved)	1,758
Skins (Seal)	364,854
Sounds and Tongues	460
Lobsters	429,681
Herring (Frozen	21,539
" (Pickled)	188,905
Total	$5,794,925

THE FISHERIES.   141

EXPORTED FROM LABRADOR.

Codfish (Dried)	$832,324
Herring	12,153
Salmon	13,034
Cod Oil	5,852
Seal Oil	1,242
Seal Skins	127
Trout . . .	228
Green fish	806
Total . . .	$865,766
Total exports fishery products from Nfld. and Labrador . . .	$6,660,691

The foregoing may be regarded as fairly representing the mean annual yield of the fisheries in recent years. When to this we add the value of the fish consumed by the people in the country, estimated at $400,000, we obtain $7,060,691 as the average annual value of the whole fisheries of the country.

CANADIAN FISHERIES.

In 1891, the total value of the Canadian fisheries, including the salt water, lake and river fisheries, was $18,978,078.

KINDS OF FISHES.

The principal commercial food fishes taken in Newfoundland waters are the cod, the herring, the salmon and the lobster. The seals are taken amid the ice-fields off the north-eastern shore of the island, and also in the Gulf of St. Lawrence, off the south-western and western coasts.

NUMBERS OF FISHERMEN.

The cod, salmon, herring and lobster fisheries are prosecuted on the shores and in the bays of the island; the cod fishery is also carried on upon the Great Bank and on the coast of Labrador. The number of men engaged in the bank fishery in 1891 was 3,269, but there has been a decrease in the number of men and vessels employed since that date. In 1891, 199 vessels, with a tonnage of 11,520 tons, took part in the bank fishery. The total number of vessels employed directly in the fisheries in 1891 was 1,242; their tonnage, 50,041 tons. The number of vessels engaged in the Labrador fishery that year was 859, with a tonnage of 33,634. In the lobster factories the number of men employed that year was 3,427 and 1,380 women. Twenty-two steam vessels took part in the seal fishery of 1893; their crews numbered 4,962 men. Those who engage in the seal fishery, which commences March 10th, afterwards are employed in the other fisheries during the remainder of the year.

COD FISHERY.

The cod fisheries of Newfoundland greatly exceed those of any other country in the world. The annual average export of cod is about 1,350,000 quintals of 112 lbs. weight. The Dominion of Canada exports an average of 450,000 quintals, and Norway about 751,000 quintals. The whole Norwegian catch averages 50,000,000 codfish. The aggregate annual catch of cod in North American waters, (including the fisheries on the banks), by French, American, Canadian and Newfoundland fishermen, is estimated at 3,700,000 quintals. The number of codfish captured to make up this weight of dried fish, allowing fifty to a quintal, would be 185,000,000. This enormous annual draft on these extensive fishing grounds has been going on for centuries without exhausting the supply, so prolific are the codfish in these waters.

EVOLUTION OF THE COD FISHERY.

For nearly four hundred years this fishery has been prosecuted. It began a few years after Cabot's discoveries in 1497. The Basque, Normandy and Brittany fishermen led the way, and for a considerable time had these newly-discovered cod-kingdoms to themselves. In the name Port-aux-Basque, the western terminus of the new line of railway, and Harbour Breton, these fishermen have left relics of themselves in Newfoundland; while the island of Cape Breton obtained its name from these ancient mariners. The English were at this time mainly occupied with a lucrative fishery on the coasts of Iceland; and though Newfoundland was discovered by their own explorers, they at first took no part in the prosecution of its rich fisheries. There is a curious letter preserved in "Purchas's Pilgrims." The writer was a certain John Rut, master of an English vessel which, by some chance, found its way to the Harbour of St. John's, where he addressed this letter to King Henry VIII. It bears the date of August 3rd, 1527. Among other things the writer informed His Majesty that he found in the Harbour of St. John's eleven vessels from Normandy, one from Brittany and two from Portugal, all engaged in fishing, but no English vessels, which honest John considered a shame, seeing that the island belonged to England, and that other nationalities were profiting by these valuable fisheries. Whether the hint thus conveyed had any effect or not, we find that a dozen years later, vessels from London, Bristol, Bideford, and Barnstaple were engaged in fishing on the Banks of Newfoundland. In 1578 fifty English vessels were engaged in the fishery on the Banks or along the shores; and when Sir Humphrey Gilbert arrived in 1583, he found thirty-six ships in St. John's Harbour of which sixteen were English. Even at that early period, so well were the extent and value of these fisheries understood, that Lord Bacon declared "they contained richer treasures than the mines of Mexico and Peru"—a remark which time has amply verified.

ENGLISH FISHERMEN.

The merchants and traders of the western counties of England speedily discovered the importance of the Newfoundland fisheries, and embarked extensively in their prosecution. They established fishing stations along the eastern coast of the island, sending out large numbers of fishermen in the spring who returned at the close of each season. When Captain Whitbourne arrived in 1615, he found 170 English vessels employed in fishing; and in 1626 Devonshire alone sent 150 vessels to engage in this industry. The French too, had greatly extended their fishing operations, and founded a settlement named Plaisance on the shore of Placentia Bay. Permanent settlements of English began to take root in various harbours on the eastern and southern shores, and these continued to grow in spite of all difficulties and discouragements.

STRUGGLE OF RESIDENT FISHERMEN.

Then began the long and melancholy struggle, described in the Historical Sketch, between "the merchant adventurers" who wanted to hold a monopoly of the fisheries and prevent a settlement of the island, and the constantly increasing resident population, which after a century and a half terminated in a complete triumph for the latter. So early as 1698, no less than 265,198 quintals of dried codfish were exported, nearly half of which quantity was taken by the resident population. The cod and other fisheries continued to expand and extended to Labrador. The population increased from year to year, and a corresponding increase in the catch of fish took place. In 1764 the resident population was 13,112, and the quantity of codfish exported was 470,118 quintals. In 1789, the population was 19,106 ; the export of cod 649,092. In 1815, for the first time, the export exceeded a million quintals. The following table shows how the export has fluctuated since that date, sometimes exceeding a million and a half quintals, and occasionally falling below a million :—

Year.	Qls. exported.
1815	1,086,266
1825	973,464
1835	712,588
1845	1,000,233
1850	1,089,182
1854	774,117
1860	1,379,804
1863	1,012,321
1870	1,164,535
1872	1,221,156
1873	1,369,205
1874	1,609,724

THE FISHERIES.

Year	Value
1875	1,136,235
1876	1,364,068
1877	1,029,064
1878	1,074,646
1879	1,387,770
1880	1,583,132
1881	1,463,439
1882	1,231,607
1883	1,642,037
1884	1,397,637
1885	1,284,710
1886	1,344,180
1887	1,080,024
1888	1,175,720
1889	1,076,507
1890	1,040,916
1891	1,244,834

1892 (Returns imperfect; some destroyed in great fire.)

1893 (Returns not yet published.)

INFERENCES.

The foregoing figures clearly indicate that the cod fishery, the grand staple industry of Newfoundland, is declining. Since 1825 the population has considerably more than trebled, so that there are three times as many hands engaged in taking fish from the water now as in the year named, and three times as many mouths to be fed. Moreover, the apparatus for taking fish is vastly increased and far more efficient than formerly. Cod-traps, huge seines, nets, bultows, jiggers, have all been introduced in modern days, and the primitive hook-and-line of earlier times is used by a comparatively small number of fishermen. But with all these, the catch has not increased; and though fresh fishing grounds have been found on Labrador and our fishermen have been extending their operations farther and farther north, on that storm-beaten coast, year after year, yet the whole catch of cod does not exceed that of 30 or 40 years ago. This is a signal of "rocks ahead." The supply even of the prolific cod is falling off. There are far fewer cod in the waters than formerly, as all the older fishermen declare. The most serious signs of exhaustion are in the shore fishery, though even on the Banks there are unfavourable indications, in recent years. In some of the bays where formerly cod were abundant the quantity now taken is very small, and the fishermen whose fathers used to fill their boats with the noble cod within sight of their own doors, have now, with great increase of toil and hardships, to search for them along the grim shores of Labrador.

CAUSES OF DECLINE IN COD FISHERY.

The causes of this decline are not difficult to discover. Reckless and destructive modes of fishing, unrestrained by any legal enactments, or proper rules and regulations, have gone on for generations. Immature fish, in countless myriads, have been destroyed before "repeating the story of their birth." Implements of a deadly and destructive nature have been used—some of these taking the gravid mother-fish in vast numbers and others, such as nets with very small meshes, have recklessly destroyed the young fish before reaching their reproductive age, and at a time when they are almost useless as articles of food. The observance of "close seasons," when the fish are spawning, was neglected. There was no minister or department of fisheries charged with the duty of supervision, and of establishing and enforcing wise rules and regulations. Laws were passed by men who were groping in the dark, being utterly unacquainted with fish-life, in any scientific sense, and such laws soon became merely dead letters, no provision for enforcement being made.

REMEDIES APPLIED.

It is not wonderful to find that under such a system, the fisheries of cod, herring, salmon and lobsters have been showing alarming signs of decline, and in some places of utter exhaustion. Five years ago the remedy was applied, and not a moment too soon. A Fisheries Commission was appointed, and this became a Department of Fisheries in 1893. At the head of it is a Commissioner of Fisheries, and a skilful scientific Superintendent of Fisheries in charge of the practical work. Well-considered rules and regulations, having legislative sanction, designed for the protection and restoration of the fisheries, are now strictly enforced. Farther on in this volume an account of the means adopted to secure these ends will be given. It may be fairly anticipated that, under this enlightened plan, not only will the present decay of the fisheries be arrested, but that in due time, the exhausted waters will be replenished, and former abundance restored. The methods of curing fish of all kinds, and preparing and packing them for market, will be improved, and consequently the value of the various products enhanced.

THE FUTURE OF THE COD FISHERY.

Thus, under the better regulations now introduced, the Newfoundland fisheries have a brighter future before them and will become increasingly a source of wealth to the country. The demand for our noble codfish is not likely to fall off. Catholic countries alone, in connection with the season of Lent and the weekly fast on Fridays, spend annually nearly a million sterling in the purchase of cod taken in North American seas. So far from declining in value, the price of Newfoundland cod has advanced from fifty to seventy-five per cent. within the last quarter of a century. While there is a difficulty, very often, in finding a market for English manufactured goods, the demand for cod never fails; and under the new and improved methods of cure and packing, as in the article known as "boneless codfish," its use is rapidly extending, while every portion of the fish is now turned to some purpose of practical utility. The improved method of manufacturing cod-liver oil has greatly enhanced its value in a medicinal point of view. The finest glue is made from the skin of the cod; and from the bones and head a valuable fertilizer. Railways, in cod-consuming countries such as Brazil, Spain and the Mediterranean countries, have cheapened its transport into their interior, and increased its consumption;

and as the railway system extends the demand is likely to grow. To the inhabitants of warm countries the dried cod furnishes a palatable article of food, and many of them regard it as indispensable. Since the days of Cervantes and Don Quixote, the dried cod, under the old Basque name of *baccalao* or *curadillo* has been in use, and is now more appreciated than ever. Thus a cod-producing country, like Newfoundland, possesses in this industry, a source of prosperity that can never fail, and which the fluctuations of trade, or the caprices of fashion cannot seriously affect. Let Newfoundland only cherish and develope her great cod fishery, and in it her people have a main-stay that will ever prove a source of national wealth.

THE ARCTIC CURRENT LIVING SLIME IT CARRIES.

There is another consideration which emphasizes the security and permanence of this cod fishery. The Arctic Current, which washes the shores of Labrador and Newfoundland, is laden with the food on which the commercial fishes live and thrive, and brings with it a never-failing supply for their sustenance. So far from being unfavourable to the production of life, the Arctic seas and the great rivers which they send forth are swarming with minute forms of life, constituting, in many places, "a living mass, a vast ocean of living slime." Swarms of minute crustaceans, annelids and mollusca feed on this "slime," and in their turn become the food of larger marine animals, even up to the giant whale. Curiously enough this ocean slime is most abundant in the coldest waters, and especially in the neighbourhood of ice-fields and ice-bergs. Thus, then, the great ice-laden "river in the ocean" which rushes out of Baffin's Bay, carrying on its bosom myriads of ice-bergs, and washing the shores of Labrador and Newfoundland, is swarming with the minute forms of marine life, from the diatom to the minute crustacean, and the crab and prawn, together with the molluscous animals and starfish in vast profusion, which contribute to the support of the great schools of cod which also find their home there. Very wonderful are these great processes of nature. These vast battalions of ice-bergs, the terror of mariners, sailing majestically past these shores, and often grounding along Labrador and in the bays of Newfoundland—bring with them the "slime-food" on which the almost microscopic crustaceans live. These in turn furnish food for the caplin, the squid and the herring which, with multitudes of other forms, are devoured by the cod. When the cod is assimilated by man, this great circle of nature is complete. So long then as the Arctic current flows the existence of the cod-fishery of Newfoundland is assured.

For the natural history of the cod, its distribution, movements, spawning, modes of its capture and cure, etc., the reader is referred to "Hatton and Harvey's Newfoundland the Oldest British Colony."

THE SEAL FISHERY.

Next to the cod fishery the most valuable of the Newfoundland fisheries is that of the seal. While the cod fishery has been prosecuted for almost four hundred years, the seal fishery is not more than ninety years old. It would appear that the attention of the people was so absorbed in capturing and curing cod that they neglected the oleaginous treasures which the vast ice-fields every year brought within their reach; and the great seal-herds were left to bring forth their young amid the icy solitudes, undisturbed by the murderous gun, club and knife of the seal hunter. But this paradisaical condition of the seal was not to last forever. The day at length came when the hunters forced their way through the crystal ramparts by which nature had so long guarded these helpless innocents. The nursery of countless mother seals was transformed into a slaughterhouse, red with the blood of their murdered darlings, slain in their icy cradles; and it became a scene of horror and death. Such is the seal hunt of to-day, involving each year a vast destruction of old and young seal life for the benefit of man.

EVOLUTION OF THE SEAL FISHERY.

The value of the seal for human uses and the right method of capturing it in these regions were slowly learned. At first, seals were taken in nets, which were placed between the shore and some island or rock at no great distance. In their migratory movements, in the early part of winter, the seals move south along the shore ; and by means of nets, in these narrow passages, a certain number were captured. The next step was shooting them from large boats, amid the ice-floes. These boats sailed about the middle of April, after the ice had broken up ; and, as at that date the young seals had left their icy cradles and taken to the water, only a few could be reached by the guns of the hunters. As late as 1795 the whole catch of seals only amounted to 5,000 per annum.

SEALING SCHOONERS.

At length an important step in advance was taken by fitting out small schooners of from thirty to fifty tons, and carrying from twelve to eighteen men, the outfit of each vessel costing about three hundred dollars. The vessels were strongly built and had appliances for encountering ice. At first they did not leave port till after the 21st of March, in order to avoid the equinoctial gales, or "St. Patrick's brush," as they were called. Soon, however, they learned by experience the advantage of making an earlier start, in order to reach the young harps before they had taken to the water. The first of March at length became the usual time for starting on the seal hunt. In these little schooners the men speedily acquired hardihood and daring and became expert in battling with the floes. The people of Conception Bay led the way in this new enterprise, and Carbonear, Harbor Grace, Bay Roberts, Cupids and Brigus became the centres of the sealing industry. The skippers of these sealing vessels, some of which were one hundred tons, became "mighty hunters" of seals, and many of them acquired considerable wealth. St. John's, the capital, followed, and had soon one hundred vessels engaged in taking seals. In those days seals were much more numerous and were taken nearer the shore than at the present time. So remunerative was the new industry found to be that its growth was wonderfully rapid. In 1805 the number of seals taken was 81,000; in 1815, 126,315; in 1821, 227,193; in 1829, 357,523; in 1830, 558,942; in 1831, 686,836; in 1833, 350,155; in 1840, 631,385.

These were the palmy days of the seal fishery to which the seal hunters of to-day look back with sad regrets as "the good old times" that can never return. Up till 1857 some four hundred vessels, of from sixty to two hundred tons, their united crews numbering thirteen thousand men, took part in the fishery. After 1850 a decline seems to have set in. There were more failures and fewer successful seasons. Occasionally the catch approached half a million, and, as in 1858, somewhat exceeded that number. Whether the falling off arose from an actual diminution in the number of seals, or the unfavourable condition of the ice and the winds, which prevented the vessels from reaching them, or from both causes, cannot now be determined.

SEALING STEAMERS.

In 1863 the great innovator, steam, entered the field and the first steamer took part in this fishery. The value of steam in connection with Arctic explorations had been previously demonstrated; and ere long its introduction completely revolutionized the seal fishery. It was soon found that steamers strongly built and sheathed for encountering ice, possessed a great superiority over the old sailing vessels. They could cleave their way through ice in which the sailing vessel would be powerless; they could hold on to a "seal patch" when the other would be blown off; and carrying larger crews, could bring in immense loads of pelts when the seals were met with in abundance. In consequence, the number of steamers rapidly increased, and sailing vessels still more rapidly diminished.

In 1866, there were 177 sailing vessels and five steamers; in 1873 there were eighteen steamers, and in 1882 twenty-five steamers. At present there are twenty-two steamers. They are from 350 to 500 tons burthen and each carries from 200 to 300 men. The larger class can bring in from 30,000 to 40,000 seals, when they obtain a full load. In one instance 41,900 seals were brought in by a single steamer the *Neptune*, the weight of fat being 874 tons ; value $103,750. Captain Blandford was commander. In 1885 the steamer *Resolute* brought in 34,628 seals, the gross weight being 772 tons ; the average weight of the pelts (fat and skin) being 50 lbs. In the same year, the str. *Ranger* took 36,112 seals, the gross weight being 755 tons ; the average weight of seal 47 lbs. When they entered port the decks of these heavily laden vessels were hardly twelve inches above water at mid-ships. Every nook and cranny was filled with pelts. The men's berths were filled ; most of the coal had been thrown overboard to make room for the precious fat ; and the decks were piled with pelts, one of them having 7,100 on her deck. These, of course, are rare instances of success. Not infrequently, however, a steamer returns to port "clean." In bad years the catch may not exceed 200,000. In 1892 it was 348,624 ; a fair voyage. But in 1893 it fell to 129,061— the poorest return on record. The cause was, not the scarcity of seals but the unfavourable condition of the ice which was very heavy, and jammed together in huge masses which never opened. In 1894, it is estimated that the united catch of all the steamers (22 in number) will not exceed 142,000 seals ; but the strong easterly winds which packed the ice on the shores and filled up the bays, brought the young seals within reach of the people on shore who took about 120,000.

Such are the uncertainties attending this perilous industry, which is dependent on the winds and waves and the movements of the great ice-fields, amid which the young seals are born and nurtured, and where they must be sought. There can be no doubt, however, that the introduction of steamers has, at least for the present, been injurious to the interests of the poor seal hunters. As in all similar cases, the introduction of machinery tends to eliminate man. The work is done by far fewer hands, and those who are thus thrown idle have to seek for employment elsewhere, and, in too many cases, can at first find none. The gathering in of the seal harvest is now done with less than half the number of hands employed in the days of sailing vessels, and every year large numbers are unable to obtain berths on board the steamers, whose united crews do not exceed 5,600. The cost of fitting out a sealing steamer is very great, and it may be doubted whether, one year with another, the capitalists find it a very profitable investment. The prizes, however, are so enormous that, in spite of failures and disappointments, the seal fishery will continue to attract enterprizing capitalists. The losses of one or two seasons are expected to be made good by the success of a third. At all events it is idle to expect that steamers will ever be withdrawn from this industry and the old sailing vessels re-introduced. As well look for the abolition of railways and the restoration of stage coaches. Men and affairs will adjust themselves, in due time, to the change; but a certain amount of suffering, in the transition stage, is inevitable, as in all similar revolutions in established industries.

THE FUTURE OF THE SEAL FISHERY.

There is no reason why the seal fishery should not long continue to be a source of wealth to the country. Wise restrictions have been, by legislative enactment, recently placed on the prosecution of this industry. Formerly every one "did what was right in his own eyes." The pursuit of the old breeding seals was followed up, after a heavy draft had been made on the young, in the earlier part of the season, and thousands on thousands of these mature seals, on which the maintenance of the species depended, were ruthlessly slaughtered. This, in the end, would have exterminated the seal. Steamers are now prohibited from making second trips, and no seals are to be killed after April 20th. This will, to a large extent, prevent the destruction of old seals; further, no steamer is allowed to leave port for the seal fishery till March 12th, and no seals can be killed till March 14th. This prevents the taking of seals that are immature. These regulations, which are rigidly enforced, will tend to the conservation of this industry, the value of which to the colony may be estimated at half a million to three-quarters of a million dollars. Its value is enhanced by the consideration that it can be prosecuted at a time when other northern countries are locked in icy fetters and their people idle. About the middle of March the hardy Newfoundland seal hunters dash out into the crashing ice-floes, and in a couple of months the work is done, and a million dollars realised. It interferes with no other industry, and the men who take part in it can follow up the summer fishery or engage in the cultivation of the soil. Formerly the average annual value of this fishery was over a million dollars, but the price of seal oil has seriously declined.

HOW SEALS ARE TAKEN.

The young seals are born on the ice which the Arctic current carries past these shores, from the 15th to the 20th of February; and as they grow rapidly and yield a much finer quality of oil than the old ones, the object of the hunters is to reach them in their babyhood, while yet fed by their mothers' milk, and when they are powerless to escape. So rapidly do they grow that by the 16th of March they are in the best condition to be taken. By the 1st of April they begin to take to the water and can no longer be easily captured. Somewhere amid these vast icy wildernesses the seals must be sought. When the vessel reaches an icefield where the seals are visible, the men eagerly bound on the ice and the work of destruction begins. A blow on the nose kills the young seal. Instantly the "sculping knife" of the hunter is at work and the skin, with the fat adhering, is detached from the carcass, which is left on the ice; the pelts are dragged over the ice to the vessel which conveys them to port. The fat and skins are then separated, the former being salted for exportation, and the latter manufactured into oil by a process in which steam is largely used. St. John's and Harbour Grace are the places where all the seal oil is manufactured.

The reader is referred to "Hatton and Harvey's Newfoundland" or to the article "Seal Fisheries of the World," by Rev. M. Harvey, in the latest edition of the *Encyclopaedia Britannica* for full details regarding the natural history of the seal and the mode in which the fishery is conducted.

The following figures show the number of seals taken in the years named:—

THE FISHERIES.

Year.	No. seals taken.
1858	507,624
1859	329,202
1860	375,282
1861	375,282
1862	268,426
1869	359,821
1871	537,084
1872	278,372
1874	398,366
1876	500,000
1877	451,678
1878	409,658
1879	457,855
1880	223,793
1881	447,903
1882	200,500
1883	322,603
1884	266,290
1885	238,586
1886	272,656
1888	230,525
1888	286,464
1880	207,084
1890	220,321
1891	364,854
1892	390,174
1893	129,061
1894 (those taken from the shore included) estimated	262,885

The following figures show the value of the products of the Seal Fishery since 1885; oil and skins being included :—

1885	$558,863
1886	529,766
1887	458,853

1888	573,984
1889	675,381
1890	555,031
1891	779,438
1892	865,784

Total in eight years $4,997,102

SALMON FISHERY.

The export of preserved salmon from Newfoundland does not constitute a large or important item, seldom reaching in value $100,000 per annum. It is either pickled or put in hermetically sealed tins. The quality of the salmon is excellent. It is taken for the most part in nets in the coves, bays and at the mouths of the rivers. The season for taking it is brief, not exceeding six or seven weeks, commencing generally in the end of May. It is often so plentiful in St. John's during this brief season, that it sells for five or six cents per pound, while at the same time it is selling in London and New York for one shilling and sixpence and two shillings sterling per pound.

SALMON RIVERS RUINED.

There are naturally no finer salmon rivers than those of Newfoundland. How comes it then that this source of wealth is so imperfectly turned to account? Why are the countless brooks and streams around two thousand miles of coast of so little value as salmon rivers? The answer is, that the proper preservation of the salmon streams has been, for generations, neglected, and human ignorance and the greed of immediate gain have wasted and partially destroyed what at this moment might be one of the valuable resources of the country. "Barring" the rivers and brooks with nets at the time when the fish are ascending to spawn; constructing weirs, traps and dams; sweeping the pools in the rivers with seine nets, and night-spearing, have been carried on for long periods by ignorant and reckless persons, till at present, in many rivers, the salmon are almost exterminated, and in others only grilse of four or five pounds weight are found.

THE FISHERIES.

RIVER WARDENS APPOINTED.

Four or five years ago the Fisheries' Commission, on its appointment, took the matter up and placed the principal rivers under wardens charged with the stringent enforcement of the rules and regulations of this fishery. The result is that the rivers have been cleared of the old "barring" obstructions; pollutions of the streams from saw-dust is prevented, and already a marked improvement is reported. The salmon are returning to their old haunts, and in a few years satisfactory progress will be made in the restoration of the salmon rivers and a vast increase in the quantity of salmon taken may be anticipated.

The best salmon fisheries at present are in Bonavista Bay, Gander and Exploits Bays, and on the west coast.

THE HERRING FISHERY.

The herring fishery of Newfoundland has been sadly neglected. Had it been prosecuted with skill and energy—had care been bestowed on the cure and packing and had it been placed, years ago, under proper regulations, it might to-day have approached the cod-fishery in value. With due care it may still do so.

The chief seats of the herring fishery are Fortune, Placentia, St. George's and Bay of Islands, while on the whole coast of Labrador the finest herrings are taken. During the last few years the Labrador herring fishery has been unremunerative.

Fortune Bay is the centre of a productive winter herring fishery, commencing generally about the first week in December. St. George's is a spring herring fishery, a small quantity being also taken in August and September. The Bay of Islands fishery is the most valuable next to Labrador, but in recent years it has proved a failure. The fish there are the Bank or Labrador herring, and of the finest quality. Bonne Bay herrings are equally good. The value of the herrings exported in 1891 was $188,905.

EFFECTS OF NEGLIGENCE.

The effect of negligence and ignorance in connection with this fishery has been that the Newfoundland herrings have lost character in foreign markets and depreciated in value. The cure was slovenly and they were shipped in badly constructed barrels. Naturally, they compare favourably with the herrings of any other country, and they appear in inexhaustible quantities. The Department of Fisheries is now taking active measures for remedying past negligences and putting an end to reckless methods of carrying on this industry. They are diffusing information as to the proper method of cure and packing; and enforcing rules for its proper prosecution. A great change for the better has commenced.

LOBSTER FISHERY.

The lobster fishery is comparatively of recent origin, the packing for export or tinning of these valuable crustaceans, having commenced in 1873.

The following figures show how this industry has advanced since that date :—

EXPORT OF LOBSTERS.

Year.	Lbs.
1874	25,814
1875	144,723
1876	290,208
1879	1,168,808
1880	1,124,580
1881	1,299,812
1882	1,265,224
1883	862,528
1884	531,226
1885	824,064
1886	1,454,912
1887	2,097,092
1888	3,360,672
1889	3,658,368
1880	3,338,512
1891	2,749,968
1892	1,560,288
1893 (estimated)	1,950,360

THE FISHERIES.

According to the Census of 1891 there were then 340 lobster factories ; employing 4,807 persons.

The Report of the Department of Fisheries for 1893 states that licenses were issued to 264 packers operating lobster factories between Cape St. John and Cape Ray. Their returns showed that the total lobster traps employed amounted to 87,720 ; the number of fishermen employed being 1,448 ; 113 smackmen ; 603 shorehands (males), and 756 females : and that they caught 5,054,462 lobsters, from which number 26,214 cases of lobsters (each case containing 48 one-pound tins) were packed. These returns apply only to the licensed lobster factories ; there were besides a considerable number of unlicensed factories such as those on the French Shore. The weather of 1893 was, in many localities, very unfavourable for taking lobsters.

The following figures show the value of the exports of lobsters in the years named :—

Years.	Value.
1888	$385,077
1889	472,524
1890	520,078
1891	429,681
1892	260,048

Total value of lobster exports in 5 years $2,067,408

THE DEPARTMENT OF FISHERIES.

Reference has already been made to the " Fisheries Commission," now named the " Department of Fisheries." Without a fuller account of its objects and methods of working, the description of the fisheries would be incomplete ; as it may fairly be regarded as the most important organization connected with these industries.

NEGLECTED FISHERIES.

It is curious to find that in Newfoundland, one of the greatest fishing countries in the world, hardly any attention was given to the supervision and regulation of the fisheries on which the great mass of its people were dependent for their bread, until about five years ago. In point of fact, these industries were left to take care of themselves. There was a popular belief that the fisheries were inexhaustible; that all which man could take from the waters would make no impression on their swarming fish-life. Good and bad seasons might come and go, but these were believed to be purely providential, and quite beyond human control. Nothing that man could do would have any effect, either to help or mar the fisheries. Fish were considered to be too prolific to permit the supposition that their number could be perceptibly diminished by human means.

COD FISHERIES DECLINING.

These proved to be the dreams of ignorance which the stern logic of events at length dissipated. Fisheries began to fail, especially around the shore. Several of the large bays, where cod were once abundant, such as Conception Bay, no longer yielded enough fish to repay the toils of the fishermen or give them bread; and they were driven to seek new fishing-grounds far from their homes. The waters were becoming depleted in many localities, and the catch in others was greatly reduced. The number of those engaged in fishing had doubled, and improved implements of all kinds had been introduced; and still no more fish was taken than formerly.

HON. A. W. HARVEY'S GOOD WORK.

These alarming facts began to impress the minds of thoughtful men, and to suggest the necessity of taking prompt and energetic measures to meet the evil and to protect and restore the fisheries. In this connection it is but just to refer to the able and praiseworthy labours of the Hon. A. W. Harvey, a member of the Legislative Council. He had made an intelligent study of the fisheries, and became profoundly impressed with the dangers which beset these industries, from the causes already referred to, and with the necessity for energetic action. In his place in the Council he had for many years kept the matter before that body and the general public. In able and exhaustive speeches, he again and again urged on the Government the vital importance of securing a thorough investigation of the fisheries, and of establishing a Bureau for their supervision. He pointed out that while all other fishing countries had found it necessary to organize departments for the collection of information regarding fish and fisheries, with a view to their conservation and supervision by wise legal enactments, we were in utter ignorance of the proper means for protecting them and turning them to a more profitable account ; while we had no scientific knowledge which would enable us to ascertain the causes of their decline and apply the proper remedies. He advocated strongly the artificial propagation of fish for restocking exhausted salt-water areas and rivers. Too much praise cannot be accorded this gentleman for the earnestness and ability with which he urged these views on the Legislature and the country. In due time his labours brought forth fruit, and he took an active part in the practical application of his views.

The author of this volume may be permitted, without incurring the charge of egotism, to say that he had long taken an interest in matters bearing on the fisheries, and that he had written extensively in support of the same views, having given considerable attention to the study of fish-life and the prosecution of the fisheries in Newfoundland. He too had urged the necessity of a Fisheries' Commission and the application of science to the fisheries.

COMMISSION APPOINTED.

At length, in 1888, the Legislature sanctioned the nomination of a "Fisheries' Commission" to make inquiries into the constitution and working of Fisheries Departments in other countries, with the view to the establishment of a similar Department in Newfoundland. The Hon. A. W. Harvey was requested to act as chairman of the Commission, and the present writer became its secretary.

WORK BEGUN.

The first step taken by the Commission was to issue a circular asking for information, which was sent to the Department of

Fisheries in the Dominion of Canada, in the United States, in England and Norway. To these courteous replies were received, embodying much valuable information. The Commission presented their first report to the Legislature in March, 1888; and in June, 1889, an Act was passed constituting a Fisheries Commission, with the same officials at its head, and defining their powers and duties. The Legislature also granted a sum of money, to be expended by the Commission in carrying on their operations.

SUPERINTENDENT OF FISHERIES.

The first step taken by the Commission was the appointment of a properly qualified Superintendent of Fisheries. They were fortunate enough to secure the services of Mr. Adolph Nielsen, Assistant Inspector of Norwegian Fisheries, a gentleman of high character, who possessed a thorough scientific and practical knowledge of fish and fisheries, and was familiar with the whole process of the artificial propagation of fish. Since his arrival in Newfoundland, he has devoted himself to the arduous duties of his office with a zeal, energy and ability which merit the highest commendation, and which have won the entire confidence of the Commission, and of those most deeply interested in the fisheries. His tact, good sense and kindness have done much to overcome the prejudices of the fishermen which they not unnaturally entertained towards new ideas and methods which threatened to upset their time-honoured traditions. They are now beginning to regard him as their benefactor. Mr. Neilsen became, of course, the right arm of the Commission; and the great value of his services is now universally admitted. He devoted himself to a thorough investigation of all departments of our fisheries, with the view of ascertaining the causes of their decline, where such had taken place, and applying the proper correctives. He also devoted much attention to the imperfect methods of cure and packing which were too often practised, pointing out and urging improvements. He drew up a paper on "The Cure of Codfish and Herrings," which the Commission published and circulated widely among the fishermen. Its value may be judged of from the fact that the Irish Department of Fisheries asked and obtained permission to re-print it, for the information of the Irish fishermen; and that the French at St. Pierre have translated and published it. The annual reports of the Commission which are printed and widely circulated each year, furnish ample details of the work done and embody all the valuable information regarding the fisheries which has been collected.

WHAT THE COMMISSION HAS DONE.

What are the results of the labours of the Commission which has now been in operation for five years? It would be impossible, in a work such as this, to do more than indicate very briefly what has been accomplished. First of all, it has been the aim of the Commission, as their investigations proceeded and accurate information accumulated, to draw up a code of rules and regulations which would conserve and improve the fisheries, and prevent injurious and destructive methods of fishing, and to make due provision for the enforcement of such regulations. This was a task of great difficulty and requiring much careful consideration. Though not yet completed, and though the rules still require amendments, it may be safely affirmed that already the fisheries of Newfoundland are as well regulated as those of any other country. The fishermen are gradually learning that these rules are devised for their benefit, and that of future generations; and are increasingly giving them a willing obedience. Wardens are appointed whose duty it is to enforce these rules and to bring offenders to justice.

ARTIFICIAL PROPAGATION OF COD AND LOBSTERS.

The Commission, however, did not confine their efforts to such investigations. They entered from the very outset on the artificial propagation of codfish and lobsters with the view of re-stocking wholly or partially exhausted sea-areas, and of sustaining the stock where it was declining under adverse influences. This was a most important departure and far-reaching in its consequences, if successful. If by artificial means the fishing grounds, which are more or less depleted of cod or other food-fishes, can be restored or more than restored to their former productiveness, and if it is possible to counteract the effects of heavy drafts, by breeding salt-water as well as fresh-water fishes, on a large scale, then a most important work is done, the value of which it would be difficult to over-estimate. Then sea-farming becomes a science, and the stock of commercial fishes may be increased indefinitely with as great certainty as cattle and sheep can be increased on land. Pisciculture promises to accomplish this; and in Newfoundland, the great experiment, on a gigantic scale, is proceeding. Other fishing countries are engaged in the same experiments; but in some respects, this country has taken the lead and maintains a supremacy.

DILDO HATCHERY.

The first step taken in the new departure was the erection of a Cod Hatchery at Dildo Island in Trinity Bay, in which also the artificial propagation of lobsters was carried on. This establishment was fitted up by Mr. Nielsen with all modern improvements and nothing was left undone to secure success. Many difficulties were encountered, and many obstacles overcome. The following figures show the number of cod ova hatched at Dildo and planted in the waters of Trinity Bay, during the four years in which the hatchery has been in operation:—

Years.	No. of codfish hatched.
1890	17,000,000
1891	39,550,000
1892	165,254,000
1893	201,435,000
Total planted	423,439,000

The following figures show the number of lobsters hatched in the same establishment during five years:—

Years.	Lobster ova hatched.
1889	4,039,000
1890	15,070,800
1891	10,274,200
1892	2,500,000
1893	1,095,000
Total	32,889,000

THE FISHERIES.

FLOATING INCUBATORS.

It is, however, in hatching lobsters by means of floating incubators, which were invented by Mr. Neilsen, that the greatest success has been achieved. This wonderful invention, which is simple, inexpensive, and easily worked, has placed Newfoundland far ahead of all other countries in the artificial propagation of these valuable crustaceans which are everywhere becoming scarcer, year after year, and in some lobster-producing countries are threatened with extinction. For four years Neilsen's floating incubators have been worked under the Fisheries Commission, in nearly all the large bays of the island. The following table shows the results :—

Years.	No. of lobsters hatched and planted.
1890	390,934,000
1991	541,195,000
1892	427,285,000
1883	517,353,000
Total	1,886,767,000

SAVING OF THE LOBSTER OVA.

It is to be observed that this enormous number of lobsters were hatched from ova collected at the various lobster factories where they would otherwise have been destroyed. The precious life-germs are saved, placed in the incubators, brought to life, and after a time liberated in the waters. The invention is of immense value not only to Newfoundland but to every country where lobsters are found. To this colony it will be worth many millions of dollars.

RESULTS.

Time is required to thoroughly test and determine the value of cod and lobster propagation, as the young cod requires three or four years to come to maturity ; and the lobster from five to seven years. It may be mentioned, however, that in Trinity Bay large shoals of small codfish and fry have been seen by the fishermen in places where they were never seen before and in such abundance that they must be the produce of the hatchery.

Similarly, vast numbers of small lobsters, from two to five inches in length, have been observed in the neighbourhood of the hatching incubators, and evidently the results of their operations. These are hopeful signs in regard to the ultimate success of these important experiments.

CURE OF HERRINGS.

It may be mentioned that the Commission devoted much attention to the improvement of the cure of herrings, as the article sent to foreign markets had deteriorated in quality and in many cases ceases to bring remunerative prices. Under Mr. Neilsen's supervision, a few hundred barrels were cured and packed according to his own method, and then shipped both to European and American markets. In every instance they brought very satisfactory prices, greatly in advance of those formerly obtained, thus demonstrating what care and skill can do in enhancing the value of this industry. He also erected a smoke-house in Placentia Bay, and turned out kippered, bloaters, and smoked herrings of the finest quality which brought excellent prices. The impulse thus given to the herring industry will greatly enhance its value.

THE FREEZING BARREL.

One other important improvement introduced by Mr. Neilsen may be mentioned. Quite recently he exhibited a freezing barrel to a number of our fishermen and "planters" in St. John's, Harbour Grace and Carbonear, designed for the freezing and preservation of bait in the prosecution of the cod fishery. One of the greatest difficulties the fisherman has to encounter is the want of bait. At times it is plentiful, and at other times the bait fishes, such as herrings, caplin and squids, disappear and the fisherman is idle ashore from the want of bait. The codfish are plentiful in the waters, but there is no bait. It often happens that a third of the fishing season is lost in this way. If then when bait are plentiful they could be frozen and preserved for times of scarcity, it is evident that the season's catch would be greatly increased. The freezing barrel accomplishes this object most effectually. It is so simple that any fisherman, having seen it in operation, can easily fit up one for his own use. All that is needed is an ordinary herring or pork barrel, some ice chopped small and coarse salt. Four wooden flanges are placed inside the barrel, in an oblique direction, so as to mix and rotate the articles to be frozen with the ice and salt, when the barrel is put in motion. The barrel is half filled with alternate layers of ice and salt, the proportions being three parts of ice to one of salt. Then the other half of the barrel is filled with fresh herrings or any other bait fishes; the head is fastened tightly and the barrel is placed on its side and rolled back and forward, at a certain speed, for about fifteen minutes. When the head is removed the fish are found to be frozen as hard as a block of wood. They are then placed in sawdust or dry mould and can be preserved for a month or longer, and used when required. The fisherman need never be without bait and the cost is trifling. The invention is a most valuable one, and will, when generally used, greatly increase the annual catch of codfish. Those who witnessed it in operation were much gratified and pronounced it a complete success. Of course this barrel can be used for freezing any animal substance, such as meats, poultry, game, etc. On an enlarged scale it could be applied to the preservation of fresh fish for use or exportation.

REFRIGERATORS.

In addition to the freezing barrel, Mr. Nielsen, last year, erected at Burin and Presque two refrigerating houses for freezing bait on a large scale, and preserving it in this condition for the use of the fishermen. In the freezing chamber twenty-four degrees of frost are obtained, which is sufficient for freezing any kind of bait. Complete success was reached, the bait being frozen as hard almost as rock, and can be kept for any length of time. These are intended as model refrigerating houses, which capitalists engaged in the fisheries may re-produce all round the coast and at each of the large fishing centres. With these and the freezing barrel, when both are brought into general use, the poorest fisherman need never be without bait. Herein we have another illustration of what science can do for the improvement of the fisheries. When, in addition to these inventions, we take into account the possible developments of pisciculture we see that aquaculture may yet become only second to agriculture in increasing the supplies of human food.

Since the foregoing was written regarding the hatching of codfish, the following appeared, under date June 19th, 1894, in the daily newspapers of St. John's, and greatly strengthens the hope of a successful issue in this new departure :—

"MILLIONS OF CODFISH—GREAT SUCCESS OF COD HATCHING AT DILDO.

"The grand experiment of re-stocking the waters of Trinity Bay by the artificial propagation of codfish, which has been going on for four years, has resulted in a magnificent success. All doubts and fears are at length dissipated, and cavillers may now hide their diminished heads. The news from Dildo is of the most gratifying description. Codfish, one, two and three years old, are in immense numbers; and older fish are visible among them. Yesterday morning the water was very calm, and the fishermen could see them at the bottom in a solid, thick mass all around and outside the island. The oldest fishermen declare they never, in all their lives, saw so much fish in the bay. One man, named John Pretty, had his cod-trap at Dildo Island. He overhauls it three times a day, and brings in a skiff-load every time, in addition to what the hatchery takes from him of spawning fish. He says he could haul it every hour and have just as much fish in it every time. Mr. Nielsen has been only two days at work and already he has four hundred and fifty fine spawning fish in the pond, with every prospect of soon getting enough fish to fill every available space in the hatchery with ova. It may be imagined with what delight he finds his toils and anxieties so nobly rewarded. What has been done in Trinity Bay can be done in every bay in the island. The depleted waters can be restored to their former abundance, and, as in the "good old times," the fishermen will be able to load their boats within sight of their own doors. Ere long, every bay will have one or two cod hatcheries in operation. Lobster hatching is equally successful. The freezing barrel, which Mr. Nielsen lately exhibited, if generally introduced, will be worth millions to the country. No fisherman need ever be without bait."

Later accounts say the fishermen of the place are delighted with the success, and declare they can catch as much fish as they like. Mr. Nielsen has 2,000 spawners in his pond and can fill every available space in the hatchery with ova. He hopes to plant three hundred millions this year.

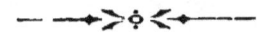

CHAPTER VIII.

INTERNATIONAL TREATIES.

THE FRENCH SHORE QUESTION.

It does not fall within the scope of a Handbook to discuss at any great length the "never-ending, still beginning" "French Shore Question." Only a few of the salient points connected with it can be referred to very briefly. It has been so long and so often debated that the subject is worn thread-bare.

TREATY RIGHTS OF THE FRENCH.

Among Great Britain's forty colonies the position of Newfoundland is in one respect unique. The sovereignty of the entire territory belongs exclusively to Britain; but the French, since the year 1713, have had the right of fishing along more than half the entire shores of the island, and of using that portion of the coasts for such purposes as may be necessary in the prosecution of their fishery. In addition to this important privilege, the French have had ceded to them possession of the two small islands of St. Pierre and Miquelon, at the entrance of Fortune Bay, "as a shelter for their fishermen," the only condition attached to the possession of them being that no fortifications should be erected, and only such buildings as are necessary in carrying on the fishery. The line of coast to which these treaty rights apply extends from Cape Ray, at the south-western extremity of the island, around the western, northern and north-eastern shores, as far south as Cape St. John, being fully half the entire coast of the island, and that by far the most fertile and valuable portion. The French have no right to occupy permanently or settle any portion of this shore, or to erect any buildings except such huts and scaffolds as may be necessary for curing and drying their fish. Their fishermen are not allowed to winter in the island.

TREATIES NOW ANTIQUATED.

At the time when the French obtained these treaty privileges, the population of the whole island was very small, and but few British subjects had settled on this portion of the coast. It was also believed then that this section of the country was worthless, as far as its soil was concerned, and that it contained nothing valuable. These notions proved to be unfounded. As years rolled on it was found that this half of the island, with a coast-line of 790 miles, contained large tracts of fertile land, valuable forests, coal beds and rich mineral deposits. The climate of the western coast is also superior to that of the eastern and southern, being free from fogs and the influence of the Arctic Current, so that it is much more favourable for colonization. Circumstances have entirely altered since these ancient treaties were made, and they are no longer applicable to the condition of the colony. Their abrogation or modification is urgently needed.

TREATY OF UTRECHT.

These concessions were first made to the French by the Treaty of Utrecht, in the year 1713. It stipulated that "The Island of Newfoundland, with the adjacent islands, should belong of right wholly to Great Britain;" that it shall be allowed to the subjects of France "to catch fish and dry them on land on that part only of the coast" defined in the treaty; and that "it shall not be lawful for the subjects of France to fortify any place in the said island of Newfoundland, or to erect any buildings there besides stages made of boards, and huts necessary and usual for drying of fish, or to resort to the said island beyond the time necessary for fishing and drying of fish."

TREATY OF 1763.

The next treaty dealing with this matter was that of Paris, 1763. It renewed and confirmed the previous treaty, and added the following article:—"The King of Great Britain cedes the islands of St. Pierre and Miquelon, in full right to His Most Christian Majesty, to serve as a shelter to French fishermen; and His Most Christian Majesty engages not to fortify the said islands, to erect no buildings upon them but merely for the convenience of the fishery, and to keep upon them a guard of fifty men only for the police." These conditions have been entirely disregarded by the French who have made St. Pierre a Colony and erected buildings of all kinds.

TREATY OF VERSAILLES.

The Treaty of Versailles, 1783, confirmed the previous treaties. Further: a Declaration was attached to this treaty in which His Britannic Majesty "in order that the fishermen of the two nations might not give cause for daily quarrels" engaged to "take the most positive measures for preventing his subjects from interrupting in any manner, by their competition, the fishery of the French during the temporary exercise of it which is granted to them, upon the coast of the island of Newfoundland; but he will for this purpose cause the fixed settlements which shall be formed there to be removed."

The Treaty of Paris, 1815, confirmed the previous arrangements, and no modification or alteration has since been made."

INJURIES CAUSED BY TREATIES.

The line of coast to which these treaties apply extends, as already stated, from Cape Ray, at the south-western extremity of the island, around the western, northern and north-eastern shores to Cape St. John. This is, in regard to its soil, climate and forest and mineral wealth, incomparably superior to the rest of the island. Had it not been by these treaties practically locked up, it would long since have been colonized, and the western coast would have been occupied by a fishing, farming, lumbering and mining population, and thriving towns and villages would have sprung up along its entire extent. To the colony these unfortunate concessions have been most injurious and have retarded its progress more than all other causes put together. The practical effect has been to exclude the people from the fairest half of their own territory; to prevent the investment there of capital in industrial enterprises; so that, for the most part, it has remained in the condition of a primeval wilderness, and the population have been cooped up in the more barren and least desirable half of the island. Of all their "historic misfortunes" this has been incomparably the greatest. Of all grievances of which the people have had reason to complain, this is the one which most loudly calls for redress.

EXCLUSIVE OF CONCURRENT RIGHTS.

Had the just and fair interpretation of the language of those treaties been insisted on and carried into practical effect from the outset by the Imperial Government, and had the unreasonable demands of the French, which were unwarranted by the terms of these documents, been promptly and steadily repudiated, the colony would not have been called upon to endure such hardships and losses, although the legitimate treaty-rights of the French would still have been felt as an embarrassment and a hindrance in the development of the natural resources of the island. It is true that the French have no territorial rights, and are prohibited from forming any fixed settlements; it is also true that their right of fishing along the line of coast is not *exclusive* but *concurrent*, and that their claim to an exclusive fishery has never been recognized by England, and has been and continues to be most emphatically repudiated by the colony itself. Still the French have so pertinaciously and unweariedly endeavoured to exercise exclusive fishing rights, and have shown such jealousy regarding them, that they have succeeded in practically preventing Newfoundland fishermen from exercising the concurrent right which the treaties warrant, and which they justly claim, by fishing within the treaty bounds. Here it is that England has failed in her duty to her colonial offshoot. Her statesmen have always recognized this concurrent right of fishing and utterly refused to admit of an exclusive right on the part of the French; yet, dreading the results of quarrels arising between the fishermen of the two nations when prosecuting their calling in the same waters, they have discountenanced all attempts at fishing on the part of Newfoundland fishermen along that portion of the shore on which the French have treaty rights.

The consequence has been that the concurrent right fell into abeyance, and for fishing purposes that portion of the coast was practically closed against the people to whom the soil of the island belonged.

EXTRAVAGANT CLAIMS.

This was not all. The French not only claimed and tried to enforce an exclusive right to the fishery, but they preferred more extravagant claims to prevent the inhabitants of Newfoundland from occupying the land within the limits defined by the treaties, whether for agricultural, mining or other purposes, thus virtually exercising sovereignty over half the island. It is true they did not pretend to occupy the land themselves, except for fishery purposes ; but they pursued only too successfully the "dog in the manger" policy, of preventing any one else from doing so. They preferred this claim on the ground that the occupation of the land by the people of the island would be an infringement of their fishery privileges. Here again the Imperial authorities inflicted a cruel wrong upon the colony by temporizing with these unfounded claims, and refusing for a long time to permit the local government to issue land grants in the disputed district, while at the same time they repudiated the French claims and declared the sovereignty of the territory to be vested solely in England.

BRITISH SETTLERS INCREASE.

Meantime, however, in spite of all difficulties and discouragements a numerous population settled on this shore. They now number nearly 12,000 people. Their condition was for a long period very miserable. They were in the position of squatters, having no title to their property ; were living without the guardianship of law ; had no roads, schools, magistrates to punish crimes, or any of the ordinary appliances of civilization. They became increasingly a source of anxiety to the local government. At length, in 1881, the representations and remonstrances of the local legislature were listened to ; the local government was empowered to make grants of land ; but these were made subject to the treaty rights of the French; magistrates were appointed; custom houses erected, and provision made for the representation of the residents, who were to send two members to the local parliament. This was a considerable step in advance. Law and order were established; the region became an integral part of Newfoundland; and the Government was empowered to exercise territorial jurisdiction over the whole, subject of course to existing treaty rights. The boon should have been granted fifty years before.

PERILS OF THE SITUATION.

The vexed question, however, of concurrent or exclusive fishing rights remains, and is as far as ever from settlement. The French endeavour to enforce their claims to an exclusive fishery as pertinaciously as ever; and the peace of the two nations is constantly in peril in consequence of these conflicting views regarding the provisions of the treaties. England, and her subjects in the Colony, maintain that they have a concurrent right to these fisheries, provided they do not " interrupt" the operations of the French fishermen. The Crown lawyers of England have declared that there is nothing in the treaties to prevent British subjects from taking fish at any places not actually occupied by French fishermen, and provided they do not disturb Frenchmen in their *bona fide* fishing operations.

VIEWS OF BRITISH STATESMEN.

The ablest British statesmen of former times, such as Lord Palmerston in his famous despatch of July 10th, 1838, have refused to acknowledge that the treaties conveyed any exclusive right to the French, and declared that had such been the intention terms far more definite and exact would have been used. In 1886 the French Government once more put forward their claims to exclusive rights, threatening to confiscate the gear of any who were found fishing on that part of the coast; to disregard the jurisdiction of local magistrates; to prevent the working of mines, and to protect French fishermen in taking salmon and lobsters as well as cod. To these preposterous claims and threats

Lord Rosebery, who was then Foreign Minister, replied in firm and dignified terms. The following is an extract from his despatch: "I have no desire to re-open the discussion on the numerous points in dispute; but I cannot refrain from deprecating more particularly the claim put forward by your government to ignore, during the fishing season the territorial jurisdiction flowing from the sovereign rights of the British Crown over the whole of the Island of Newfoundland, expressly conferred by the terms of the 13th article of the Treaty of Utrecht; nor can I pass in silence the reiterated assertion, in your note, of an exclusive right of fishing on the part of the coast on which the French treaty rights exist. There can be no doubt that the inhabitants must not 'interrupt by their competition' the French fishermen; but Her Majesty's Government can hardly believe that the French Government could intend to apply to them the term 'foreigner;' or to question the right of the colonists to procure the means of subsistence by fishing on their own coast, so long as they do not interfere with the Treaty Rights of the French fishermen. Such a claim has no precedent in history, and would be not only repugnant to reason, but opposed to the practice of years, and to the actual terms of the Declaration of Versailles, which provide that the old methods of fishing 'shall not be deviated from by either party,' showing conclusively that the French right to the fishery is not an exclusive one."

THE LOBSTER DISPUTE.

In 1889 a new and very serious complication arose in connection with the French-shore question, which "made confusion worse confounded." On the treaty shore the British residents had several years before commenced the new industry of canning lobsters. It prospered so well that by 1889 some forty lobster factories had been erected on the shore. Then it suddenly occurred to the French that they had a right to share in this industry, and they erected a small number of factories. Their views expanded rapidly, and speedily they preferred an exclusive claim to the lobster fishery and began to use active measures for the removal of British lobster factories, claiming that they were an interference with their treaty rights and that they required the places occupied by them for their own uses. This preposterous claim, so entirely unwarranted by the letter or spirit of the treaties, proved to be the "last straw" in the case of the patient, long-suffering Newfoundlanders. Public feeling was aroused and soon reached fever heat. Mass meetings were held in the capital and elsewhere, and delegates were despatched in 1890 to Canada and England to appeal to the people of both countries for sympathy and assistance in their struggle to get rid of these French claims. The agitation was not confined to the lobster question. The whole bearing of these antiquated treaties, which for a century and a-half had been an incubus on the colony, retarding its progress, was now discussed in the light of recent events. The grievances of years had now become intolerable; and it is not wonderful to find that a deeper conviction than ever before took hold of the minds of the people that these French rights in Newfoundland were incompatible with the prosperity and progress of the colony and that they must be terminated, not by a violation of the treaties, but by an equitable purchase or compensation, or exchange of territory, as might be agreed on.

COLONISTS APPEAL TO ENGLAND.

To the Parliament and people of England the colonists appealed for justice. England had originally made these treaties and she alone could solve the difficulties. This coast had really become of little or no value to the French. Their fishery had declined till now only seven or eight fishing vessels, manned by three or four hundred men, visited the coast annually. For the sake of this handful of fishermen this half of the island, rich in a variety of resources—agricultural, lumbering and mining—must be locked up. While useless to the French, these resources were invaluable to the people of the colony. This was such a manifest grievance to the colonists, and such a preposterous absurdity in an economical point of view, that the appeals of the delegates both in Canada and England met with a warm sympathetic response, and the press of both countries sustained their claims. It seemed but simple justice that the colonists should be masters in their own territory and free to develope its resources.

LOBSTERS NOT INCLUDED IN TREATIES.

But the French had to be reckoned with and they refused to yield an inch on the lobster question. In vain did the British diplomatists remonstrate and point out that when the treaties were made and gave the French the liberty of "taking and drying fish," lobster canning was unknown, and lobsters could not have been included; that only cod-fishing could have been in view when "taking and drying fish" was specified, lobsters not being fish, and canning a very different process from "drying;" that lobster factories are not the "temporary huts and stages" allowed in the treaties, but permanent buildings which the French were forbidden to erect. The French still obstinately clung to their claim; and probably wearied with their pertinacity, the British Government offered to submit the lobster question to arbitration. This temporizing policy paved the way for the host of troubles which speedily followed.

MODUS VIVENDI.

The French accepted arbitration; and without submitting the matter to the local legislature, the British Government arranged with the French a *modus vivendi* pending the results of the arbitration. As soon as this was made known popular indignation burst forth afresh. The Legislature in the Session which opened March 6th, 1890, unanimously adopted resolutions condemning the *modus vivendi*; and mass meetings of the people followed denouncing it in the strongest terms. It was too late, however, the British Government having been committed to the arrangement; so that the *modus vivendi* went into operation and the naval officers engaged in the protection of the fisheries received instructions to enforce it.

MODUS VIVENDI OBJECTIONABLE.

The most objectionable feature in this *modus vivendi* was that it gave formal permission to the French to erect lobster factories on certain conditions, thus apparently admitting their claims, and casting a doubt on the *exclusive* rights of the colonists to all the lobsters on the French shore, as to which no doubt whatever existed in the minds of British statesmen and lawyers. This was done, moreover, without the knowledge or consent of the colonists, and in opposition to the position taken previously by the British Government. It had the appearance of conceding to the French certain territorial rights which they never enjoyed before, as lobster factories were permanent establishments. The *modus* allowed all lobster factories in existence on July 1st, 1889, both French and British, to continue, pending an arbitration, but prohibited all new erections, unless by joint consent of the commanders of British and French naval stations.

STRANGE DISCOVERY.

The unpalatable arrangement, however, had to be enforced by the naval officers on the station. Ere long a strange and startling discovery was made, namely, that the Act of Parliament enabling British Governments to enforce these treaties, by orders issued to naval officers, had expired by virtue of one of its own provisions in the year 1834, and had never been renewed; so that from that time till the present no legal authority had existed for the enforcement of Her Majesty's instructions to naval commanders upon the coast of Newfoundland.

MR. JAMES BAIRD VERSUS SIR BALDWIN WALKER.

It was an unpleasant surprise to the British Government to be reminded of this fact, and told that their illegal enforcements had been going on for 56 years. But to make such a discovery, which no one at first credited or even noticed when announced, was one thing; and to work it out practically for the benefit of the colony, was quite another thing. Mr. James Baird, a merchant of St. John's, who was embued with a large amount of public spirit, resolved to bring the matter to a practical issue. One of his lobster factories on the French shore had been seized, as he believed, illegally, under the provisions of the *modus vivendi*, and operations were ordered to be discontinued. Mr. Baird at once took an action against the British naval officer—Sir Baldwin Walker—who issued the order, estimating his damages at $5,000. The case was argued at great length and with much legal acumen before the Supreme Court of Newfoundland, with the result that judgment was given in favour of Mr. Baird. The officer had no legal authority to confiscate the factory.

COERCION BILL IN THE HOUSE OF LORDS.

The British Government then, for the first time, realized that they had no legal authority for the orders issued to the naval commanders for the enforcement of these treaties. The treaties, however, were binding, and nothing remained but to ask Parliament for power to enforce them. Accordingly a Bill was introduced into the House of Lords for this purpose. It was a re-enactment of the provisions of an old Act 5, Geo. IV., with a new application.

DELEGATION TO PARLIAMENT.

As soon as its nature and scope were made known popular feeling was aroused afresh in the Colony. The Legislature of Newfoundland at once despatched a joint delegation composed of members of both Chambers, to present a remonstrance to the British Parliament with the view of arresting an obnoxious coercive measure which was regarded as an interference with the rights and liberties of the people of the Colony. The names of these delegates deserve to be placed on record as they discharged their duties ably and fought the battle of their country bravely. The following is a list of these deputies:—From the Legislative Council—Hon. A. W. Harvey and Hon. M. Monroe; From the House of Assembly—Sir William V. Whiteway, Premier; Hon. Speaker Emerson, and Mr. A. B. Morine, Leader of the Opposition.

DELEGATES AT THE BAR OF THE LORDS.

The delegation claimed to be heard at the Bar of the House of Lords, and this rare privilege was granted. Then occurred that memorable historic scene when the representatives of England's oldest Colony stood before the most noble and august assembly in the world, and in a document marked by high ability, moderation and wisdom, set forth the long array of their country's wrongs and grievances, in words which made a deep impression on that great assemblage. The House of Lords was crowded to an extent rarely witnessed before. The appeal of the delegates was listened to with deep sympathetic interest; and generous applause was given to it by speakers of both political parties. The press of England joined in approval of the dignified and judicious position assumed by the delegation. They wisely offered, on behalf of the Legislature by whom they had been accredited, to pass the necessary enactments to enable England to fulfil her treaty obligations. The obnoxious measure before the House was then withdrawn, arrangements were made for arriving at an agreement between the British Government and the delegates as to the nature of the enactment which the Colonial Legislature would be asked to sanction for the enforcement of the treaties. In regard to what followed it is only necessary to say that misunderstandings arose. A complete and satisfactory enactment has not yet been passed by the local legislature; but such an understanding has been reached as has removed many difficulties out of the way, and leaves little doubt that a measure will ere long receive the sanction of the Imperial authorities and the local legislature, which will secure the objects in view. Meantime, the *modus vivendi* has been continued, by local enactment, till the close of 1895. This will give time for further negotiations.

HARDSHIPS OF TREATIES.

It is very clear from the foregoing narrative of events, that this "French Shore Question" is about as far as ever from a solution. What the people of Newfoundland want is to be made masters in their own territory, and to get rid of these French claims. They have no wish to disturb the French in their possession of St. Pierre and Miquelon, or to interfere with their fishery on the Banks for which these islands furnish a basis. But they keenly feel the injustice of shutting up half of an island larger than

Ireland in order that six or seven small French fishing vessels may use it for drying their fish for three months in the year.

THE FRENCH REFUSE COMPROMISES.

It is necessary, however, to look existing facts in the face. France has again and again declared, through the mouth of her foremost statesmen, that she will not accept a money compensation or even a territorial exchange for her treaty rights in Newfoundland. They say no French Government dare propose any such arrangement in face of the popular indignation it would kindle. The national sentiment will not allow them to listen to such a proposal as giving up the last relic of French Empire in the New World. The maintenance of the French navy is somehow immovably associated in the Gallic mind with the nursery for her seamen which France holds in these waters. It may be too that her statesmen look upon these treaty rights as affording them a fine vantage ground in dealing with England on the Egyptian question, or other disputed subjects.

DIFFICULTIES OF SETTLEMENT.

Whatever may be the explanation, France will not relax her hold on Newfoundland ; and further, except by going to war, which no one desires and all parties shrink from, England has no power to compel her. The published correspondence between the two Governments shows that English statesmen have spared no efforts to bring about a settlement of this old dispute favourable to the colony ; but have laboured in vain. France is impracticable, and will concede nothing. Both England and the colonists are willing to submit the whole questions connected with the treaties to arbitration ; but France will accept arbitration only on the lobster claim. This does not indicate that she has full confidence in the justice of her demands on other points, or in her own interpretation of the treaties. With all his diplomatic skill, Lord Salisbury has failed to bring her to reason. He has been met at all points by a *non possumus*.

CO-OPERATION WITH ENGLAND.

What is the wisest policy for Newfoundland to adopt in the present crisis in her affairs ? The colonists have amply vindicated their rights as freemen by making known their grievances and wrongs, and they have won the sympathy of England and the respect of her leading statesmen of both political parties. They may rest assured, therefore, that as soon as opportunity presents itself their wrongs will be righted. But England cannot accomplish impossibilities. She cannot disregard her treaty obligations, and she has no power to compel France to forego her treaty rights. England is in honour bound to enforce observance in Newfoundland of her treaty engagements, whatever they may be. The despatch received from Lord Ripon, Secretary of State for the Colonies, in March last, indicates an earnest desire to adopt conciliatory measures, and to make such concessions in regard to the provisions of an Act to be submitted to the local Legislature, as will smooth the way for its acceptance. Under such circumstances, it will be evident to most thinking men that the duty and interest of the colony lie in co-operation with the Imperial authorities, both in securing a proper measure for the enforcement of the treaties and also in the settlement of the whole question in the future. The present time calls for moderation, self-control, and the exercise of that good sense which will look facts in the face calmly, and not indulge in hysterical demands for the immediate abrogation of all French rights, refusing every compromise which falls short of this. Nothing can be gained by shrieking for such extreme measures as tearing up the treaties, and the immediate withdrawal of the French.

SELF-RESTRAINT AND PATIENCE.

Whatever may have been the conduct of the Imperial Mother towards the first-born of her colonies, in the rough days of the past, she has now nothing but the kindest intentions and the most sincere good will. She has every desire to atone for the harshnesses and negligence of the past, and to help us in our hour of need. We may learn a lesson from the conduct of Canada in dealing with the Behring Sea trouble. She trusted the Imperial Authorities and cordially co-operated with them, in a spirit of "sweet reasonableness;" and the result has been an arbitration which secures for Canada all that could be fairly expected. If the colonists are patient and wise, while firmly holding on to their rights, the day may not be distant when all present difficulties may admit of an easy solution.

NEW RAILWAY AS A FACTOR.

To the present writer it seems that the new line of railway is destined to be an important factor in the settlement of the French Shore Question. Once those solitudes are peopled by a busy thriving population— farming, mining, lumbering, manufacturing,—once the smoke of homesteads fills the air and the whistle of the locomotive is heard amid the " forests primeval," our French fishing friends will find that there is no room for them ; and the last pale ghosts of the old treaties will vanish for ever. It may be found that the great innovator—the railway—is destined to make Newfoundlanders masters in their own house.

Before closing this chapter it may be well to allude to another serious evil inflicted on the colony by the concessions already described. St. Pierre, which at the nearest point is but fifteen miles from the Newfoundland shores, has long been a smuggling centre, very large quantities of wine, brandy, rum, tobacco, tea, sugar, drapery and other goods, are every year smuggled into the southern and western portion of the island. The revenue is is thus defrauded ; the honest traders are placed at a disadvantage ; and the worst of all, the people are demoralized. So many small vessels are constantly running to St. Pierre, carrying bait for the French Bankers, and bringing back contraband goods, that it is found to be quite impossible to prevent smuggling on a large scale. The evil might be checked by a British Consul resident at St. Pierre ; but though asked for, again and again, the French steadily refuse to permit a consul to exercise his functions on their island. Doubtless the French traders find it profitable to supply the smugglers, and do not want to be disturbed. This grievance has long been felt, but no redress has ever been attempted. Taking into account the whole effects of these treaties, it is not wonderful that the colonists should have at times discovered impatience, and always cherished an irritable discontent with their hard lot.

THE WESTMINSTER REVIEW ON THE SITUATION.

Subjoined are a few extracts from an able article in the *Westminster Review* for April, 1892. The writer, Mr. E. R. Spearman, is thoroughly in sympathy with Newfoundlanders in their hard struggles :—" It behoves Englishmen to make themselves masters of the whole story of the Newfoundland difficulty, and to be thus prepared to deal with it intelligently whenever the crisis comes. To begin with, it must be understood by Englishmen that the great bulk of Frenchmen do not care two straws about Newfoundland itself, but do care a great deal about other sore subjects of controversy with England's empire elsewhere, and so seize on any available grievance like Newfoundland to manifest international ill-will whenever the Gallic cock desires to give the English lion a prod with his angry spurs." * * * "Though enough physical mists surround Newfoundland, there is still no real reason why any political mists should envelope it, so far as Englishmen are concerned. Every verse in the great epic of Newfoundland should be fresh in every Englishman's brain, for it is that epic which marks his race's march to world-wide empire and glories unequalled in the record of mankind."

ENGLAND'S NEGLECT AND CRUELTY.

"England is a cruel mother. Most of her colonial children have been born against her will, and she has often tried to strangle them, both before and after birth. Though thus begotten, they strangely enough have invariably regarded their parent with unquenchable love, seeking her favour with rich gifts and valuable services, only to be insulted and plundered. Fostering care of her colonies has never been the rule of the greatest colonizing nation the world has ever seen. On the contrary, the colonists have generally been such as have fled from England in bitterness of spirit, and the dominant policy of England has always been to treat these exiles as a herd of condemned spirits, who must not be allowed to escape torture by shifting their quarters, but be harassed without remorse. Hard as has been the measure meted to all her colonies by England, to none has she been a more unnatural parent than to the first-born, the child of her youthful maternity as a breeder of other commonwealths from the bosom of her own, and a child, too, who has paid a tribute for nearly four hundred years far exceeding 'the wealth of Ormuz or of Ind,'—the harvest of the sea, more precious to our island than the diamonds of Golconda or the gold of Peru.

TOILERS OF THE SEA.

"No English Homer has yet arisen to tell the tale of Newfoundland, shrouded in mystery and romance; the daring invasion and vicissitudes of those exhaustless fisheries; the battle of life in that seething cauldron of the North Atlantic—"the Western Ocean" as the sailors say with a shiver and a shrug—where the swelling billows never rest, but cross and criss-cross in roaring rivalries, and the hurricane only slumbers to bring forth the worse dangers of the fog-bank and the iceberg. Fierce as have been during the four centuries the fight for the fisheries by European rivals, their petty racial quarrels sink into insignificance before the general struggle for the harvest. The Atlantic roar hides all minor pipings. The breed of fisher-folk from these deep-sea voyagings consist of the toughest specimens of human endurance. All other dangers which lure men to venture everything for excitement, or for fortune, the torrid heat or Arctic cold, the battle against man or beast, the desert or the jungle, all land adventurers are nothing compared to the daring of the hourly existence of the heroic souls whose lives are cast upon the Banks of Newfoundland. The fishermen may seem wild and reckless, rough and illiterate, but supreme danger and superlative sacrifice breed noble qualities; and beneath the rough exterior of the fisherman you will never fail to find *a man*, no cheap imitation of the genuine article. None but a man can face, for the second time, the frown of the Atlantic—that exhibition of mighty all-consuming power, beside the sober reality of which all the ecstacies of poets and of paintings are puny failures.

NEWFOUNDLAND THE NURSERY OF ENGLAND'S NAVY.

" Among these heroic children of the sea England's sons have always been foremost. We should expect England to be especially proud of such offspring, familiar with their struggles, and ever heedful of their welfare, lending an ear to their claims or complaints before all other suitors. Strange to say it has always been the exact reverse. In the great fisheries, England, from her position and the nature of her people, has taken the leading part. *The fisheries of Newfoundland have been the origin of all our most cherished triumphs. From Newfoundland has been nursed the whole of that navy, mercantile or warlike, which makes us masters of the seas. From Newfoundland has sprung the whole inspiration which has led the English empire to cover the globe.*

" It was pre-eminently the New Found Land — the first garner of English discovery. It was in 1497 that the Anglo-Venetian, John Cabot, with his genuine English sons,

> " Sailed away,
> From Bristol Bay "

to find more gems for the conqueror of Bosworth Field to add to his diadem. John Cabot's voyage was the first of many Bristol expeditions ; and the West Country men came to consider the Banks of Newfoundland as almost their watery homestead.

CAPABILITIES OF THE ISLAND.

" Bearing these facts in mind, one would expect Englishmen to take a most lively interest in a possession next to Ireland in proximity, larger than Ireland in area, and far exceeding Ireland in potential product. Besides the fisheries (which themselves must ever remain unrivalled as a national inheritance, and were the most important gift furnished to Europe by the discovery of the New World) Newfoundland also possesses a perfect treasure-house of minerals,—almost all the metals, and coal and petroleum. In fact there is every reason to expect that the fame of Newfoundland as a mining field would be world-wide, were attention given to developing the resources of the island; but everyone hitherto has considered fishing as the object of their existence; and England has so treated her colony as to prevent the growth of a population extensive enough to attend to all industries opened to man in such a favoured spot. At the present crisis, one of the chief hardships suffered by the Newfoundlanders is interference with any attempt at mining operations by the French patrols, who have in fact, if not in theory, the power foolishly conceded by England, of practically nobbling all industry for about a thousand miles of coast line. In fact the monstrosity of the French case, in this respect, would be ludicrous in its audacity were it not so exasperating."

* * * * * * *

NEWFOUNDLAND ALWAYS BELONGED TO ENGLAND.

"Degenerate indeed must be the Englishmen who read the record and fail to claim the absolute supremacy of English rights in Newfoundland in all particulars. For be it remembered that this early possession has been fortified by uninterrupted occupancy "to make assurance doubly sure." The island has been invaded by the French and others in war-time, *but never conquered*; and such invasions give no shred of title in time of peace. The French visitors have been from the first (as all other foreigners, even from the start,) merely guests on the shores of Newfoundland; and if they become obnoxious, England has every right, moral and legal, to refuse them further hospitality."

ARRANGEMENT OF 1885.

"The French have undoubted claims in Newfoundland; but experience has shown that a continuance of the exercise of these claims is impracticable. They should be bought out in the interests of peace."

* * * * * * *

"It is well to understand that the Newfoundlanders have always been most patient and reasonable. Ignorant people have often called the islanders otherwise, because such people never reflect that the Newfoundlanders, being on the spot, have the best means of judging of the merits of the dispute. Thus the Newfoundlanders have been abused by 'inspired' pens and high officials in England for refusing to accept the treaty of 1885, alleged to be so favourable to the island. The true reason for such a rejection was this: France had, from time immemorial, had more clever surveyors and negotiators than England in those parts. Thus her accomplished French surveyors made a plan which looks delightful on paper to the uninitiated. The English settlers were surrendered parts of the disputed coast; but, here a bit and there a bit was reserved absolutely to France. Now, these bits happened to include all the good harbours of the coast. All settlement and mining ventures would be impossible. No wonder Newfoundlanders rose in wrath against such a sacrifice."

THE END OF THE MATTER.

"Newfoundlanders must be absolutely masters in their own land, and for this happy release they will doubtless be both willing and able to pay a sufficient price. Way back to Edward VI., an Act of Parliament declared the Newfoundland fisheries an unlicensed privilege of every Englishman. We practically allow the said fisheries to be to-day the unlicensed privilege of all mankind. But Newfoundland itself is our own, our eldest born. We should deserve to be wiped away from the list of honourable nations if we do not stand by the island in this hour of her distress."

TREATY OF UTRECHT.

Thirteenth clause of the Treaty of Utrecht (1713) presents in clear and brief terms the whole matters in dispute, and those who wish to understand the French Shore question should never lose sight of it. This treaty was drawn up in English and French and then translated into Latin, in which language it was signed, so that this version is official and authoritative. Here is a correct translation of the 13th clause from the Latin text:—

"The Island called Newfoundland, with the adjacent islands, shall from this time forward belong wholly to Great Britain;

and to that end the town and fortress of Placentia, and whatever other places in the said island are in the possession of the French, shall be yielded and given up within seven months from the ratifications of this treaty, or sooner if possible, by the Most Christian King, his heirs and successors, to those who have a commission from the Queen of Great Britain for that purpose. Nor shall the Most Christian King, his heirs or successors, or any of their subjects, at any time hereafter lay claim to any right to the said island and islands, or any part of it or them. Moreover it shall not be lawful for the subjects of France to fortify any place in the said Island of Newfoundland, or to erect any buildings there besides stages made of boards and huts necessary and usual for drying of fish, or to resort to the said island beyond the time necessary for fishing and drying of fish. But it shall be allowed to the subjects of France to catch fish and to dry them on land, on that part only which stretches from the place called Cape Bonavista to the northern point of the said island, and thence running down by her western side, reaches as far as the place called Pointe Riche. But the island called Cape Breton, as also others both in the mouth of the River St. Lawrence, and in the Gulf of the same name, shall hereafter belong of right to the French, and the Most Christian King shall have all manner of liberty to fortify any place or places there."

FISHERY TREATIES BETWEEN GREAT BRITAIN AND THE UNITED STATES.

The treaties between Great Britain and the United States, bearing on the fisheries in British-American waters—Newfoundland included—have been the subject of lengthened disputes and voluminous diplomatic correspondence, and the difference in opinion regarding their proper construction has given rise to much irritation and international jealousy. The treaty of 1783, which recognized American Independence, in its third article conferred upon the people of the United States the right to take fish of every kind on the Grand Bank and all the other Banks of Newfoundland; also in the Gulf of St. Lawrence, and on such part of the coast of Newfoundland as British fishermen shall use;

but not to dry or cure the same on that island, and also on the coast, bays and creeks of all other of His Britannic Majesty's dominions in America ; also liberty to dry and cure fish in any of the unsettled bays, harbours and creeks of Nova Scotia, Magdalen Islands and Labrador, so long as they remain unsettled.

CONVENTION OF 1818.

The rights guaranteed by this article were enjoyed to the war of 1812 which terminated the Treaty of 1783. The Treaty of Ghent contained no reference to the fisheries, and disputes having arisen between the fishermen of the two nations, the Convention of 1818 was agreed on. Its first article provided that "The inhabitants of the United States shall have for ever, in common with the subjects of His Britannic Majesty, the liberty to take fish of every kind on that part of the southern coast of Newfoundland, from the said Cape Ray to the Ramean Islands ; on the western and northern coasts of Newfoundland, from the said Cape Ray to the Quirpon Islands, and on the shores of the Magdalen Islands"—also on Labrador ; also that, "The American fishermen shall have liberty for ever to dry and cure fish in any of the unsettled bays, harbours and creeks of the southern part of the coast of Newfoundland here above described, and of the coast of Labrador," such right to terminate when any portions become settled. Further : the United States in this article agreed to " renounce any liberty heretofore enjoyed or claimed by the inhabitants thereof to take, dry or cure fish on or within three marine miles of any of the coasts, bays, creeks or harbours of His Britannic Majesty's dominions in America ;" and were only to enter such bays or harbours for shelter, or to obtain wood or water.

RECIPROCITY TREATY, 1854.

This convention did not work satisfactorily, and in 1854 a Reciprocity Treaty was agreed on. By the terms of this agreement the entire sea fishery was thrown open to Americans, as well as certain rights to land and cure their fish. The Americans in turn gave British subjects reciprocal privileges on their eastern coasts. This treaty was to continue for twelve years. At the end of that period it was terminated in 1886 at the instance of the American Government. In 1871 the Treaty of Washington was concluded. It dealt with the complications arising out of the "Alabama Claims," and also with the fishery rights of both nations. It threw open the fisheries to the Americans in almost the precise terms of the Reciprocity Treaty. It was further agreed that commissioners should determine the respective value of the fishery privileges mutually granted. When these commissioners met in Halifax, five and a-half million dollars were awarded to the Dominion of Canada and Newfoundland as compensation for the concessions made by them to the Americans, in throwing open to them fisheries of greater value than those conceded by the United States to British fishermen. Of this sum Newfoundland received one million dollars.

The Americans were dissatisfied with the award and the treaty was terminated, at their instance, in twelve years, ending in 1883. Since then the Convention of 1818 has been in force. Several attempts have been made to establish another Fishery Treaty between the United States and Canada, but without success. Newfoundland endeavoured to make a separate treaty with the United States, and the Bond-Blaine Convention was the result. Hitherto the British Government have failed to sanction this arrangement.

CHAPTER IX.

CHARACTERISTICS OF THE PEOPLE—THE CLASSES AND THE MASSES.

MERCHANTS AND THE SUPPLYING SYSTEM.

WE come now to glance at the characteristics and general qualities and endowments of the people who have to fight life's battle on this sea-girt isle, and by whom its destinies must be largely determined.

IMPORTANCE OF RACE.

There is a great deal in race. Climate, modes of life, general environments, may do much to modify racial characteristics and tendencies, but can never wholly efface them. That a people or an individual should be descended from a sound, good stock, is a matter of vast importance. "Blood" must ever count for much. The people who are doing the work of to-day are the epitome of their respective long lines of ancestry—the summing up of whole generations whose labours and moral and intellectual attainments have culminated in themselves and made them what they are. "Can the Ethiopian change his skin or the leopard his spots?" We can no more throw aside our race peculiarities and characteristics than we can get clear of our own shadows. The crossing and intermingling of races may go a certain length in effecting changes in the resulting progeny; but the "Ethiopian" cuticle is ineffaceable and will re-appear in spite of all superficial varnishings. Ancestry is an important factor in shaping the destinies of a people.

A GOOD STOCK.

Now the two hundred thousand people who at present constitute the whole population of Newfoundland—an island much larger than Ireland—are come of a good stock, or rather stocks, for they are derived entirely from the Saxon and Celtic races. Moreover, the blood, in this isolated region, has been kept pure from any undesirable intermixtures; and, so far, this blended race has been developed under favourable circumstances. The intermingling of Saxon strength, energy, endurance and capacity for "toiling terribly," with Celtic swiftness, brilliancy, imaginativeness and emotional activity, ought to produce a superior race, having the best qualities of the stocks from which they originated.

SAXON AND CELTIC ELEMENTS.

Newfoundland enjoys the distinction of being Great Britain's oldest Colony. This was the first portion of the western world on which the Saxon set his foot. It was here that the nation which was destined to discover the North-West Passage and the sources of the Nile, and to plant American, Indian and Australian Empires first raised its flag in the west and tried its first experiment in colonization. And the first colonists who settled here were not men who were forced to "leave their country for their country's good." Some of them were men born in the "Spacious times of great Elizabeth"— men brave, enterprising, true sea-kings who could fearlessly "lay their hands on ocean's mane." Many of them were Devonshire men—the country that produced Sir Walter Raleigh and his half-brother Sir Humphrey Gilbert, and Drake and Hawkins, and many another old English worthy. To these were added, at a later date, some of Ireland's best blood; for the men who were brought here by Sir George Calvert, Viscount Falkland and Sir David Kirke from Ireland, were of the right stamp for colonists; while the Irish emigrants who arrived at a later date were those who sought new homes beyond the Atlantic, in order to escape from persecution and evil days in their native land. Thus, on the soil of Newfoundland, the tough enduring Saxon and the more lively, versatile Celt have met, in proportions not far from equal; and from this wholesome amalgamation of races have sprung the stalwart men and comely matrons and maids whom the traveller of to-day looks on with admiration. The race has taken kindly to the soil and thriven. Reared in one of the most salubrious climates in the world, breathing an invigorating atmosphere, engaged largely in open-air employments, many of them constantly battling with the billows, a hardy, energetic race has grown up, in whom the red corpuscles of the blood predominate and who are well fitted for the world's rough work. In the historical sketch the early settlers were depicted and the hardships they had to encounter,—fighting cold and hunger in their "tilts," battling with the ice-floes, drawing a scanty subsistence from the stormy ocean, and pursuing their ill-remunerated labours amid sore discouragements of all kinds. But in the struggle with difficulties they gained energy, courage, self-reliance, all that constitutes true manhood ; and they transmitted these as an inheritance to their posterity who have now "entered into their labours," and find their lot cast amid happier surroundings.— They and their fathers have buffeted the billows and drunk in the health-giving sea-breezes, and now we find the present generation of Newfoundlanders, in their general physique, a powerfully built, robust and hardy race. The noblest nations of the earth, past and present, were not nurtured amid the flowers of the South, but in the cold and stern North, where nature had to be conquered by sweat of brow, and where the barren wilderness had to be transformed by hard toil into the fruitful field.

MENTAL ENDOWMENTS.

It is quite true that the intellectual development of the people in the past was not cared for as, under happier auspices, it might have been. When men are "living from hand to mouth," and struggling for the daily bread, mental pursuits are impossible and education is little considered. A great change for the better, however, has taken place within the last quarter of a century. The people are learning to appreciate the value and importance of education, for which State provision is now made and in which great improvements have been effected. Many have now attained a position of comfort and even wealth ; so that leisure is secured for the cultivation of the mind and attention to refinements in taste and habits of life. When young Newfoundlanders go to other countries for the professional training not yet attainable at home, they are able, in many instances, to compete successfully with other youths and to win honours at school and college. Indeed, anyone who comes into contact with the masses of the people cannot fail to be struck with their mental quickness and general intelligence. Let education do its work and it will be found that here is a people who, when duly cultured, will play no unworthy part in the world of the future, and will compete with the brain-workers of the coming age in all departments of life.

MORAL QUALITIES.

It is admitted on all hands that a more moral, orderly and law-abiding people cannot be found elsewhere. Serious crime is rare and the proportion of offenders against the law to the whole population is very small. Temperance has made great progress among them, and on the whole they are a sober people. Their kindness and hospitality to strangers who visit the country are proverbial. A traveller finds himself at once at home in Newfoundland whether in the capital or the more distant settlements, and all vie with each other in showing him attention and kindness. Quiet, orderly, church-going, attached to their religious faith, the people live peaceably among themselves, and outbreaks of bigotry or fanaticism are now almost unknown. Kindness to the poor and indigent is a marked feature in the character of the people; and when through failure of the precarious fisheries, distress occurs, the fishermen help each other to the full extent of their means, and often share to the last morsel with those who are more destitute than themselves. Charitable societies for the relief of the poor are organized in the capital and the chief towns. In no other country is there a more generous liberality shown to sufferers when overtaken by calamity or misfortune.

SIR R. BONNYCASTLE'S OPINION.

Sir Richard Bonnycastle, who resided for some time in Newfoundland, and knew the country and people well, in his book entitled " Newfoundland in 1842," bears the following testimony to the character of the people :—" I declare, and I am sure I shall be borne out by every class of people in this country, and by all those whose domicile is merely a transient one, that a more peaceable, respectable, loyal, or kinder-hearted race than the Newfoundland English and Irish, whether emigrant or native-born, I never met with. All they want, now that temperance has so beneficially operated upon them, is education, agriculture, roads, and the quiet which a firm, decided and impartial government promises to have in store for them." Many similar eulogies might be quoted, did space permit, for all writers agree in admiring and commending the natural qualities of Newfoundlanders.

THE UPPER CLASSES.

There is, of course, no distinction of ranks other than that arising from wealth, education or official or professional position. The upper class is composed of the officials of the Government, members of the Legislature, judges, clergy, merchants, doctors, lawyers, and wealthy individuals who have retired from business. The middle class is composed of the newer merchants, importers, commission agents, shop-keepers, tradesmen, farmers, and that large class who by industry and economy have acquired a modest competence. This middle class, well named "the shield of society," is steadily increasing, and is making its influence for good felt extensively. On its growth and permanence largely depends the future of the country ; and one of the most hopeful signs of the present time is that its ranks are swelling. The middle class who look to Newfoundland as their home and that of their children, must be regarded as the mainstay of the country. It is among them that the sentiment of progress has taken deepest root ; and that a strong desire for the development of the resources of the island is most keenly felt. The fishermen and the working classes generally welcome the prospect of new industries for the support of themselves and their children, feeling that the fisheries alone are insufficient for their increasing numbers.

MERCHANTS.

The capitalists of the country are the merchants, numerically a small class, but vitally important to the interests of the community and the prosecution of the staple industries on which the bulk of the people depend for a subsistence. They collect, export and dispose of the various products of the fisheries; and import the supplies of all kinds, food, clothing, fishing gear, etc., required by the fishermen. Their vessels carry the dried fish, oil, etc., to the consuming countries, such as Brazil, Spain, Portugal and Italy. They own most of the large steamers which prosecute the seal fishery. There are now but about ten of the large mercantile firms engaged in the exporting business, all but one having their establishments in St. John's. There are a number of other firms who give out supplies to the fishermen at the beginning of each season, and take the products of their labours in return, but who sell the fish thus collected to the large exporting firms. These import their own goods, but do not generally engage in the export trade.

THE CREDIT SYSTEM.

In the historical sketch, the evils of the long contest between the "merchant-adventurers" of the olden times who claimed a monopoly of the fisheries and carried them on from England and the resident fishermen who had settled in the country are depicted. The latter had much to bear, and were cruelly wronged and trampled on. The conflict was long and bitter, and it is not wonderful that the fishermen regarded the merchants as tyrants and oppressors and reckoned them, for generations, as their natural enemies. The antagonism between the two classes was violent; and the memories of what their forefathers suffered long rankled in the minds of the sturdy settlers. Traditions of the "bad old times" were handed down from generation to generation. The colonists at length won the day and gained their liberties. The migratory fishery from England ceased, and all monopolies at length ended.

CAPITALISTS NEEDED.

Still capitalists were found to be indispensable. The fisheries could not be carried on without them. Ships were needed to carry the fish to market; boats, coasting vessels, fishing gear, must be procured. The fishermen were poor and most of them required advances in food and clothing at the commencement of each fishing season. Labour must be organized or the fishermen would starve. Capital was needed to put the wheels of industry in motion. Thus a new race of merchants sprung up. Many of them were men who by their superior energies, skill and perseverance, rose from the ranks, and accumulated wealth which they used in the business of the country. Others were men who represented business firms in the old country and invested their capital in the fisheries. Thus grew up the "credit" or "supplying system" as it was called. The merchants made advances in the necessaries of life, and at the close of the fishing season received the products of the fishermen's labours in payment. It is a system fraught with many evils; but under such circumstances, its growth and ramifications were inevitable. It was injurious to the industries of the people. Many became hopelessly plunged in debt, and men so circumstanced lost heart and hope, and became dependent, and too often indolent, careless as to the cure of their fish, and indifferent as to the payment of their advances. On the other hand the capitalists having great risks to run, and bad debts and precarious fisheries to reckon on, are compelled to charge higher rates than those of the ordinary market, otherwise he would speedily become bankrupt. The "supplying system" is quite as bad for the merchant as the fisherman; and it is a great mistake to suppose that the merchants are accumulating large fortunes in this line of business, which is as bad for him who gives as for him who takes. In fact the merchants have done much in recent years to curtail the "credit system" and keep it within the narrowest possible bounds. Its extinction, however, must be a matter of time. To attempt to terminate it abruptly would create wide-spread misery, and derange the whole business of the country.

CONSERVATISM OF THE OLDER SCHOOL OF MERCHANTS.

What is needed now is to promote a good understanding between capital and labour—between employer and employed. Twenty-five or thirty years ago most of the capitalist class were non-resident. Many of them came here to make money and then to return to their homes in the old country to enjoy it.— Their interest in the people and in the advancement and prosperity of the country could not be the same as in the case of those who regarded it as their permanent abode and the home of their children. In many cases the wealth they amassed did not remain as capital to extend industries and develope the resources of the island, but went to enrich other lands. This older order of merchants looked upon the island as solely a fishing country, and were more or less opposed to all changes and innovations, or the promotion of other forms of industry. Hence the working class regarded them very much in the light of absentee landlords, whose interests were not identical with their own. An unfriendly relation between capital and labour thus grew up.

NEW SCHOOL OF MERCHANTS.

The last quarter of a century, however, has witnessed a wonderful change. Not only has the middle class increased in numbers and wealth, but the ideas and position of the merchant class have been entirely altered. More and more they are becoming permanent residents in the country and are looking to it as their home. They are erecting tasteful and costly residences. The present generation of merchants and capitalists are thoroughly convinced of the necessity of turning to account the rich natural resources of the country and opening up new industries for the employment of the people, for whose support the fisheries are insufficient. They are men of intelligence, energy and progressive views, and prepared to do their part in advancing the interests of the country and opening it by railways. They identify themselves with the people, and their help and guidance will be valuable. The old prejudices and the spirit of antagonism on the part of the working classes towards the merchants —the product of former times and of old memories and traditions—will disappear when they are found doing their duty, and confidence and friendly relations between the "classes and the masses" will be restored. But, that this may be realised, a kindly and friendly interest must be manifested in the well-being of the poor toiling fishermen, whose lot has been hard enough; and no efforts must be spared to improve their condition and raise them to a higher level. They are naturally a warm-hearted people, who will respond to kindness. Their faults of character, it must be remembered, are chiefly the results of their surroundings and the hard and harsh struggles through which they have been obliged to pass. Let the upper classes show that they have the welfare of the people at heart and do their part in a patriotic spirit in promoting the advancement of the Colony, and friendly relations between capital and labour, which is especially desirable here, need not be disturbed.

THE PLANTERS.

There is another class of smaller capitalists, called "planters," to be found in all the principal fishing centres. This term carries us back to the days when all colonies were "plantations," and the colonists were "planters." The "survival" of the name here is curious, for it does not at all indicate a man who plants or cultivates anything, but simply a sort of middle-man who stands between the merchant and the fisherman. He takes his supplies of goods and fishing requisites direct from the merchant, to whom he is accountable, and distributes them among a number of fishermen who look to him for advances; and at the close of the fishing season they hand over the proceeds of their labour as payment. The price of fish is, of course, determined by the demand in foreign markets, and by the quantity taken. The larger the sea-harvest here and in Norway, the great rival of Newfoundland, as a rule, the lower the price. The planter again passes on the fish he has collected to the supplying merchant. Many of the planters are independent and pay cash for their supplies. Others have but small means, and are simply more enterprising fishermen who own a "fishing-room" with a few boats and seines. They engage a number of hands for the season and the fish are made on their own premises.

THE FISHERMEN.

In the height of the fishing season, if fish are abundant the labours of the fishermen are severe and incessant; but during the long winter, the bulk of them are in a state of enforced idleness. In the fall of the year, after the fish are disposed of, there are boats, nets, etc., to repair, stages and flakes to look after, and fuel to be cut in the woods and hauled over the snow. Much of the work of handling and drying fish is done by women and girls, whose work is often very heavy. If the fishery has proved successful, the fisherman has a snug balance coming to him, after paying for his summer supplies and is enabled to lay in a stock of provisions for the winter. Should the fisheries prove a failure, the poor fisherman after all his toil has perhaps only a few quintals of fish to hand over in payment of his advances. He is then dependent on the liberality of the merchant or planter for a supply of the necessaries of life to carry him through the winter. Should he have done his best, and acted honestly, such supplies are rarely refused. The merchant or supplier has to take the risks of the voyage as well as the fisherman, and in bad seasons his losses are often very heavy. Should a second or third bad season follow on the back of the first, the unfortunate fisherman too often becomes hopelessly involved in debt. The merchant finds himself at the end of the year with a long list of bad or very doubtful debts in his ledger, and suffers quite as much as the fisherman. It is easy to see that the business of supplying for the fisheries is far from being a bonanza. One bad season may sweep away the gains of several good ones. The more the credit system is curtailed the better for both parties. The merchants would be glad to abolish credit and pay the fishermen in cash for their fish when taken; but the practice is deeply engrained, during by-gone generations, in the habits and ideas of the people, and the bulk of them are too poor to dispense with advances. The more distant fisheries, such as on Labrador and the Banks, could not at present be carried on without large outlay of capital. To withdraw advances suddenly would be to entail starvation on thousands. The present class of merchants and capitalists are not accountable for a system which originated when the fisheries were first worked and is the growth of many generations. They can only get rid of it by slow degrees.

FISHING POPULATION IMPROVING.

Late years, however, have witnessed a marked improvement in the condition of the fishermen. They are becoming more provident and thrifty ; and far larger numbers than formerly can now afford to dispense with supplies on credit, and pay in cash for what they require. There is every reason to hope that this will be a steadily increasing class, as education spreads. Those who combine farming with fishing are invariably the most independent and comfortable of their class. On the whole the fishermen of Newfoundland, though they have not much of this world's goods, compare not unfavourably, as to their condition, with the labouring classes of other countries. If they have privations and hardships they have many compensations for these, in their free open-air life, their robust health, their capabilities of enjoying simple pleasures. There is perhaps as much genuine happiness among them as among any similar number who toil for the daily bread. Compared with the pale factory workers, the toilers in the great cities of Europe and America who breathe a pestiferous atmosphere in crowded tenements, too often amid foul conditions that depress the spirits and shorten life, the condition of these hardy fishermen is an enviable one. Their passionate attachment to the land of their birth, their love for it when settled in other lands and their frequent longings to return, —all indicate that their life has been on the whole a happy one.

SOCIAL ENJOYMENTS.

Winter is the fishermen's season for enjoyment. In their homes, however poor, life vindicates its right to gladness and relaxation. The season for "fireside enjoyments, home-born happiness" is welcomed. They have their social pleasures, outdoor sports, games, shooting, hunting, trapping, etc. Dancing is a favourite winter amusement among the fishermen and their families ; and to the music of the fiddle, the flute or fife, or in the absence of any other instrument, the Jew's Harp, they dance for hours with a vigour and honest heartiness which brings them more real pleasure than is experienced in the refined and artificial entertainments of more advanced communities. Weddings in particular are celebrated with an amount of gaiety and festivity which at once indicates exuberance of animal spirits, and a kindly sympathy with the " happy couple." Winter is also the season for tea festivals, religious and secular *soirees*, lectures, concerts, readings with music, &c. St. John's, the capital, of course, takes the lead in such matters, and there winter is considered by far the pleasantest season. A taste for theatricals and concerts has been developed among its people; clubs, reading rooms, libraries, furnish social and intellectual enjoyments. With balls, skating rinks, snow-shoeing, tobogganing, sleighing, the winter passes pleasantly among the well-to-do classes. In the larger towns and villages similar social enjoyments, on a smaller scale and of a simpler character, are multiplying; and newspapers, books, periodicals, now find their way among the lonely "dwellers by the sea" where formerly they were entirely unknown, and are stirring intellectual life among the toilers of the sea.

If it be true, as some one has stated it, that "the law of the world's progress is an advance from the warmer to the colder latitudes,"—from the enervating heat of the tropical and semi-tropical lands to the invigorating climes of the bracing north, we may ask whether the day is not coming when these stalwart islanders, nurtured amidst storms and grim north-easters, battling with the billows amid ice-laden seas, will take a high place among the world's workers and leaders, and outstrip the less capable inhabitants of warmer regions. The most flourishing and densely peopled parts of New England States and Canada were, two centuries ago, looked upon, from outside, very much as those regions of Newfoundland we have been describing, are now regarded by the outside world. If the latent possibilities of the former have developed so marvellously, in a few generations, may we not regard such an advance as a precedent for the progressive capabilities, at present dormant, in the comparatively small population who occupy this island.

CHAPTER X.

POPULATION—RATE OF INCREASE.

CENSUS OF 1891.

The earliest estimate of the resident population of the island was made in 1654, when it was ascertained that about 350 families were scattered in the different harbours. Allowing an average of five persons to each family, the total population was, at that date, 1,750. In 1680, the commanders of the convoy frigates, on duty in connection with the fisheries, collected statistics of the population which gave 2,280 as the number of residents. The West Country merchants, who carried on the fisheries from England, had in the same year nearly 4,000 men employed in the various fishing ports of the island, who all returned to England at the close of the season. They had 97 ships of the burden of 9,305 tons; 793 boats; 133 stages. Besides they had 99 ships of 8,123 tons, navigated by 1,157 seamen and employed in carrying the produce of the fisheries to Europe, the West Indies and South America. Their annual take was 133,910 quintals of dried codfish, and 1,053 hogsheads of train-oil. In 1698, the resident population reached 2,640, who that year caught 101,152 quintals of fish.

The following table shows the resident population in the years named :—

Year.	Population.
1654	1,750
1680	2,280
1698	2,640
1763	7,000
1780	8,000
1785	10,000

Year.	Population.
1804	20,380
1825	55,719
1827	59,571
1832	60,000
1836	75,094
1845	98,703
1857 (Labrador included)	124,288
1869 "	146,536
1874 "	161,374
1884 "	197,589
1891 "	202,040

RETURNS OF THE RELIGIOUS DENOMINATIONS.

It was not till 1845 that the different religious denominations were distinguished in the census returns. The following table shows the respective numbers of the two leading divisions of Roman Catholics and Protestants in the years named, according to the census returns :—

Year.	Protestants.	Roman Catholics.
1845	49,505	46,983
1857	67,743	57,214
1869	85,496	61,040
1874	97,057	65,317
1884	122,259	75,330
1891 (Labrador inc.)	127,947	72,696

The following table gives, in detail, the numerical strength of the different denominations at the various periods named :—

1845.

Church of Rome	46,983
Church of England	34,294
Methodists	14,239
Presbyterians	478
Congregationalists	539
Remainder unknown.	

1857.

Church of Rome	57,214
Church of England	44,285
Methodists	20,229
Presbyterians	838
Congregationalists	347
Baptists and others	44

1869.

Church of Rome	61,040
Church of England	55,184
Methodists	28,990
Presbyterians	974
Congregationalists	338
Baptists	10

1874.

Church of Rome	64,317
Church of England	59,561
Methodists	35,702
Presbyterians	1,168
Congregationalists	461
Baptists and others	165

1884.

Church of Rome	75,330
Church of England	69,646
Methodists	48,943
Presbyterians	1,478
Congregationalists	768
Baptists and others	65

1891.

Church of Rome	72,696
Church of England	69,824
Reformed Church of England	487
Methodists	53,276
Presbyterians	1,449

Congregationalists	782
Salvation Army	2,092
Baptists and others	37
Moravians on Labrador	1,397

The last named returns include Labrador.

The total population of Newfoundland and Labrador in 1884 was 197,335. The census of 1891 gives 202,040 as the population of both; showing an increase of 4,705 in seven years, or at the rate of 2.38 per cent. in that time, or at the rate of 3.40 per cent. in ten years. From 1874 to 1884 the increase was 36,209, or at the rate of 22.4 per cent. in ten years. The falling off in increase from 1884 to 1891 was caused by emigration to the United States and Canada, owing to deficient fisheries. The emigration has almost ceased during the last two or three years, so that probably the increase of population has now resumed its normal proportions.

The Labrador population in 1891 stood as follows in regard to denomination :—

Church of England	1,749
Church of Rome	354
Methodists	604
Presbyterians	2
Moravians	1,397
Micmac Indians	20

The Moravians are christianized Esquimaux.

POPULATION. 209

The following table shows the population of Newfoundland according to denomination, census of 1891 :—

POPULATION OF NEWFOUNDLAND ACCORDING TO DENOMINATION, CENSUS OF 1891.

DISTRICT.	Church of England.	Roman Catholic.	Wesleyan.	Presbyterian.	Other Denominations.
St. Barbe	3,362	1,784	1,627	14	3
Twillingate	3,916	2,449	9,661	58	696
Fogo	2,829	1,174	2,692	4	1
Bonavista	8,550	3,069	6,045	14	171
Trinity	9,947	1,613	6,888	11	413
Bay-de-Verde	506	2,135	7,062	....	5
Carbonear	1,011	1,896	2,734	10	114
Harbor Grace	8,033	5,494	1,964	157	233
Port-de-Grave	2,999	1,991	2,722	1	273
Harbor Main	2,157	6,814	218	....	....
St. John's East	5,376	11,644	2,767	652	337
St. John's West	3,174	9,112	2,368	378	219
Ferryland	169	5,673	5	5	1
Placentia	1,643	10,614	527	13	5
Burin	1,797	2,930	3,845	2	485
Fortune	5,292	1,817	120	4	438
Burgeo and La Poile	5,162	138	1,166	4	1
St. George	2,252	3,995	261	121	3
Labrador	1,749	354	601	2	1,397
Total	69,834	72,696	53,276	1,449	4,795

Factories, mills, &c., in Newfoundland, Census of 1891 :—

  No. of Saw Mills 53
  " Tanneries 3
  " Breweries and Distilleries . . 2
  " Iron Founderies 2
  " Bakeries 4
  " Furniture Factories . . . 4

210 POPULATION.

Value of Other Factories	24
Value of above Factories	$893,860
" Goods produced	$1,450,456
No. of hands employed	1,209
" Lobster Factories	340
" persons employed	4,807
Value of Lobster Factories	$179,288
No. cases Lobsters, 1890	77,580

Agricultural Stock and Produce, &c., in Newfoundland, Census of 1891:—

Acres Improved Land	64,494
" in Pasture	20,524
Wheat and Barley—bushels	491
Oats—bushels	12,900
Hay—tons	36,032
Potatoes—brls.	481,024
Turnips—brls.	60,235
Horses	6,138
Milch Cows	10,863
Other Horned Cattle	12,959
Sheep	60,840
Swine	32,011
Fowl	127,420

Professional men—Census 1891:—

Clergymen	180
Teachers	601
Lawyers	43
Doctors	62
Government officials	608

Census 1891—According to employment:—

Merchants and Traders	767
Clerks and shop hands	1,948
Mechanics	2,681
Factory hands	1,058
Lumberers and Miners	1,923
Engaged in curing fish	53,502
Farming	1,545

POPULATION. 211

According to place of birth :—
- Natives 193,353
- Foreign
- British 3,049
- Colonies 1,163
- Other countries . . . 369

Census of 1891 shows that there are of
- Deaf 159
- Deaf and Dumb 136
- Blind 187
- Crippled and Disabled Paupers . 2,485
- Lunatics 280
- Orphans 690

The Sexes stand to each other thus :—
- Males 100,684
- Females 97,259

AGE.

There are from 65 to 70 years of age 1,536 males.
    "   " 65 to 70   " 1,486 females.
    "   " 70 to 75   " 1,062 males.
    "   " 70 to 75   " 983 females.
    "   " 75 to 80   " 608 males.
    "   " 75 to 80   " 587 females.
Upwards of 80   " 376 males.
Upwards of 80   " 468 females.

The following are a few more items of interest which appear in census of 1891. In the twelve months preceding the census year there were 6,599 births ; 4,362 deaths ; 894 marriages. The number of males engaged in curing fish 35,931 ; of females engaged in curing fish 17,571. Number of males who can read, 47,077 ; of females who can read, 47,803 ; of males who can write, 36,877 ; of females who can write, 36,273. There are 31,983 married males ; and 38,098 married females ; 2,973 widowers ; and 5,800 widows. There are 33,644 inhabited houses and 37,299 families.

The number of churches is as follows :—
- Church of England 156
- Church of Rome 131
- Methodists 128
- Other Denominations . . . 12

CHAPTER XI.

MODE OF GOVERNMENT.

REVENUE, TRADE, PUBLIC FINANCES.

In 1832 the boon of Representative Government was granted to Newfoundland. In 1855, in compliance with the strongly expressed desire of the people, what is commonly known as "Responsible Government" was, after a lengthened agitation, conceded to the Colony. This was simply the application of the principles of the British Constitution to the government of the island. It provided that "the country should be governed according to the well-understood wishes of the people." The party who are sustained by a majority in the Legislature have at their disposal the appointments to the principal offices in the Colony. They also select the Executive Council. The House of Assembly is elected by the people; the Legislative Council is nominated by "the Governor in Council."

CONSTITUTION.

This form of government consists of a Governor who is appointed by the Crown, his salary of $12,000 a year being paid by the Colony; an Executive Council chosen by the party commanding a majority in the Legislature, and consisting of seven members; a Legislative Council of fifteen members nominated by the Governor in Council, and holding office for life; and a House of Assembly at present consisting of 36 members, elected every four years by the votes of the people. In the governing body thus consisting of the Governor, representing the Queen, the Legislative Council and the House of Assembly, is vested collectively the legislative power. They have also exclusive jurisdiction over such matters as the public debt and property; raising money on the credit of the Colony by loan, taxation,

MODE OF GOVERNMENT.

postal service, trade, commerce, fisheries, etc. The General Government is also the custodian of the public funds, from which are disbursed the expenses of the public service. There are 18 electoral districts sending 36 members to the House of Assembly, as follows:—

	Members.
Bay-de-Verds	2
Bonavista	3
Burgeo and La Poile	1
Burin	2
Carbonear	1
Ferryland	2
Fogo	1
Fortune Bay	1
Harbour Grace	3
Harbour Main	2
Placentia and St. Mary's	3
Port-de-Grave	1
St. Barbe	1
St. George	1
St. John's East	3
St. John's West	3
Trinity	3
Twillingate	3
Total	36

HOUSE OF ASSEMBLY.

The members of the House of Assembly are now elected by ballot. All males, on reaching the age of 21, are entitled to vote. The members of both branches of the Legislature are paid. Members of the House of Assembly, if resident in St. John's, receive $194 per session; if resident elsewhere $291 per session. The members of the Legislative Council receive $120 per session; the President $240. The Speaker of the House of Assembly receives $1,000 per session.

MODE OF GOVERNMENT.

POWERS OF THE GOVERNOR.

The Governor who is also Commander-in-Chief in and over the Colony and its dependencies, has the power, in the Queen's name, to commute the sentence of a court of justice; to summon, open, prorogue and on occasions dissolve the local Parliament; to give or withhold assent to, or reserve for the Royal consideration all bills which have passed both Chambers.

THE LEGISLATURE.

The Legislature must meet once a year, and is usually summoned "for the despatch of business" in the month of February. Thus the Colony is practically self-governing. Its history shows the steady growth of government by the people. The electors, in reality, govern the country, as they choose the members of the Assembly who by their votes maintain in office or overthrow the Government of the day. Newfoundland, like England, enjoys "Responsible Government;" that is, each government is responsible to the people, through the members of the Legislature they elect, to carry out their wishes.

SUPREME COURT.

The Supreme Court was instituted in 1826 by the promulgation of a Royal Charter. To it and to magistrates belong the correct interpretation and proper enforcement of the laws of the country. It is composed of a Chief Justice and two Assistant Judges. It holds two terms or sessions each year, on the 20th of May, and the 20th of November. There are circuits of the Supreme Court held in the northern, southern and western districts of the island, at such times and places as may be fixed by the proclamation of the Governor. These are presided over by Chief Justice or one of the Assistant Judges, in rotation. The salary of the Chief Justice is $5,000; of each Assistant Judge, $4,000. They hold their appointments for life.

COURT OF LABRADOR.

The Court of Labrador has civil and criminal jurisdiction over such parts of Labrador as lie within the jurisdiction of Newfoundland. It is presided over by a judge who is nominated by the Governor in Council. His salary is $1,154.

CENTRAL DISTRICT COURT.

The Central District Court is a Court of Record, held in St. John's, for the said district, for the adjudication of civil causes, and sits whenever business requires. There are two Judges appointed by the Governor in Council. There is also a District Court in Harbour Grace with jurisdiction over the electoral districts of Conception Bay. It is presided over by a Judge, who is *ex officio* a justice of the peace. There is a sheriff for each judicial district of the island who is appointed by the Governor in Council.

QUARTER SESSIONS.

Courts of general and quarter sessions are held in the island, in such places as may be determined by the proclamation of the Governor. They are presided over by the stipendiary magistrates or justices of the peace.

LAW SOCIETY.

"The Law Society of Newfoundland" is constituted by statute, and is under the inspection of the Judges of the Supreme Court for the time being. "No person is admitted by the Supreme Court to practice as an Attorney unless upon actual service of five years with some practising Attorney of the island ; or, if a regular graduate of any college in Her Majesty's Dominions of four years ; or who, having been entered on the books of 'The Law Society' as a student-at-law, shall have been subsequently called to the Bar in England, Scotland or Ireland, or any of Her Majesty's Colonies." Any person who has been called to the Bar in England Scotland or Ireland, or any of the colonies, upon producing evidence thereof, and undergoing a satisfactory examination, may be called by the Law Society to the degree of Barrister.

REVENUE, TRADE, PUBLIC FINANCES, SHIPPING.

The following table shows the revenue and the value of the exports and imports for the last twenty years:—

Year.	Revenue.	Exports, Value.	Imports, Value.
1872	$812,752	$7,166,443	$6,716,068
1873	801,412	7,700,739	6,766,603
1874	841,588	8,569,960	7,354,689
1875	830,219	8,214,768	7,058,372
1876	855,228	8,168,540	7,205,907
1877	872,913	7,625,441	7,363,634
1878	839,640	6,594,807	6,868,723
1879	962,921	7,168,924	7,261,002
1880	897,474	7,131,095	6,966,243
1881	1,003,803	7,648,574	6,863,708
1882	1,119,385	8,228,291	8,350,222
1883	1,262,702	7,058,738	9,131,464
1884	1,209,316	6,567,135	8,075,792
1885	1,009,222	4,726,608	6,698,500
1886	1,042,424	4,862,951	6,020,036
1887	1,272,660	5,676,720	5,397,408
1888	1,370,029	6,582,013	7,420,400
1889	1,362,893	6,607,500	6,122,985
1890	1,454,536	6,099,686	6,368,835
1891	1,824,206	7,437,158	6,869,458
1892	1,883,790	Records destroyed in great fire.	
1893	1,764,791	Not yet published.	

The following table shows the public debt of the Colony:—

Year.	Debt.
1882	$1,498,777
1883	1,549,313
1884	2,149,153
1885	2,149,597
1886	2,287,391
1887	3,005,040
1888	3,335,589
1889	4,133,202
1890	4,138,627
1891	5,223,363
1892	6,383,367
1893	8,053,127

INCREASE OF DEBT.

The increase of the public debt within the last ten years has arisen mainly from the building of about 311 miles of railway, now completed and in operation ; and which, in the future, by the development of the resources of the Colony, will yield ample returns, and increase the revenue. The debt is represented by these lines of railways, and also by the St. John's Dry Dock which cost over $600,000 ; the new Post Office, a very creditable building, and other public works such as light houses and breakwaters. The remarkable expansion of the public revenue gives ample assurance that in the construction of public works the Colony has not gone beyond its means and can well afford to pay the interest on its debt without any undue strain. The investment in railway building, without which the rich natural resources of the Colony must remain dormant, has been already fully justified. Within twenty years the revenue has doubled ; and is now quite sufficient for the maintenance of the civil service and payment of the interest on the public debt. Judging from the experience of the past there is every reason to anticipate a further steady increase of revenue. These public works, while in progress, distribute money in the shape of wages ; and by increasing the imports add to the revenue. If we take the gross debt of $8,053,127 it amounts to nearly $40 per head for the entire population. The gross debt of the Dominion of Canada is $205,333,000, and the amount per head is $60. In Belgium the public debt is $63 per head ; in France $146 per head ; in Italy $75 per head ; United Kingdom $86 ; New South Wales $225 South Australia $330 ; and New Zealand $292 per head of the entire population.

TAXATION.

If we take the revenue of last year at $1,764,791 this shows a taxation of $8 per head for the entire population. But it must be taken into account that there are no direct taxes in Newfoundland, except in St. John's which is now under a Municipal Council. The local taxation for water, sewerage and street improvements is small. The greater part of the revenue is derived from Customs' Duties on imports ; so that $8 per head represents nearly the whole amount of taxation. In the United Kingdom the taxation is $6-62 per head ; in Victoria the taxation is $15-35 per head ; in New South Wales $12 ; in Western Australia $22 ; in New Zealand $16-91 ; in Canada $5-81. In all these countries there are direct taxes in addition, which greatly swell the amount paid.

If you take the revenues for 1889, 1890 and 1891, the average amount is $1,580,545, which would give a little over seven dollars per head for taxation. This cannot be reckoned excessive when it represents almost the entire per capita taxation. The duties are partly *ad valorem* and partly specific, but only to a slight extent differential, the tariff being designed for revenue purposes only, not for protection. All expenses for making and repairing roads, streets, bridges, breakwaters, public wharves, etc., are defrayed out of the general revenue, the Board of Works having charge of that department. The provision for the poor, for education, for the maintenance of a police force, and for the whole Civil Service is also chargeable on the general revenue. The Crown lands and the postal service are the only other sources of revenue besides the Customs duties. In 1891 the whole volume of trade amounted in value to $14,306,616.

The following table shows the principal countries with which trade is carried on, and the amount in each case, in year 1891 :

Country.	Value of Imports therefrom.	Value of Exports thereto.
United Kingdom	$2,341,706	$1,930,991
Dominion of Canada	2,499,945	779,634
British West Indies	319,560	377,301
Italy	9,258	450,047
Spain	104,708	718,591
Portugal	30,044	1,051,839
St. Pierre	12,027	10,115
United States	1,526,674	568,540
Brazil	....	1,102,995

SHIPPING, 1890.

Number of Steamers owned in the Colony	35
Tonnage	6,178
Number of Sailing Vessels, 20 to 60 tons	1,421
Number of Sailing Vessels, 60 tons and upward	271
Tonnage	25,740
Number of Boats from 4 to 30 quintals	20,452
Number of Vessels built in 1890	52
Tonnage	1,812
Number of Vessels engaged in Bank fishery	199
Tonnage	11,520
Number of Vessels engaged in Labrador fishery	859
Tonnage	93,634

CHAPTER XII.

EDUCATION.

It was not till within the last fifty years that any serious attention was given to the cause of education in the Colony, or any aid granted from the public funds towards the establishment and maintenance of schools and academies. The circumstances under which the colonization of the country was carried out, as described in former chapters, sufficiently account for this neglect in regard to the means of education. When the people were poor and engaged in a hard struggle for the daily bread, and when settlements were small and widely separated, physical wants were too pressing to permit much attention being given to educational claims. As a consequence, in those early days many of the young grew up ignorant of the very rudiments of knowledge, especially in the smaller and more distant settlements.

COLONIAL AND CONTINENTAL CHURCH SOCIETY.

The beginning of common school education dates from 1823, when "The Newfoundland School Society" was founded in London by Samuel Codner, a Newfoundland merchant. Its name was afterwards changed to "The Colonial and Continental Church Society." The schools it planted were maintained mainly by the liberality of the members of the society, aided at a later date by a grant from the public funds of the Colony. It has still about twenty schools in operation. Its Central School, in St. John's, is used by the Church of England Boards of Education as a training school for their teachers. This Society has done excellent work in the cause of education.

ACADEMIES AND COLLEGES.

It was not till 1843 that the local Legislature granted the annual sum of £5,100 for the promotion of common school education. In the same year the Legislature made a provision for the higher education by establishing an Academy in Saint John's. This institution did not succeed and was discontinued in 1850. In its room three Academies were founded on the denominational principle, and a fourth was added at a later date. These four institutions, which are connected respectively with the different religious denominations, have expanded and greatly elevated the standard of education. They are conducted by teachers of ability and high character, and give an excellent training to the pupils. They have now obtained the designation of "Colleges," and are known as the Roman Catholic, Church of England, Methodist, and Presbyterian Colleges. The two last-named lost their buildings in the great fire of 1892; but the Methodist Buildings are restored and will soon be ready for use; and they are more spacious and better built than those destroyed in the general conflagration, and do much credit to the body to which they belong. The Presbyterian College has also resumed operations in a new building having excellent class-rooms.

PUPIL TEACHERS—LONDON UNIVERSITY CENTRE.

The training of pupil teachers is carried out at the Colleges. After going through a course of education, these teachers must pass examinations, and are graded according to merit, before they are eligible to take charge of schools. Pupils are also prepared for the Universities at most of the Colleges. St. John's has been made a centre of the London University, so that pupils can here prepare for and pass the matriculation examinations. Openings are thus provided for the more talented and aspiring of the young to attain distinction and fit themselves for the higher posts of duty.

JUBILEE SCHOLARSHIP.

As a further encouragement to those who aspire after the higher education, "The Newfoundland Jubilee Scholarship" has been founded. The Governor in Council appropriates the annual sum of $480, "for the institution of a scholarship in the London University to be given and awarded to the student who shall take the highest place among competitors in and from this Colony, at the matriculation examination holden in June and January of any year ; and where there shall be no competition, then such scholarship shall be awarded to the student who shall pass in the first division in such examination : Provided that such student shall be a native of this Colony, or shall have re-resided in it for five years preceding such examination : and shall have studied under masters of the Board Schools or colleges of this Colony ; and provided that such student shall, for two years thereafter, prosecute his or her studies at some British University. Such scholarship shall be tenable for only two years by the student winning the same."

COUNCIL OF HIGHER EDUCATION.

In 1893, an Act was passed to Provide for Higher Education. This Act makes provision for the appointment of a Council of Higher Education, with the view of promoting a higher standard of education throughout the Colony by the holding of examinations and the awarding of prizes and diplomas and scholarships to successful candidates. The Council is to consist of 23 members ; and the Superintendents of Education and Headmasters of Colleges are members *ex officio*. The sum of $4000 annually is appropriated for the purposes of this Act ; and the Jubilee Scholarship is made subject to the regulations of the Council.

EDUCATION DENOMINATIONAL.

The whole educational system is carried on upon the denominational principle, each religious denomination receiving a grant for education from the public funds, in proportion to its numbers. Separate boards of education in the different districts have charge of the elementary schools. Four Superintendents of Education are appointed by Government—for Roman Catholic, Church of England, Methodist and Presbyterian schools and colleges respectively. In recent years, the progress made in education has been of a very satisfactory character, though, of course, much yet remains to be done, especially in the more distant settlements. It may be alleged that this plan of separate education is attended with much waste of means and power; and no doubt this is true. A united education, if practicable, would possess many advantages. It may be doubted, however, in the present state of denominational feeling, whether united education is possible. Denominational zeal perhaps furnishes a stimulus to educational effort which would otherwise be wanting. United education may come in the future when denominational interests occupy men's minds to a less extent; but the best policy surely is to accept the system now established and try to make the most and the best of it. It must be admitted that very considerable improvements have taken place in recent years, and that a far greater amount of zeal and interest in the cause of education than formerly is felt and manifested. That the separate system is much more costly must be allowed; but as things now stand, it probably gives the best results that could be at present attained. The recent appointment of a "Council of Higher Education," composed of the representatives of all denominations, is a step in the right direction, and will tend to promote greater unity of action in connection with the higher branches of education. It will also bring together men from all parties who take an interest in education, and lead them to feel that here is a common ground on which they can meet and act for the good of all. The necessity of educating the masses who through universal suffrage are made "the masters," should be more keenly felt by those who have the direction of public affairs and by whom the destinies of the future are, to some extent, shaped. When, by law, every man on reaching the age of twenty-one, is entitled to vote in the election of members of the House of Assembly, the safety and well-being of the commonwealth require that such a power should not be exercised by an uneducated people. More than ever the thorough education of the whole is now called for, as their votes are to control the government of the country. It is no doubt true that

"The crowning fact,
The kingliest act
Of Freedom is a Freeman's vote."

It is, however, equally true that it is all-important that the voters should be men of intelligence and integrity, who will not be influenced by low and base considerations, if they are to wisely control and protect the liberties and the life of the country. Freedom should be combined with intelligence and a sense of moral responsibility, and then the "kingliest act"—the casting of the ballot—will be regarded as a sacred trust and will be at once safely and beneficially performed. The call for universal education, of a wise and elevating kind, is emphatized by the boon of universal suffrage.

The following table shows the provision made by the Legislature for education?—

Legislative grant in 1893 for Colleges, Grammar Schools and Elementary Schools . .	$151,891 22
Amount *per capita* for the entire population of 202,040	75.17 cents.
Legislative grant for Elementary Schools . .	$97,753 15
" " Pupil Teachers . .	5,610 84
" " Encouragement of Teachers .	25,297 87
" " Inspection . .	6,060 00

Legislative grant for Colleges :—

Church of England . . .	$3,328 53
Church of Rome . . .	3,465 49
Methodist . .	2,539 72
Presbyterian	990 00
Grammar and Superior Schools . .	7,604 07

Number of Elementary Schools in 1893 :—

Church of England . . .	194
Church of Rome . . .	200
Methodist	144
Presbyterian	1
Others	10
Total . . .	549

EDUCATION.

Number of Pupils attending Elementary Schools in 1893 :—

Church of England	11,808
Church of Rome	10,265
Methodist	8,465
Presbyterian, Congregational and others	296
Total	33,834

Number of Pupils attending Colleges, 1893 :—

Church of England	141
Church of Rome	250
Methodist	252
Presbyterian	80
Total	723
Grand total of pupils attending Colleges and Schools	34,557

CHAPTER XIII.

POST OFFICE DEPARTMENT, CONSTABULARY, LIGHT HOUSES, BANKS, NEWSPAPER PRESS.

POST OFFICE DEPARTMENT.

Postal communication between St. John's, the United Kingdom and European countries, the United States and Canada, is maintained by the *Allan Line* of steamers; the *Canadian and Newfoundland Line*, whose steamers "Barcelona," "Moruca" and "Clunda" touch at St. John's in their outward and homeward trips; by the steamers of *The Red Cross Line*, plying between New York and St. John's *via* Halifax; also by the steamer "St. Pierre," plying between Placentia and other western ports in Newfoundland and Halifax *via* St. Pierre, and by the steamer "Harlaw" plying fortnightly between Halifax and the west coast of Newfoundland, calling at ports in Cape Breton.

Full information as to the sailings of these steamers will be found in a subsequent chapter containing directions for tourists. By all these lines of steamers mail communication with the outside world is regular and frequent during the summer months. During three winter months the Allan steamers do not call at St. John's, but go direct to Halifax. A fortnightly steamer during those months runs between St. John's and Halifax carrying mails and passengers; but the steamers of the Canadian and Newfoundland Line call at St. John's, on both their outward and homeward voyages, throughout the winter months. The "St. Pierre" makes fortnightly trips between Halifax and Placentia during winter months.

Local postal communication between St. John's and the various towns, villages and settlements, is maintained by railways, coastal steamers and steam-launches, vehicles and couriers.

The railway to Harbour Grace conveys the mails for the towns and settlements of Conception Bay, Bay de Verde District, and the south shore of Trinity Bay. The Placentia railway carries the mails for Placentia and St. Mary's Bays to Placentia, whence they are distributed by the s. s. *Alert* which plies round the Bay, her route extending to Grand Bank in Fortune Bay. The Northern and Western Railway carries the mails for the northern districts, which at various points are transmitted to their destination either by steam-launches or couriers.

The coastal steamer on the northern route carries mails fortnightly to all the ports of call ; and in summer as far as Red Bay, Labrador, where it connects with the Labrador mail steamer which plies on that coast during the fishing season.

The coastal steamer plying on the western route conveys mails to all the ports of call as far as Bonne Bay during the summer months and as far as Channel in winter. For the sailings of these steamers see the chapter for tourists.

The postal service, under the direction of the present energetic Postmaster-general, J. O. Fraser, Esq., has been brought to a condition of great efficiency, and compares not unfavourably with that of any other British colony. The Post office is fitted up with all modern improvements, and the building itself with its various arrangements is creditable to the colony. A parcels post with the United Kingdom, the United States and Canada, is of very great advantage to the whole community. There is also an inland parcels post. The book post, post cards, stamps, post office boxes, branch offices and pillar boxes throughout the city, money orders, letter carriers, delivery, present every facility that could be reasonably desired, and prove that this service is managed with a view to meet the wants of the general public. The improvements introduced in recent years have been of great value.

The total number of post offices in the colony is 846. The number of postmasters or mistresses being the same.

Postal rates are as follows :—Inland postage : letters not over one ounce in weight, three cents ; for city delivery, one cent.

Newspapers, local and foreign, free, if under four ounces ; if over they are charged at book-rate. Books, pamphlets, magazines, are charged one cent per two ounces. Post cards (local) one cent ; for foreign countries, two cents ; return cards, four cents.

Letters—for England, and most European countries, and the United States, 5 cents if not over half ounce in weight. To Canada the letter rate is three cents per ounce.

During the summer months mails are despatched direct to Liverpool on alternate Saturdays by steamers of the Allan Line, and by the steamers *Ulunda*, *Moruca* and *Barcelona* when convenient.

CONSTABULARY.

The Constabulary consists of an Inspector and General Superintendent ; a Sub-Inspector ; a clerk and store-keeper ; three head constables ; fourteen sergeants ; six acting sergeants ; ninety-five constables, and nine mounted police. The total force numbers 129 ; of which 61 constitute the St. John's staff, the rest being in outports.

STATIONS.

The force is organized, equipped and disciplined in every respect similar to the Royal Irish Constabulary ; and properly speaking it is a military as well as a civil force, being thoroughly drilled in the use of arms, etc. The force was first organized after the withdrawal of the military in 1871, and is a fine body of men, thoroughly drilled and instructed in their various police duties at Fort Townsend, the head-quarters, the best and most efficient men being always selected for the outport stations.

LIGHT HOUSES.

The coast of the island is well lighted and almost every year witnesses an increase of light-houses and other means of securing the safety of its large sea-faring population. At present there are thirty-nine light-houses and beacons erected and maintained by the Newfoundland Government, and nine by the Government of Canada. There are three fog-signals, one whistling buoy and one bell buoy at the most dangerous points around the coast, under the Newfoundland Government, and seven fog-signals at the Canadian light-stations. The erection of nearly all these light-houses has been the work of the last fifty years.

In 1813 a light-house was placed at Fort Amherst, at the entrance of St. John's Harbour. No further effort was made to light the coast till 1835, when the local Legislature passed an Act for the erection of a light-house at Cape Spear, five miles south of St. John's, and for another at Harbour Grace Island in 1836. Cape Bonavista light-house was built in 1843; Cape Pine in 1851; Cape Race in 1856, (now under the Government of Canada); Baccalieu in 1859; Cape St. Mary, 1860; Fort Point, Trinity, 1874; Carbonear Island, 1878; Cape St. Francis, 1867; Long Point, Twillingate, 1876; Cabot Island, Bonavista Bay, 1880; Gull Island, (Cape St. John), 1884; Brigus Head, 1885; Penguin Island, 1890; King's Cove Head, 1893.

In 1872 a ten-inch steam whistle was placed at Cape Race, and in thick weather is sounded for ten seconds with intervals of silence of fifty seconds in each minute. At Cape Ray, in 1877, a steam fog horn was erected, giving a blast of ten seconds every minute; in 1884 a steam fog horn was placed at Cape Bauld, and another at Cape Norman in 1890. At Belle Isle, in the Straits of the same name, a fog-bomb was placed in 1891, which fires cotton-powder signals every twenty minutes from a point near the upper light, 400 feet above the sea, in thick weather. In 1877 a Siren trumpet was placed at Cape St. Francis, and at Fort Amherst a three-pound charge from a 32-pounder gun is discharged every hour and on the stroke of the hour, during daylight or when Cape Spear is enveloped in fog. Here also is placed a mechanical fog horn. At Cape Spear, in 1878, a Compressed Air Trumpet was placed; at Powles' Head (near Trepassey) a Courtnay automatic whistling buoy was placed; and in 1890 a bell buoy at Port-au-Basque.

To sustain the light-house and alarm system light-dues are collected to the extent of one shilling per ton on all vessels entering any port or harbour of the Colony, except coasting, sealing or fishing vessels, but not to be levied more than once a year.

Sealing and coasting vessels pay six pence per ton on registered vessels of forty tons and upwards; vessels under forty tons pay fifteen shillings per ton. No greater sum than £25 can be levied in any year on any steamer or vessel entering any port of the Colony; and no steamer plying between Europe and any port of North America, and entering any port of the Colony as a port of call, is liable to pay any light-dues or any port charges except pilotage.

A sum of about $45,000 annually is required to maintain the system, of which about $30,000 are collected as light-dues.

BANKS IN NEWFOUNDLAND.

The Savings' Bank is a Government establishment, and it is enacted by statute that "the general revenue of the Colony is liable for all moneys deposited in the bank and all interests payable thereon." This gives absolute security to depositors. Being thus a Colonial institution, the Governor in Council appoints the Cashier and eight governors, five of whom are selected from the members of the House of Assembly and three from the Legislative Council. Three directors are annually elected by these governors from among themselves, and by them the affairs of the bank are superintended. Depositors of any amount over four dollars for a period of not less than six months, receive interest at the rate of three per cent. per annum. By an Act of the Legislature the reserve fund is constituted a sinking fund for the liquidation of the public debt of the Colony, the annual profits of the Savings' Bank being added to this fund from year to year. Already this fund has wiped out no less than $350,942 of the Public Debt. This has been the work of the last fifteen years—a fact which speaks volumes for the excellent management of the Savings' Bank.

On the 31st December, 1893, the amount of deposits in the Savings' Bank was $3,068,288. The profits for the year were $20,337. There are at present 6,620 accounts and the same number of depositors. There are Branch Banks in Harbour Grace, Heart's Content and Placentia. Hours of business from 10.30 a. m., to 3 p. m.

The following figures show the deposits in the Savings' Bank in the years named :—

Year.	Deposits.
1878	$1,092,659
1879	1,134,555
1880	1,219,787
1881	1,291,162
1882	1,429,428
1883	1,544,547
1884	1,660,492
1885	1,787,554
1886	1,749,616
1887	1,860,968
1888	2,028,033
1889	2,184,723
1890	2,292,076
1891	2,460,663
1892	3,033,356
1893	3,068,288

It will be seen from the foregoing table that in the last sixteen years the deposits in the Savings' Bank have increased by nearly two millions of dollars, or in the period named are not very far short of having increased three-fold. As the great majority of depositors belong to the middle and working classes, this shows a gratifying advance among them of thrifty, economic habits, and a substantial increase in their means of subsistence. It also proves that the Colony is steadily advancing along the path of progress, and that the policy adopted of developing the natural resources of the country, by railway construction and other means, is improving its material condition. There is no better test of progress than the amount deposited in the Savings' Bank from year to year.

It must be remembered also that the other two banks have large amounts on deposit at 3 per cent.,—probably together as large as those in the Savings' Bank.

THE UNION BANK OF NEWFOUNDLAND.

Hours of business from 10 a. m. to 3 p. m. Discount days—Mondays and Thursdays.

The Union Bank is a prosperous and well-managed institution. It was established in 1854. During the first 18 years it paid an average dividend and bonus of 11½ per cent. per annum. The reserve fund was then so large that the Directors declared a special bonus of 50 per cent., which was taken by the shareholders in paid up shares. On this increased capital the dividends and bonuses were for many years twenty per cent. per annum, or to original shareholders equivalent to twenty-seven per cent. on their investment.

At the close of 1893 the stock of this Bank was $456,000 in shares of $100; Reserve, $300,000; Dividend and bonus for last complete year was 15 per cent. Notes in circulation 31st May, 1893, $606,162.

COMMERCIAL BANK OF NEWFOUNDLAND.

Hours of business from 10 a. m. to 3 p. m. Discount days—Tuesdays and Fridays. The Commercial Bank is also a very prosperous and well-conducted establishment. It was established in 1847.

At the close of 1893 its Stock was $306,000, in shares of $200; Reserve, $100,000. The dividend for last complete year was 10 per cent. Notes in circulation 30th June, 1892, $550,717.

THE NEWSPAPER PRESS.

The following newspapers are published in St. John's:—*The Royal Gazette*—weekly; *The Times*—bi-weekly; *The Evening Telegram*—daily; *The Evening Herald*—daily; *The Daily News*—daily, and also a weekly issue; *The Trade Review*—fortnightly.

The following papers are published elsewhere:—*The Harbour Grace Standard*—bi-weekly; *The Twillingate Sun*—weekly; *The Trinity Record*—weekly; *Weekly News*, Carbonear—weekly.

CHAPTER XIV.

SCENERY.

ATTRACTIONS FOR TRAVELLERS AND TOURISTS.

Not many years have elapsed since the discovery was made by the outside world that Newfoundland contains some of the grandest and most picturesque scenery in all this beautiful world. Formerly the idea of associating "the land of fog and codfish" with the sublime and beautiful in nature would have been scoffed at. All that was known about the island was summed up in Burns' lines in his "Twa Dogs" :—

"Some place far abroad
Where sailors gang to fish for cod."

The prevalent idea was that it was mostly shrouded by a curtain of fog, and that the interior was a region of dismal swamps, grim repulsive rocks and strips of land covered at intervals with a stunted forest growth. Gradually, these mistaken ideas were dispelled; and now every year witnesses an increasing number of visitors from the outside world—tourists in search of the picturesque—travellers, explorers, health-seekers, sportsmen—who carry back with them glowing reports of the wonderful attractions of this "gem of the western world." Now that railways and steamships are affording easy access to its shores, fiords, rivers and lakes, an increasing throng of such visitors, especially from the United States and Canada, will find their way to this newly-found land, to revel in its unique scenic beauties, and drink in its health-giving breezes laden with the breath of ocean. No traveller or tourist ever returns disappointed; but on the contrary they declare "the half has not been told."

LIKENESS TO NORWAY.

Newfoundland has well been named the "Norway of the New World." In many points it strikingly resembles that country to which tourists now flock from all lands. Its deep fiords, which indent the shores everywhere, guarded by lofty cliffs whose forms are reflected in the clear bright waters of the bays, have a remarkable resemblance to those of Norway, and are often not less magnificent in their scenery. Many of these great watery ravines, running inland for eighty or ninety miles, and exhibiting a wonderful variety of scenery along the great arms which they project in all directions; and in the islands which stud their bosoms, are on a much grander scale than the famous Norwegian fiords. The two great bays of Trinity and Placentia, which almost cut the island in two, have no parallel in respect of size, among the fiords of Norway. Then, in their short but beautiful summers, their bright skies, their exhilarating atmosphere, their population of fishermen, so abundant in insular peculiarities and primitive characteristics, hidden away in nooks remote from all the outer world, quaint in manners, gracious to strangers, the two countries resemble each other very strikingly. Norway was once as little known as Newfoundland, and its beauties as little appreciated. Now it is the resort, each summer, of many hundreds of travellers, and by its fine system of roads, it has been rendered everywhere accessible. The turn of the Norway of the New World has come at length. The artist and the photographer have been at work; and pictorial illustrations of its scenery—about which there can be no deception—are making it widely known, and thus the stream of visitors is swelling. Till Sir Walter Scott, in his poetry and romances, raised the curtain, and made known the marvellous beauties of the Highlands of Scotland, who thought of penetrating those unknown wilds! Now many thousands annually find pure and elevated enjoyment and add to the happiness of their lives by rambling among the romantic scenes of the Scottish Highlands.

NEWFOUNDLAND AS A HEALTH RESORT.

To the millions of the United States and Canada, in the near future, Newfoundland will become what Norway and the Highlands of Scotland now are to European nations. In this sea-girt isle Americans will find a welcome escape from the burning heat of their own summers; scenery novel and attractive; and a bracing exhilarating air that imparts new vigour to the frame and sends back the smoke-dried denizens of the great cities with the tide of health coursing through their veins, and life made incomparably better worth living. As a sanitarium—a pleasant health-resort—Newfoundland is destined to take a high place, when the accommodation and comforts which travellers or invalids require are provided—as unquestionably they will be—at the most desirable places, throughout the island. In fine summer days the heat is never oppressive, and nights are always cool, so that after the day's ramble, sleep comes sweet and refreshing. There is something peculiarly balmy, soothing and yet invigorating, in the summer breezes, whether on sea or land, cooling the fevered brain and smoothing the wrinkled brow of care. After a few weeks near the coast, inhaling the salt-sea breezes and exposed to the life-giving sun's rays, the invalid who has come with shattered nerves and fluttering pulse, returns with a new supply of iron in his blood and a sense of well-being which makes it a luxury to live. To escape from the sweltering summer heats of New York, Boston or Chicago, and after a pleasant sea-voyage, to breathe the pure air of Terra Nova; to climb its rocky heights, or wander over its plains and "barrens" bright with wild flowers; to ply the angler's rod or bend the oar in the clear water of its countless lakes; or to explore one of the great fiords which stretch their arms far inland, amid the wildest and grandest scenery,—all this is like passing into a new and better state of existence and enjoying for a time a purer and better life.

THE PEOPLE FRIENDLY.

One thing the tourist may safely reckon on is the sensation of novelty. Not only are the aspects of nature, indeed the whole character of the scenery, such as are not to be met with elsewhere, but here the traveller finds himself among a "peculiar people" —the hardy fisher-folk, quaint in their manners, having their own ways of looking at things;—unaffected by the fashions and conventionalities of the outside world; primitive in their modes of living, kindly, fearless, friendly. Travellers will find such a people abundantly interesting and worthy of a careful study. They are not dull, commonplace repetitions of the people among whom travellers are accustomed to meet, but original, quaint, unique. While they are friendly to all comers to their shores, to none do the hospitable Newfoundlanders, of all grades, extend a heartier welcome than to the citizens of the Great Repulic. A traveller has only to say "I am an American" and every door is open to him and every hospitality is placed at his disposal. This kindly feeling towards the Stars and Stripes is not caused by any Anti-British sentiment, for the people are thoroughly loyal to the Crown of England and have no desire to renounce their allegiance to the Mother-Country—but arises mainly from admiration for the people of the United States and their free institutions, and partly also from the fact that a large number of Newfoundlanders have, from time to time, found a home in the Western Republic, and thus there is a constantly increasing communication between this island and the States. The mails from the United States are larger than from any other country; and a large number of families have representatives or connections living under "the Star-Spangled Banner." To many of the young generation the United States is the land of promise. A large amount of business lies with the States, and the commercial union is steadily extending. Thus, among the people, Americans find themselves thoroughly at home, not only in the capital but throughout the island.

PROFESSOR ALBERT BICKMORE.

A distinguished American professor—Albert S. Bickmore—of the American Museum of Natural History, New York, spent a few weeks, in 1891, in Newfoundland and on the coast of Labrador. He said, after his extensive tour, "In regard to beauty and grandeur of scenery, health-giving climate and general attractiveness for those whose energies have been lowered by city life, and who seek to recuperate, few countries could surpass

Newfoundland. But it is not sufficiently known. Few know even the way of reaching it. A guide-book setting forth its attractions, should be published, giving such information as tourists require in order to see the country to advantage. Many hundreds of Americans would every year find their way here were the country only known. In the future, if proper steps are taken, Newfoundland may become one of the most popular summer resorts. In addition to the scenery and pure air, you have salmon and trout-fishing to an unlimited extent ; and in the fall snipe, curlew, and ptarmigan shooting, as well as deer-stalking. Boating on the lakes, driving or walking over your breezy hills ; pic-nicing in such places as Petty Harbour, Middle Cove or Topsail ; sketching or photographing your rare scenery, drinking in the oxygen of an atmosphere which at every breath quickens the pulses and puts colour in the cheek—what more could the heart of man or woman tourist ask for ?"

PROFESSOR HYATT'S EXPERIENCE.

Another eminent scientific man,—Professor Hyatt, of Boston, —spent the summer of 1885 on the West coast of the island. With a number of other scientists, he was engaged in collecting fossils and studying the geology of the district. He wrote of his excursion in the following terms :—" Certainly one can rarely see in this world more remarkable and picturesque villages than those of Burin, Burgeo and Rose Blanche. The effect of the pond-like harbours, surrounded by rugged hills, often of considerable height, is rendered exceedingly pleasing, often lovely, by the habit of building the cottages anywhere and everywhere, according to the fancy or fortune of the owner. Burgeo was especially remarkable, and an artist could spend many summers on this coast and become its pictorial historian with great gain to himself." The Professor found Port-au-Port a geological paradise, rare and curious fossils being abundant. " I have one endoceras" he wrote " two feet six inches long and with the living chambers nearly perfect—one of the finest things I have ever seen in any collection, not even excepting Hall's or Barrande's. We also found abundance of fossils at Ingornachoix Bay, where the fossil cephalopods are marvellous in size and number. We have revelled for ten days with hammer and chisel in digging out these."

HIS OPINIONS OF THE SCENERY.

In regard to the weather and scenery on the West Coast the Professor said:—"The weather favoured us while in Newfoundland. We were not detained by fogs and had very few adverse winds. *The scenery was superb, and has made all the countries we have passed through since seem tame and unpicturesque,* except indeed the steep mountainous cliffs of Cape North and the vicinity, in Cape Breton. *I never expect to get so much pleasure combined with intellectual profit out of any future trip.* Port-au-Port is a paradise for the artist as well as for the geologist; and the same may be said of Bonne Bay and Bay of Islands. From Cape Ray to St. John's Island, for the space of 250 miles on the western coast of Newfoundland, the principal mountain ranges whose general course is north-east south-west, approach the sea more or less closely. They are so arranged that they present their ends to the sea on the south coast, and are seen more from the side on the west coast. From St. George's Bay to St. John's Island, on the western coast, they form a series of steep cliffs, cones and domes, which also greatly enhance the beauty of the deep and branching fiords of Bay of Islands and Bonne Bay. The climate, vegetation and lovely harbours made the trip along this part of the route a series of delightful surprises."

GEOLOGIZING.

At the close of his trip at Anse-au-Loup, the Professor wrote: "The collection now on board contains many large and remarkable specimens of the fossils of the Quebec group, more especially the cephalopods. Some of them are certainly unique and could not be re-placed from the same localities. We have used a method of cutting out which has enabled us to remove slabs two and three feet long and six inches to a foot broad from the face of the solid rock. We have often failed in getting specimens of large size out whole; but in many cases we have entire ortho ceratites, piloceratites, endoceratites and ormoceratites of huge size, from a foot to over two feet in length. The coiled nantaloids have also been collected in considerable numbers; and the materials on hand will enable me to work out many obscure points in the structure and relations of these forms. Our collections are also rich in other fossils which we have collected as opportunity served." One of the Professor's party took photographic views of the most striking scenery as they passed along the coast. These form a series of most beautiful pictures of scenes which were never before photographed.

COMMANDER KENNEDY, R. N.

Captain Kennedy, R. N., commander of H. M. S. *Druid*, who spent several years in Newfoundland engaged in the Fisheries' Protection Service, and who knows the island thoroughly, published about ten years ago "Sporting Notes on Newfoundland." The following extract from this interesting work will show his opinion of the climate and scenery :—"To one who, like the writer, has had the opportunity of seeing the country, of mingling with its warm-hearted inhabitants, of penetrating into the vast and almost unknown interior in quest of sport, Newfoundland presents a deeply interesting aspect, whether it be from a sporting, an artistic or a social point of view."

THE WEATHER.

"The fogs on the east and south coast seldom if ever penetrate inland; and I have no hesitation in saying that for four or five months in the year, namely, from June to October, inclusive, the climate is far superior to that of Great Britain, while the winters are undoubtedly milder than those of Nova Scotia, Canada or New Brunswick. During the months of July, August, September, and part of October, the weather is magnificent, the thermometer ranging occasionally as high as 85°. At this time the country presents a most beautiful appearance, resembling in parts the Highlands of Scotland. The mountains are clothed to their tops with many kinds of woods, conspicuous among which are the fir, the pine, maple, birch and hazel. The "barrens" are covered with a rich carpet of moss of every shade and colour, and abound in all sorts of wild berries, pleasing both to the eye and taste. The banks of the rivers are also at this time fringed with wild strawberries, raspberries, currants, blue-berries, and adorned with many kinds of lovely ferns and wild flowers ; while foaming torrents and tumbling cascades complete a picture delightful to the eye of the artist and the salmon-fisher. The scenery of the south coast is of the grandest description ; deep gorges in the coast-line lead through narrow entrances, with precipitous cliffs on either hand, to magnificent harbours where the navies of Europe may float secure from every gale." " In the interior of the islands are thousands, aye, millions of acres of good land, suitable for growing crops, or raising cattle or sheep, as shown by the magnificent wild grass which grows in all the swamps, and upon which the deer feed unmolested, save when the solitary hunter intrudes upon their sanctuary." " As regards salubrity of climate, Newfoundland has no equal. On our visits round the coast the doctor's duties were absolutely *nil*." " I believe that few countries have such advantages as are possessed by Newfoundland, with her magnificent harbours and her boundless stores of wealth ; but no country has ever yet progressed without railroads, or even roads. With the completion of the railway to Hall's Bay and the probability of its ultimate extension to the west coast ; with copper mines in full blast along her shores, and other industries in like activity, the proud boast of every Newfoundlander, " This Newfoundland of Ours," will be no idle one, and the sovereignty of the island will be assured, not only in name but in reality." (The foregoing was written eleven years ago. Captain Kennedy's anticipations are receiving rapid realization.)

AN ARCHBISHOP'S OPINION.

The late Roman Catholic Archbishop of Halifax, N. S.,—a gentleman of high attainments and culture—paid a visit to Newfoundland some years ago. On his return he published an account of his trip in which he spoke in rapturous terms of the country, its scenery and its people. The following are the opening paragraphs of his paper:—"It is strange how ignorant we often are of the beauties and attractions of places near our shores, while thoroughly conversant with the lesser grandeur of historic lands far away. Thousands from the United States and many from Canada yearly flock to Europe, and write rapturous accounts of the scenes over which poetry or fiction has thrown a glamour. For a trifling outlay, and without the discomforts of a long sea voyage, they could, by visiting Newfoundland, enjoy a cool and healthy summer, and revel in all the wild grandeur of Alpine scenery, or dream away the hours by lakes and bays compared with which Killarney and Loch Katrine are but tame and uninviting pools.

COUNTRY EASY OF ACCESS.

"It was my good fortune to pay a short visit to that romantic land, and to enjoy the hospitality of its most hospitable people. The country is now easy of access, either by the Allan steamers plying between Baltimore, Halifax and St. John's; or by boats from Montreal, Pictou and Charlottetown, or by those of a line between New York and St. John's. By any of these routes you can enjoy just a taste of the great Atlantic, and then you find yourself in a land where the virgin forest still fringes the noblest bays in the world; where codfish actually swim within a yard of the shore, and salmon bask on the ledges of secluded inlets. Yet it must not be thought that the country is a howling wilderness, devoid alike of civilizing influences and local refinement. You have all these; but the population is so small compared with the vast extent of the island, that primitive nature still holds sway over hundreds of miles of country."

THE "LONDON TIMES" ON NEWFOUNDLAND.

Some fourteen years ago, when Newfoundland was less known than at present, and its attractions for tourists and travellers less favourably presented, the London *Times*, after a visit to the island of one of its ablest correspondents, in a leading article, gave utterance to some kindly words regarding the oldest of England's colonial brood. Here are a few extracts:—"An

Englishman from Middlesex or Yorkshire, set down in Newfoundland, would, for the method of thought and the way of regarding things which he would discover in those about him, be conscious of little difference between the society he had left and that on which he had been engrafted. It is to be regretted that more from these shores do not make the experiment, at any rate for a time. Newfoundlanders can doubtless exist very comfortably without the constant intercourse of Englishmen. But they not unnaturally take a little umbrage at being set down, in pure ignorance, through being left out of the track of British tourists, as a population resembling, in locality and habits, the Esquimaux. Canada and the Cape and Natal, and even the sequestered Shetlands, have each, for its especial class of taste and imagination, its traits of peculiar interest and fascination. They have at all times had their delights and graces remarked. Newfoundland alone has been left to the chance of one or another of its people caring to expatiate on its merits and being so importunate or skilful as to gain an audience. Were but a single trial given, to borrow the language of advertisers, the British public is assured that Newfoundland would soon become a favoured resort. It is guarded by as many terrors and obstructions as if it were the cave of a dragon and his treasure. Yet behind the barrier of cloud and ice lies a land of pleasant airs and radiant sunshine. There are woods and meadows and flowers. There are cathedrals, concert rooms and libraries, with all the luxury attendant upon dwellers in villas.

* * * * * *

"Newfoundland as a Colony is dwarfed by its relation to two continents as a central fish-market. For itself it has promising mines which would reward capital and enterprise, were not both monopolized by the hereditary pursuit. It has fertile belts which will bear wheat in profusion. It has vast expanses of practicable pastures. Railways would open up tracts of agricultural territory which are now presumed to be irreclaimable marshes and wildernesses. In the meantime there is hunting as good as in the great American North-West, without the distance to travel, and with hospitality and friendly English fellow-citizens to welcome the sportsman. What is wanted is just a little sunshine and countenance from the Mother Country, to stir the islanders themselves to develop Newfoundland for Newfoundlanders. Life is easy yet not too easy. Nature affords a sufficiency of opportunities without enervating the population by doing its work herself. Travellers who have the courage to penetrate the veil of fog and winter, and the more obstinate barrier of discouraging presumption of perennial gloom, will discover that life is well worth living among Newfoundland balsam poplars; and that the oldest English Colony has with age only deepened and intensified its English characteristics."

After fourteen years, it is pleasant to know that the anticipations of the great English journal have been fully verified. Newfoundland, every year, attracts greater attention and the stream of travellers drawn to its shores is constantly swelling. The railways built and in course of construction will greatly increase among the outside world the desire to know more of this mis-known country, and to make acquaintance with its novel, picturesque scenery. Its coast scenery is of course better known than that of the interior. Many voyagers have seen, in passing, its dark frowning cliffs, its miles on miles of rocky walls, three to four hundred feet in height, its bold promontories and headlands, sculptured into grim fantastic forms by the blows of Atlantic billows—shapes massive and awe-inspiring in their stern grandeur. These external ramparts engaged in ceaseless conflict with the watery battalions which are ever rushing on them, are apt at first sight to be repellant to the traveller. But within these rocky outworks, up the great fiords, with their countless branches, along the banks of the rivers and brooks, among the rolling hills and great barrens are scenes of rarest beauty, and over all a sky blue and serene as that of Italy and more varied in its changing aspects. No element of nature's sublimity and beauty is wanting. In drives or rambles along the shores of bays, the roads now scale the lofty hills, then dip down into silent dells, and ever and anon break out to the sea through wood-skirted ravines. There, in the distance, are the glittering icebergs sailing majestically past; or here, aground in some quiet cove, lies one of the white wanderers, the waves gently laving its sides, while cascades are pouring from its top as it melts under the fierce rays of the summer's sun. Everywhere the eye is greeted with some new, fantastic form of cliff, or rich colouring of porphyry rock; while the softness of delicate mosses contrasts at intervals with the ruggedness of bare rocks on which the gnawing tooth of time has been operating for countless ages. At almost every turn of the road little gem-like lakes flash into view, their waters clear as crystal, many of them with moss-clad islets sleeping in their bosoms. Such a drive, in a bright summer's day, around these great sea-arms, is something to be remembered till the close of life.

CHAPTER XV.
DIRECTIONS FOR TOURISTS.

HOW TO SEE THE COUNTRY—ROUTES OF TRAVEL.

NEWFOUNDLAND is now easy of access to the outside world, whether from the United States, Canada or Europe. Three fine steamers of the Allan Line—the *Corean*, *Siberian* and *Carthaginian*—under contract with the Government for the conveyance of mails—ply between Glasgow, Liverpool, and Philadelphia, calling on their westward trips, fortnightly, at St. John's and Halifax, and on their eastward trips at St. John's only. Fares from Liverpool to St. John's—saloon, $48; second cabin, $28–30; steerage, $19–20; from St. John's to Halifax, $20. They leave Liverpool and Philadelphia fortnightly. The accommodation for passengers on board the Allan steamers is excellent. The average passage from Liverpool to St. John's is seven days. Messrs. Shea & Co., Agents in St. John's; Allan & Co., Liverpool. For list of sailing see advertising pages.

CANADIAN AND NEWFOUNDLAND STEAMSHIP CO.

The steamers of *Canadian and Newfoundland Steamship Co.* also sail between Liverpool and Halifax, calling at St. John's. A steamer of this line leaves Liverpool and Halifax every ten days, touching at St. John's on both the outward and homeward trips. The *Mornea*, *Barcelona* and *Ulunda* are excellent steamers, and every attention is paid to the comfort of passengers. Fares—saloon, from Liverpool to St. John's, $48; from St. John's to Halifax, saloon, $15; steerage, $9. Agents—St. John's, J. & W. Pitts; Liverpool, J. J. Langley, Bank Chambers, Cook Street; London, Thos. Ronaldson & Co., 37 Leaden Hall St.; Glasgow, Donaldson Bros., 165 St. Vincent Street; Halifax, James Hall, P.O. box 215. These steamers usually reach St. John's from

Liverpool in seven or eight days, and Halifax in two days from St. John's. They carry mails.

RED CROSS LINE.

The steamers of this line—the *Portia* and *Sylvia*—ply between New York and St. John's, calling at Halifax each trip. The usual passage from New York to St. John's is five to five and a half days, with a "stop-over" of a day or half a day at Halifax. They sail every ten days. Fares: from New York to St. John's, saloon $34, steerage $18; from St. John's to Halifax, saloon $18; steerage $9. Agents in St. John's, Harvey & Co.; in Halifax, Corbett & Co.; in New York, Bowring & Archibald, 9 Stone St. They usually carry mails between Halifax and St. John's. The *Sylvia*, in the summer season, goes to Pilley's Island (280 miles from St. John's) for a cargo of ore, taking passengers who wish to make the round trip, which usually is very pleasant and enables them to see an interesting part of the coast scenery. The *Portia* does not go further than St. John's. The *Sylvia* calls at St. John's on her return from Pilley's Island. The Red Cross steamers are favourites with the travelling public, and are well managed.

ST. JOHN'S AND MONTREAL.

From Montreal St. John's is reached in four days (1070 miles) by steamers of the Black Diamond Line—*Bonavista* and *Coban*—sailing fortnightly. They are safe and comfortable. Fares: $30 saloon, $15 steerage. Agents—St. John's, Harvey & Co.; Montreal, Kingman, Brown & Co., 14 Palais Royal.

Also by steamers of the Ross Line—*Thames*, *Greetlands* and *Polino*—sailing weekly from Montreal and St. John's during the season, from April till the close of navigation. Fares, $25 saloon. The S. S. *Tiber* also plies between Montreal and Saint John's. Agents for all four, St. John's, Shea & Co.; Montreal, Dobell & Co. The accommodation for passengers is fairly good.

STEAMERS ST. PIERRE AND HARLAW — WESTERN COAST.

The s. s. *St. Pierre* plies between Halifax, Sydney, (C. B.), Channel and Placentia, calling at Trepassey, St. Mary's, Placentia, Burin, St. Lawrence, Lamaline, Fortune, Grand Bank, St. Jacques and Belloram alternately; Harbor Briton, Gaultois, Hermitage Cove and Pushthrough alternately; Ramea, Burgeo, La Poile, Rose Blanche, Channel, Bonne Bay. The *St. Pierre* also touches at the port of St. Pierre, both going from and returning to Halifax. Her sailings are fortnightly. She carries mails.

The s. s. *Harlaw* plies between Halifax and the principal western ports of Newfoundland, making fortnightly trips.

Both the *St. Pierre* and the *Harlaw* are well fitted up, safe and comfortable. Travellers speak in high terms of both. Tourists who wish to see the magnificent scenery of the western coast and enjoy its delicious summer, would find it advantageous to take either of these boats at Halifax, and they will thus get a glimpse of St. Pierre and of the noble scenery of St. George's Bay, Bay of Islands and Bonne Bay. This is now becoming a favourite route, and is rapturously spoken of by those who have taken the round trip. When the new railway is completed to Bay of Islands, which will probably be the case by the end of 1894, travellers who voyage by these boats can land at Bay of Islands, and take the railway for St. John's, making a stay at any of the intermediate places; and thus greatly enhance the pleasures of their trip, and enjoy any amount of trout and salmon fishing, or shooting in the proper season. (See chapter on Roads and Railways.)

COASTAL STEAMERS.

The steamers *Grand Lake* and *Virginia Lake*, of the Newfoundland Coastal Co., leave St. John's fortnightly, one taking the southern and western route to Bonne Bay and calling at intermediate ports to land and receive mails and passengers; the other running north to Battle Harbour, Labrador, there connecting with the Labrador mail steamer, and calling at all intermediate ports to land and receive mails and passengers. These steamers are strongly built, well officered, and the food and accommodation are very good. (For their sailings see advertisement at the end of this volume; also trips by them subsequently given.)

ST. JOHN'S—FINE ENTRANCE TO ITS HARBOUR.

For picturesqueness of situation there is no other city in North America to compare with St. John's, the capital of the island. All travellers who visit it admire the striking approach to the harbour, and the fine view on entering its waters. As the voyager, coming northward from Cape Race, sails along the grim, iron-bound coast whose rocks, two to four hundred feet high, fling back in defiance the great Atlantic rollers, the steamer suddenly turns her prow shoreward as if to dash herself against the dark cliffs. In a few minutes a narrow opening in the rocky wall is seen, as if, by some convulsion of nature, the great rampart had been rent asunder and the sea had rushed in. As the vessel glides through this cleft the traveller looks up, not without a touch of awe, at the great cliffs of dark red sandstone piled in broken masses on a foundation of gray slate rock. On his right he sees an almost perpendicular precipice, 300 feet in height, above which rises, with almost equal steepness, the crest of Signal Hill, 520 feet above the level of the sea, on which stands the "Block House" for signalling vessels as they approach the harbour. On the left, the rugged hill attains a height of 600 feet. From its base a rocky promontory juts out, forming the entrance of the Narrows on one side. On the summit of this projection is Fort Amherst Light-house, where is heard the hoarse music of the restless Atlantic whose waves break on the rocks beneath. The scene is grand and impressive.

THE NARROWS.

Formerly batteries, armed with formidable Armstrong guns, rose one over the other, on the projecting shoulders and narrow platforms of the surrounding cliffs; but years ago the small garrison was withdrawn, and the cannon removed. The Narrows, or channel leading to the harbour, is nearly half a mile in length; and it is not till two-thirds of it are passed that the city itself opens to view. At the termination of the Narrows the harbour trends suddenly to the west, thus completely shutting out the swell from the ocean. In ten minutes after leaving the Atlantic the steamer is safely moored at the wharf, in the still waters of a perfectly land-locked harbour. Vessels of the largest tonnage can enter at all periods of the tide, the rise of which does not exceed four feet. Between Signal Hill and Fort Amherst, at the entrance, the Narrows are about 1,400 feet in width; but at the narrowest part between Pancake and Chain Rocks, the channel is not more than 600 feet wide. The harbour is about a mile in length, and half a mile in width. It is deep with a mud bottom, and in the centre it is said to be 90 feet in depth. Of its size, it would be difficult to find a finer harbour.

STREETS, ETC.

The city is built on the northern side of the harbour, on a site which could hardly be surpassed. From the water's edge the ground rises with a slope till the summit is reached, where there is a large level space. Along the face of this slope the main streets run, and the city is rapidly extending itself in all directions. An excellent system of sewerage is laid out, which when completed will render the sanitary condition of the city superior to that of any other on the Atlantic seaboard. Already it is a very healthy city. Three principal streets—Water, Duckworth and Gower Streets—run parallel with the harbour and with one another, and are intersected by a number of cross-streets, running north and south. The former follow the sinuosities of the harbour, so that they are irregular and winding. The new part built since the great fire of 1892 is considerably improved, and the large shops and stores in the eastern half of Water Street are a great advance on those destroyed by the fire. Duckworth Street has also been better laid out and much improved.

HOUSES, VILLAS, ETC.

On the south side of the harbour the hills spring so abruptly from the water that little more than a sufficient site for a range of warehouses and oil factories could be scooped out. From the waters of the harbour the city presents a fine appearance, climbing the slope of the hill which is crowned by the Roman Catholic Cathedral, a noble structure which overlooks the whole. There is ample space in every direction for expansion. Already the tendency is to build dwelling houses in the suburbs, or on the summits of the rising grounds overlooking the harbour, and to leave the large stores and shops solely for business purposes, instead of having as formerly residences over them. Many of the new houses erected outside the city on the higher grounds are of a superior description, and these as they increase will form squares and crescents, and become the fashionable quarters. The leading roads in all directions, to the distance of two miles from the city, are getting lined with handsome villas, the residences of the wealthier classes. Water Street, the principal business street, presents a very substantial appearance, the houses being of stone or brick. The shops, stores and counting-houses occupy the ground floors, while some of the merchants and many of the shop-keepers still reside in the upper storeys. Fish-stores and other warehouses project from the rear on the side next the harbour. Many of the shops, especially in the recently re-built part of Water Street, present a very handsome appearance, and compare not unfavourably with similar establishments in the large cities of Canada and the United States. In other parts of the city the bulk of the houses are built of wood, and many of the streets are exceedingly dingy and commonplace.

PURE WATER—FIRE BRIGADE.

St. John's has the immense advantage of possessing an abundant supply of the purest water which is obtained from Windsor Lake, four and a-half miles from the city and standing at a height of 400 feet above the sea-level. The pressure is thus so great that water can be thrown from the hydrants to a height of fifty feet, or 150 feet along a street. Taught by sad experience, the Government and Municipal Council are now organizing a fire brigade of a highly efficient order, equipped with all modern improvements, which will render the recurrence of a great fire, like that of 1846 or 1892, an improbable event.

DISTANCES FROM OTHER CITIES.

The city is situated on the east side of the peninsula of Avalon, which presents a wide frontage to the sea, and on the portion of American land which approaches nearest to the Old World. It is 60 miles north of Cape Race ; 600 miles from Halifax ; 1,170 miles from Montreal; 1200 miles from New York; and 1700 miles from Queenstown—being 1,000 miles nearer it than New York. It is in 47° 33' 33" N. latitude, and 52 45' 10" W. longitude.

OBJECTS OF INTEREST IN ST. JOHN'S WORTHY THE ATTENTION OF TOURISTS AND VISITORS.

A walk along Water street, the main business thoroughfare, about a mile in length, will enable a stranger to form an idea of the style of business and the mode of conducting it. Handsome shop-fronts, tastefully "dressed" and exhibiting all kinds of fancy goods and more substantial articles, are everywhere conspicuous. The visitor will be specially struck with the beauty and solidity of the new blocks erected since the fire—such as Baird's Building ; Marshall and Rodger's ; Ayre and Sons ; Garland's ; Goodfellow's Buildings. These, in architecture and general arrangements, do not suffer by comparison with similar establishments in any other city of the same size. The thronged shops, crowded streets, and general bustle and activity show that a large business is done here. This is especially the case in the early summer and in the Fall.

FISH STORES, ETC.

A glance at one of the large fish-stores—such as Baine Johnstone's, Job's, Monroe's or Thorburn and Tessier's—is interesting as showing how the dried cod-fish are sorted, stacked in huge piles, and made up in "drums" for foreign markets. To see the process of manufacturing the fish-oils and the complicated machinery used, it is necessary to cross the harbour in a boat, and walk through one of the great oil-factories on the South Side, where the seal oil is refined and prepared for market.

OFFICES—MUSEUM.

In the Exchange Building, near the foot of McBride's Hill, the Anglo-American Telegraph Co. have recently opened a new office which is well arranged and creditable to the Company. Hours of business from 8.30 a. m to 9 p. m. There is a branch office in the eastern end of the city, and also in the Post office. The Post office, already referred to, is a fine building towards the western end of Water street. Its arrangements for the accommodation of the public are all that could be desired. The upper portion of it is devoted to the purposes of a Public Museum which will well repay a visit. Here are arranged specimens of all the minerals and coal found in the island, together with specimens of the building-stone, marbles, granites, etc., and of the timber. The geologist can here study the fossils found in the various formations of the country which are named and classified. The antiquarian will find here a most interesting collection of the relics of the extinct aboriginal inhabitants of the island. Here are skulls, bones, almost entire skeletons of the unfortunate lost tribes of Beothiks. The skeleton of a boy found in a grave in Pilley's Island, with the skin and nails perfectly preserved, is regarded as a great curiosity. Their stone implements, arrow-heads, gouges, hatchets, etc., are objects of much interest. Local objects of natural history are in great profusion —such as stuffed specimens of caribou, bears, seals, birds, fishes. There is also a collection of the mollusca of the island. Here too is preserved an arm of the now celebrated "Devil Fish" or gigantic Cuttle Fish—named after its discoverer, the present writer, *Archetuthis Harveyi*. When first discovered, in 1873, it made a sensation in the scientific world. Its body was ten feet in length, and its longest arms each thirty feet. (For full particulars of this Giant Cuttle see "*Hatton and Harvey's Newfoundland*," or article "Newfoundland" in the *Encyclopædia Britannica*.) A forenoon spent in the Museum will well reward the tourist.

DRY DOCK.

Continuing the walk westward along Water Street, the Long Bridge is reached, near the head of the harbour, where is the

Dry Dock, built of wood and opened in 1884. It is 600 feet long, 83 feet broad, with a depth of 25 feet on its sill at low water. It is thus able to accommodate all but the very largest steamers afloat. It cost $550,000.

LUNATIC ASYLUM.

Three miles further out, on the Waterford Bridge Road, is the Lunatic Asylum, a handsome structure, beautifully situated and excellently managed. Visitors are admitted by an order from the doctors in charge of the institution. The walk or drive to it along the Castor's Valley, as the little brook is called, is very pleasant. Victoria Park is passed on the right.

CATHOLIC CATHEDRAL.

There are many more objects of interest in the city. The most conspicuous building is the Roman Catholic Cathedral, which occupies a commanding site on the summit of the hill on which the city is built. It is in the form of a Latin Cross, 237 feet in length, and 180 feet wide across the transepts, with two towers 138 feet in height. It is richly ornamented with statuary, the finest being "The Dead Christ," by Hogan, under the altar, and those of St. John the Baptist and of the Virgin, in front of the Cathedral. The view from the Cathedral grounds is specially fine. Adjacent to it are the Bishop's Palace, Saint Bonaventure's College and a Convent. The whole group of buildings cost about $500,000. The general appearance is very fine.

CHURCH OF ENGLAND CATHEDRAL.

The Church of England Cathedral, about half way up the slope, will when completed be one of the finest ecclesiastical buildings in British America. It was designed by Sir Gilbert Scott, and is in the early English style. Unfortunately it was terribly injured in the great fire of 1892, only the bare walls being left. The walls of the transept were not seriously injured but the arches were ruined. This portion of the Cathedral has now been roofed and the arches restored, and it soon will be available for services; but the nave which suffered more is still in ruins. Its entire restoration is most desirable.

On Military Road running along the crest of the ridge stands the Colonial Building or House of Parliament, containing chambers for the two branches of the Legislature, and most of the public offices. It is 110 feet long and 85 feet wide and was built in 1847 at a cost of £100,000. Its Ionic portico is borne by six massive columns, 30 feet high. Near it is Government House, an unpretentious but substantial and comfortable abode, where the representative of Royalty resides. It is surrounded by well-kept grounds. The Imperial Government erected it in 1828 at a cost of £30,000.

ATHENÆUM AND OTHER BUILDINGS.

The Athenæum was a handsome building near the Union Bank in Duckworth Street. It was totally destroyed, with its fine public library, music hall, reading room and the Savings' Bank in the fire of 1892, and is now in ruins, awaiting restoration. A fine building for the accommodation of the Savings' Bank is to be erected opposite the Athenæum, on the site of St. Andrew's Presbyterian Church which is in course of re-erection on a more commanding site higher up the slope, where the Masonic Temple stood before the fire. The last named building is to occupy a fine site a little above the new Savings' Bank. The Athenæum reading-room and library are in Tobin's Building toward the eastern end of Duckworth Street. They are open to strangers on the introduction of a member. The Penitentiary, a solid granite building, and the Public Hospital, an excellent institution remarkably well cared for, are on the Quidi Vidi road, on the outskirts of the city. Both will repay a visit.

INDUSTRIES.

Although the chief business interests of St. John's are in the exportation of the grand staple, the codfish, and its seal-oil refineries, yet in recent years there has been a wonderful development of local industries of various kinds. There is now a large and well-equipped Rope Walk at Mundy Pond, half a mile from the city, which gives employment to about 400 persons, and is equal in all respects to any other establishment of the kind in British America or the United States. There are also three iron foundries, nail foundry, machine shops, railway work-shops, two biscuit bakeries of a superior description, breweries, tanneries, furniture, tobacco, soap and butterine factories—all of which give employment to a large number of hands.

NATIVE BERRIES.

One recently introduced native industry deserves special mention—the preserving, on a large scale, for exportation, of the delicious wild berries which grow in unlimited quantities all over the island. Only one firm has yet taken a prominent part in this new and promising industry—Mr. W. H. Davidson, Grocer, Water Street, to whom the credit of introducing it belongs. If generally carried out, thousands of idle hands—especially women and young persons,—might be profitably engaged in gathering the wild straw-berries, rasp-berries, capillaire, partridge-berries, bake-apples, "hurtz" or blue-berries, which cover hundreds of thousands of acres and can be gathered in the vicinity of every settlement. The article produced by Mr. Davidson is delicious. Some two years ago he sent a package of these preserved berries to the Queen who was pleased to accept the same, and to express her great satisfaction with the contents. To make this industry a success, a drawback on the sugar used should be allowed by the Government, as the duty on that article is nearly 100 per cent., greatly interfering with the success of such an enterprise.

DRIVES AND WALKS IN THE VICINITY OF ST. JOHN'S.

By making St. John's headquarters, the tourist can enjoy many delightful excursions by vehicle, or for short distances on foot. Cabs can be hired for the day or half day at the rate of four dollars per day, or eighty cents per hour. Short drives through the city cost from thirty to fifty cents, according to distance. There are numerous lakes and ponds at moderate distances from the city where excellent trout fishing can be had;

but there is no good salmon stream nearer than Salmonier, at a distance of fifty miles. It is reached by rail to Holyrood, thence by vehicle. In the season the salmon fishing there is excellent.

VIEW FROM SIGNAL HILL.

All visitors speedily find their way to the top of Signal Hill overlooking the narrows, where a magnificent view is obtained. It can be reached by a walk of half an hour, or by a short carriage drive. The road leading to it starts from the eastern end of Duckworth Street. At the height of 350 feet two small and deep lakes are passed. When the summit is reached, if the day be clear, a noble view is enjoyed. On the one side is the broad Atlantic "with all its terror and mystery"—not a rock or shoal in the great expanse till the Irish coast is reached. Looking northward we see *Sugar Loaf, Logie Bay, Torbay Head* and the serrated range of hills on the south side of Conception Bay. The dark perpendicular sea-wall, with numerous indentations, runs up to Cape St. Francis. A fine sweep of country, dotted with numerous glittering lakelets and farm-houses and fringed with sombre groves of fir, stretches away to the north-west. The great chasm which forms the entrance to the harbour is seen below, guarded by precipitous rock-masses. The remains of the batteries which once commanded the narrow entrance are visible on their rocky platforms. Fort Amherst and Cape Spear lighthouses and Freshwater Bay, with its fishermen's cottages, are seen to the south. A bird's-eye view is presented of the harbour and its shipping, with the whole city lying along the northern slope, crowned by the Roman Catholic Cathedral. A lower peak called Gallows Hill stands out prominently.— Here, in the olden time, criminals were hanged in sight of the whole city.

BATTLE OF SIGNAL HILL, 1762.

In 1762 Signal Hill was the scene of a brief but bloody struggle. For the third time in sixty-six years the French had got possession of St. John's. Lord Colville was sent from Halifax with a squadron to drive them out. Colonel Amherst landed a force from the fleet at Torbay, and marched overland to Saint John's. Up the rugged heights from Quidi Vidi the English soldiers charged to capture Signal Hill, the key of the position. The French fought desperately, and having a great advantage from their position, succeeded several times in repulsing their foes. At length Captain MacDonald, leading a company of Highlanders with fixed bayonets, dashed up the height and swept all before them. The brave leader and his lieutenant were both severely, but not mortally wounded. Signal Hill being won, the French saw that all was lost. Their fleet managed to escape by creeping out of the harbour in a thick fog. The English lost twenty men; the French loss was heavy, but the number is unknown. St. John's never again fell into the hands of the French.

GEOLOGY OF THE HILL.

Looking around the summit of the hill it is seen to be capped by dark red sandstone belonging to the Huronian system of rocks, corresponding to the English Cambrian which is developed all over the peninsula of Avalon. The hill itself is strewed with large boulders holding jasper and other water-worn pebbles, showing that they once formed the margin of an old Silurian sea, and that by foldings and various earth-movements, the sea-bottom has become a hill of 520 feet above the level of the water. Here too are seen striations on the rock-surfaces, showing that at a later period they were under glacial action. Geologists tell us that the whole island was once, during long ages, in the same condition in which Greenland now is—under a great ice-cap many hundreds of feet in thickness. Most travellers allow that the view from Signal Hill is rarely surpassed elsewhere.

QUIDI VIDI.

A second interesting walk is to the picturesque fishing village of Quidi Vidi, half a mile from the city. The road to it leads past the Penitentiary and Hospital, along the margin of the pretty little Quidi Lake, on which an annual regatta is held.

The village is a typical fishing-village where can be seen in perfection the stages projecting over the water of the little harbour, at which the fishermen land their fish, and the "flakes" on which the cod are dried. During the fishing season, the whole process of "splitting," "heading" and salting can be seen. The small harbour is connected with the ocean by a narrow gut only wide and deep enough for fishing boats. All around rise steep red cliffs in fantastic shapes. Very frequently an iceberg or two are grounded close by the mouth of the little harbour—their dazzlingly white pinnacles and spires contrasting strikingly with the dark frowning rocks. These, with the fishing boats, stages and flakes make a strikingly characteristic picture. Artists are strongly attracted to this spot. A little river flowing through the lake forms a pretty cascade as it tumbles over the rocks into the harbour. Visitors will enjoy calling at some cottages of the fishermen, where they will receive a warm welcome, and can have a pleasant chat with the sturdy fishermen and their wives whose oddities of speech and quaint views of things form an interesting study. A walk over the White Hills from the village, for two miles, brings the visitor to the beautiful Virginia Water.

TO TORBAY, ETC.

Another delightful drive is to Torbay, a village six or seven miles from St. John's. The road runs to the north, passing near Virginia Water, a pretty little lake embossomed in woods, and abounding in fine trout. Then Logie Bay (four miles) is reached, famous for its grand coast scenery. Outer and middle Cove, two miles farther on, are scarcely less remarkable for rocky scenery. Torbay is a thriving village picturesque in situation, having a handsome Roman Catholic church, a Convent, excellent schoolrooms and a large public hall. The drive may be extended a few miles further on the road to Pouch Cove. Along this coast, up to Cape St. Francis, are no pebbly beaches on which the summer waves gently break, but there is the massive grandeur of perpendicular cliffs, often sculptured into forms of stern beauty.

TO PORTUGAL COVE.

Portugal Cove, nine miles north-west from St. John's, is a spot which no tourist should omit visiting. The road is excellent and for the first four miles presents a continual ascent ; but when the summit or "height of land" is reached, if the day be clear, a splendid panorama presents itself. Away in the distance, on the right, is the grand old ocean, heaving gently, under the summer breeze, like "the bosom of an infant asleep." A white sail or two are visible, or perhaps half a dozen lonely wanderers of the deep that were born of Greenland glaciers and are now as towering icebergs sailing past to meet their doom in the warm waters of the Gulf Stream. The whole range of dark cliffs and headlands from Cape Spear to the entrance of Conception Bay, is visible from this eminence. Two miles further Windsor Lake is passed, from which the city is supplied with water. Then comes a gradual descent, by a winding road, through a little valley of rare beauty with a brook flowing at the foot of its encompassing rocks, till at a sudden turn of the road, Conception Bay in all its beauty bursts into view. The whole scene can be taken in at a glance — Belle Isle (6 miles long) ; the whole range of the northern shore of the bay, 30 miles distant, and the lonely rocky isle of Baccalieu, dimly visible in the distance at the mouth of this noble sheet of water. On the south shore is the quaint fishing village of Portugal Cove, with its wooden houses nestling amid the clefts of the rocks, and its little water-fall tumbling over the cliffs into the sea. The bold navigator Cortereal discovered this bay in 1501, and named the roadstead after his country. Half a day may be pleasantly spent here admiring the great over-hanging cliffs, the huge boulders scattered all around, the rugged hills ; and chatting with the primitive people who here fight life's battle. The sea has been the grave of many of their kindred ; but is it not too, with all its wild restlessness, their bountiful mother from whose prolific bosom they derive their means of subsistence! The return to St. John's is best made *via* Broad Cove, by the Thorburn Road, which affords a change of scene and many delightful views. A visit to Portugal Cove is a matter that will be remembered.

PETTY HARBOUR.

Perhaps even a finer drive from the city is to Petty Harbour (7 miles distant). It lies south of St. John's. The road runs *via* Waterford Bridge past the Lunatic Asylum, and for most of the distance is within sight of the Atlantic. Countless little lakes are passed on the way, each more beautiful and charming than the last, and at length Petty Harbour with a population of about a thousand, is reached. It is situated at the mouth of a deep ravine through which flows a clear stream falling into the snug little harbour, fringed all around with fish-flakes, and shut in by towering precipices. This is a scene for the artist or photographer. The drive by the old road, returning by the more modern road, through the Goulds, is one of the most charming in the neighbourhood of the city. At a short distance south of Petty Harbour is "The Spout"—a funnel-shaped opening from above into a cavern which the sea has scooped out. In stormy weather the sea, rushing into this cavern, hurls the spray and foam aloft through this opening, presenting to the eye of the traveller a most curious sight, visible at times for miles around.

A LONGER EXCURSION—ST. JOHN'S TO RENEWS.

Tourists who are inclined for a more extended excursion may make arrangements for a drive from the Capital to Renews, 54 miles south of St. John's. It is possible to reach Renews by getting a seat in the mail-conveyance which leaves St. John's twice a week — on Mondays and Fridays;—but a better plan would be to hire a carriage (fare about $4 per day) and make the journey one day returning the next. As the hotel accommodation is somewhat primitive, it would be advisable to start with a well-filled luncheon-basket. The drive will amply reward the tourists. The road is excellent, and at many points the views are superb. The "barrens" along the route are famous for ptarmigan shooting, (willow grouse); and after September 15th, when this sport begins, is much frequented by sportsmen. Countless lakelets and trout-brooks are passed, in which fine trout are abundant. Striking views of the ocean are obtained at various points on the way, and the coast scenery is magnificent, the hills having a strong resemblance to the Cordillera peaks. The road first winds through a pretty, well-cultivated little valley, over Waterford Bridge, passing near Blackhead (four miles from St. John's) from which Cape Spear can be reached—the most eastern point of North America, the summit, crowned by its lighthouse, being 264 feet above the sea-level. Petty Harbour, already referred to (population 953) is next passed and Bay of Bulls (20 miles from St. John's) is reached. The name is supposed to be a corruption of the French Baie de Bois (Bay of the woods). The population is about 700, nearly all fishermen. Bay of Bulls is a harbour of refuge where vessels find shelter when the ice or stormy winds render it impossible to double Cape Spear and reach the Capital. It was the scene of several skirmishes in the olden days when English and French fought for supremacy in the island. The last of these was in 1796 when a French squadron appeared off the harbour of St. John's; but finding that a hot reception was prepared for them, they passed on without challenging a shot. They avenged themselves, however, by burning the defenceless settlement of Bay of Bulls, and after this small exploit disappeared. This was the last attempt made by the French to get a hold on Newfoundland. At an earlier date (1696) the French were more successful. Brouillan, Governor of Placentia, with a squadron attacked Ferryland. On his way he met a solitary English man-of-war which he chased into Bay of Bulls. Captain Cleasby, its Commander, determined to defend his vessel to the last. The gallant captain placed all his guns on the broad-side next the enemy and fought furiously till his vessel took fire, when he escaped to the shore. The French followed him, and he and his men had to surrender. Ferryland was destroyed by Brouillan. The famous French Commander D'Iberville joined him and St. John's, then defended by a feeble garrison, was captured and burned.

The next settlement on this route, two miles further, is Witless Bay (population 866). Then in succession come the small villages of Mobile, Toad's Cove, La Manche, Brigus, Cape Broyle (population 511), and Ferryland, forty-four miles from St. John's, (population 549). Ferryland is a historic spot. Here in 1624, (see Historical Sketch), Sir George Calvert, afterwards Lord Baltimore, planted a colony, built a fort and a fine mansion, in which he resided with his family for a number of years. Here too Sir David Kirke took up his residence in 1638, armed with the powers of a Count Palatine over the whole island. These famous leaders and warriors have long since vanished, "like the snow-flake on the river"; but the curious traveller can still trace the remains of the fort and houses. Continuing this southern route, Aquaforte and Fermeuse (population 637) with its deep and safe harbour, are reached. Three miles further comes Renews, fifty-four miles from St. John's, (population 538). The scenery around these harbours is most picturesque. At Renews are the tall rugged hills called the Butterpots, the range running thirty miles north to Holyrood at the head of Conception Bay where is another hill named Butterpot. Ten miles further south is Cape Race, but the road or track beyond Renews is not passable for a carriage. Round the grim rocks of Cape Race (a corruption from the Portuguese name Capo Razo, or Bare Cape), swift conflicting currents circle; dark fogs in summer and autumn often brood for weeks together, so that the navigator has to shape his course mainly by the soundings. In recent years the dangers of this spot, where many a ship has been dashed to pieces, have been greatly lessened by the erection of a powerful fog-whistle.

EXCURSIONS BY SEA.

Two trips from St. John's by steamer can be recommended to those who enjoy the sea, and wish to make acquaintance with the various localities and to view the grand coast scenery which is unsurpassed elsewhere. The fine steamers of the Coastal steamship Company—the *Grand Lake* and *Virginia Lake*—make fortnightly trips, during summer and autumn, the former taking the southern and western route, and the latter the northern route to Battle Harbour, Labrador, touching at the various intermediate ports. Those who do not class themselves as invalids, but who want to breathe the bracing sea-air and benefit by the stimulus imparted to mind and body by constant change of scene, will find either or both of these trips, in the Coastal steamers, enjoyable and beneficial. The accommodation for travellers, especially in the *Grand Lake*, is excellent; the table good, and the captains and officers are experienced careful men, noted for their attention and courtesy to travellers. Almost the entire round of the island can be made in these steamers. Those who do not care to make the whole round can land at any of the intermediate ports where there are sufficient attractions, and spend a few days fishing, shooting, sketching and photographing, awaiting the return of the steamers, thus greatly enhancing the pleasures of the trip and securing the opportunity of making a closer acquaintance with the country and its people. After reaching Battle Harbour, the tourist can extend his trip along the whole coast of Labrador as far as Nain, as the Labrador mail steamer connects there.

THE WESTERN ROUTE PER "GRAND LAKE"—ST. JOHN'S TO BONNE BAY DISTANCE 651 MILES.

From St. John's to Bonne Bay the fare for cabin passage is $15—meals included,—the same rate in returning; for intermediate ports the rate is proportional according to distance. From St. John's to Battle Harbour the fare for cabin is $12. On the Labrador steamer $2 per day. On each route there are about 24 ports of call, so that ample opportunity of viewing the scenery and obtaining an idea of the country is afforded.

PORTS OF CALL—WESTERN ROUTE.

After leaving St. John's the steamer makes her first call at Ferryland, and rounding Cape Race she passes (25 miles farther) St. Shotts, where many a mariner has gone down, "unknelled, uncoffined and unknown," and enters the fine harbour of Trepassey. Her course thence is up St. Mary's Bay, 25 miles wide at the mouth, and 35 miles in length. St. Mary's, the port of call, (518 inhabitants) is a busy fishing village and somewhat of a farming district. Placentia Bay, the largest in the island, being

90 miles in length and 55 miles wide at its mouth, is next reached. It contains clusters of islands, one of them, Great Merasheen Island, being 21 miles long. The scenery of this bay is very fine. The steamer makes four calls here—at Placentia, St. Lawrence, Lamaline and Burin. Burin is a very prosperous place, having extensive fisheries and a large trade with St. Pierre Its land-locked harbour is one of the finest in the island. Fortune Bay is next reached, noted for its fine herring fishery and is a great resort for American fishing vessels. The French Islands of St. Pierre and Miquelon are visible, in the mouth of the Bay. Fortune, Grand Bank, Belleoram, St. Jacques, Harbour Briton are touched at in succession. The scenery of Bay D'Espoir (corrupted into Bay Despair) and of Hermitage Bay, arms of Fortune Bay, is pronounced by many travellers to be the most magnificent in the island. Burin, Harbour Briton, Burgeo and Rose Blanche are most picturesque in situation. Artists will here find the most striking materials on which to work, and might spend here with profit many weeks studying nature's varied forms.

FORTUNE TO CAPE RAY.

From Fortune Bay there is a straight line of coast 100 miles in length, terminating at Cape Ray. It is indented with numbers of small bays and harbours, the most important being La Poile and Rose Blanche Bays. Numerous clusters of islands are seen in passing, such as the Penguin Islands and the Burgeo Islands. From the largest of the latter Captain James Cook, the celebrated navigator, observed an eclipse of the sun in 1765. Port-au-Basque, a splendid harbour, deep, and perfectly sheltered, is destined to be a place of great importance as the western terminus of the trans-insular railway now in course of construction. Close to it is Channel, a thriving place, with a population of 723.

CAPE RAY TO PORT-AU-PORT.

Rounding Cape Ray (165 inhabitants) the steamer now passes along what is popularly known as the French Shore. Opposite Cape Ray, on the Cape Breton shore, is Cape North, the two capes sentinelling the entrance of the Gulf of St. Lawrence. From Cape Ray to Cape Anguille the coast is singularly rugged and inhospitable. The Great and Little Codroy Rivers discharge their waters between these two points after flowing through a fertile valley 50 miles in length. The noble bay of St. George's Bay, 516 miles from St. John's, now opens, having according to the Census of 1891 a population of 6,632. Its fertile shores, as we have already seen, are rich in forest and mineral wealth. The steamer makes a short stay at Sandy Point, then rounds the peninsula of Port-au-Port famous for its fossils, and latterly for its asbestos mines. The packing of lobsters is here carried on extensively. Geologists come here to chisel the great cephalopods out of its rocks.

BAY OF ISLANDS.

Ninety-four miles farther north the Bay of Islands (population 1,500) is reached. As the name indicates it has numerous islands. It has three great arms running twenty miles inland, one of which receives the Humber, the second largest river in the island. The scenery of this bay is spoken of by all travellers in rapturous terms. A paper contributed by Mr. G. S. Benjamin to the *Century Magazine*, giving an account of his trip to this region, contains the folowing :—"The day was superb as if this noble bay wished to fix a favourable impression upon the memory of the voyagers who had come so far to see it. Blomidon soared majestically above us, the monarch of that mountain land, crowned with a wreath of roseate clouds, and the surrounding isles were suffused with the glow of a peaceful sunset. The water of the Bay of Islands is as blue as that of the Mediterranean. In this case it cannot be due to a larger proportion of salt which is the cause of the intense blue of the sea in warm climates, so it must be attributed to the greater depth of the Newfoundland Bay. As I gazed entranced at the lovely scene before me I was able for the first time to realize, by the aid of the golden haze veiling the long slopes and tumbling steeps the grandeur of the sierras which enclosed the Bay of Islands. The silence was intensified by the silvery waterfalls dropping from crag to crag many hundred feet with an etherial motion and yet giving forth no echo or sound of their dashing, so distant were they from our ship."

BONNE BAY.

Forty miles farther north Bonne Bay is entered. Another traveller says of it, "if anything it is even more magnificent in natural beauty than the Bay of Islands. A lovelier scene cannot be imagined. Great hills in the foregrounds and beyond ; mountains peeping over each others' shoulders ; and away up in the blue sky the snow sparkled on the higher storm-lashed peaks which reared their heads far inland, all robed in a beautiful transparent atmosphere utterly unknown elsewhere. To the north the hills were bare, rugged, precipitous ; but on that particular morning the glorious sunshine made them lose half their desolate bleakness. We climbed the nearest hill, but only for a short distance. Cliffs towered above us on every hand, over which poured cascades of melting ice (the time was early May) thundering in the deep chasms below. The hoarse roar of waterfalls came from far and near. The heat was almost unbearable —and this in a land known only for its fogs!! We left Bonne Bay with regret."

RETURN.

The *Grand Lake* at Bonne Bay is 651 miles from St. John's and usually reaches it on the fourth or fifth day after starting from the capital, returning by the same route and calling at the same ports as on the outward trip. The round trip is usually made in nine or ten days.

RETURN BY RAIL.

When the Northern and Western Railway reaches Bay of Islands, probably by the close of the present year (1894) tourists can land there and enjoy the railway journey back to St. John's, thus obtaining greater variety. This will probably become a favourite route for visitors.

NORTHERN ROUTE—ST. JOHN'S TO BATTLE HARBOUR, LABRADOR.

Distance about 500 miles. Cabin fare (meals included), $12 ;

same amount returning. The *Virginia Lake*, of the Coastal Steamship Co., leaves St. John's fortnightly, during the summer and autumn months, for Battle Harbour, Labrador, calling at intermediate ports to land and receive mails and passengers. In some respects the trip is even more enjoyable than that previously described. The sea-breezes are more bracing; the atmosphere clear from the entire absence of fog. The bright sunshine, the impressive coast scenery, the frequent stoppages at the various harbours breaking the monotony of the voyage, and affording glimpses of the people and their ways of living; the great bays across which the steamer ploughs her way—all combine to render the excursion stimulating and pleasant. Then should the trip include the Labrador coast, a strange wild land is reached, and a new experience is gained amid its icebergs and towering cliffs, its hardy fisher-folk gathering in the sea harvest and battling with the billows. There is something entirely out of the ordinary track of travellers in such an excursion. All is fresh, awakening, "bracing brain and sinew."

ST. JOHN'S TO TRINITY--HATTON'S "UNDER THE GREAT SEAL."

After clearing St. John's Narrows the *Virginia Lake* passes Torbay Head, Cape St. Francis with its restless waves breaking upon the "Brandies," as the outlying rocks are called; the mouth of Conception Bay; the grim cliffs of Baccalieu Island, the resort of myriads of sea-fowl; and Grate's Point. It then enters the noble bay of Trinity, seventy miles in length; and after touching at Old Perlican on the southern shore (forty-seven miles from St. John's) it crosses to Trinity (sixty-eight miles) one of the finest and most beautiful harbours in the world. Round the shores of Trinity Bay more than 18,000 people are clustered, nearly all engaged in the fisheries; many of them spend the summer on Labrador. At the head of this bay, the first Atlantic Cable was landed in 1858; and the cables, now in operation, emerge from the ocean at Heart's Content, on its southern shore, after traversing the great submarine plain of 1,600 miles between Newfoundland and the coast of Ireland. A few miles farther up the bay is Heart's Delight, a small fishing village, having 430 inhabitants, now famous as the scene of Mr. Joseph Hatton's popular novel "Under the Great Seal." This accomplished novelist has depicted in his exciting story the magnificent scenery of Heart's Delight and Heart's Content, and the ways and speech of the fisher-folk, with marvellous accuracy and touching effect. All who wish to realise what Newfoundland was in the days of the Fishing Admirals should read this fine tale, rich in pathos and dramatic effects.

CATALINA TO TWILLINGATE.

The next call of the steamer is made at Catalina (87 miles) — a harbour of refuge at the north entrance of Trinity Bay—(over 1,900 inhabitants). The name Catalina, like Kathleen in Irish, is the musical Spanish term for Kate or St. Catherine, after whom it is named. Bonavista Bay is now entered, having around its shores a population of 17,849. Its largest town, (Bonavista), (107 miles) has a population of 3,550, being a thriving place. Around the bay is much excellent land ; a large quantity being under culture. King's Cove (116 miles) is next touched at (population 589). Then a call is made at Greenspond (148 miles) on an island with fine fishing grounds around it, (population 1,317). The steamer's course is then shaped for Fogo (815 inhabitants), a harbour on an island of the same name in Notre Dame Bay. The prosperous town of Twillingate (French *Toulinguet*) also on an island, having a population of 3,585, is next reached, (distance from St. John's 232 miles.)

THE MINING REGION.

The voyager is now in the famous copper-mining region. Calls are made at Exploits, Pilley's Island, (population 411), noted for its splendid iron-pyrites mine (see chapter on Mineral Resources), the ore being pronounced the finest in the world for the manufacture of sulphuric acid. Little Bay Island, Little Bay, Nipper's Harbour, Bett's Cove, Tilt Cove—317 miles— (1,004 inhabitants).

TILT COVE TO BATTLE HARBOUR.

Proceeding on her northern route the steamer now approaches an important landmark—Cape St. John—the northern headland of Notre Dame Bay, and the north-eastern terminus of the French Shore. From this point she glides along a vast wall of rock 400 to 500 feet high and six miles in length, the summits presenting every immaginable shape into which rocks can be torn or sculptured. The ports touched at after passing Cape St. John are Coachman's Cove (349 miles from St. John's); Conche (399 miles), St. Anthony (435 miles), Griquet (450 miles), Great Kirpon (450 miles). Cape Bauld and Cape Norman, dreary and desolate spots, the most northern points of the island are then passed. Here at times a great procession of stately icebergs may be seen moving to the south through the Straits of Belle Isle, across whose eastern entrance the steamer now shapes her course, passing Belle Isle, a treeless, barren little island nine miles long and three miles broad. Early mariners called it the "Isle of Demons," imagining that they heard here "a great clamour of men's voices, confused and inarticulate, such as you hear from a crowd at a fair or market-place." The grinding of the ice-floes and the crash of the lofty bergs during a gale would be quite sufficient to give rise to these superstitious fancies. After passing Belle Isle the steamer soon reaches her terminus at Battle Harbour, 495 miles from St. John's. Battle Harbour is a sheltered roadstead, between Battle Island and Great Caribou Island. It is a great fishing centre for Labrador vessels, and during the season is crowded with craft of all sorts, presenting a very lively scene.

LABRADOR TRIP.

From Red Bay or Battle Harbour to Nain, Freestone Island and Ramah—distance about 450 miles fare on board the Labrador steamer $2 per day.

To those who do not fear to rough it a little, a trip in the Labrador mail steamer *Windsor Lake* can be recommended. The invigorating atmosphere, the sternly grand scenery, the wild but novel surroundings render this excursion attractive to all who can dispense for a little with the mere luxuries of civilization, and who are not over squeamish as to "what they eat, drink and avoid" and are content with plain wholesome fare. Admirers of icebergs will revel in a scene where they can at times be counted in hundreds. This "great and terrible wilderness"—to use an Old Testament phrase—stretches for more than a thousand miles to Cape Chidleigh, at the entrance of Hudson's Straits. The coast is indented by countless fiords, one of them, Hamilton Inlet, is 30 miles wide at its mouth, while its head is 150 miles from the sea. Fortunately, on this grim storm-beaten coast, there are numerous and safe harbours. It is under the jurisdiction of Newfoundland along its Atlantic coast line; but the interior and the Gulf Side of the coast from Blanc Sablon are under Canada.

Formerly the St. John's mail steamer connected at Battle Harbour with the Labrador steamer, but a change has been made this year, the southern terminus of the Labrador steamer's route being Red Bay where connection is made. The route is also extended beyond Nain to Ramah, the most northern of the Moravian Mission stations. As, however, the *Windsor Lake* calls at Battle Harbour on both her northern and southern trips, no difficulty will be experienced in joining her there; but it is at Red Bay the steamers meet for connection. Only two trips in the season are made to Nain and Ramah, on which occasions Battle Harbour is the southern terminus.

LABRADOR PORTS OF CALL.

The principal ports of call in Labrador are Francis Harbour, Square Island, Dead Island, Venison Island, Punch Bowl, Batteau, Domino, Indian Tickle, Grady, Pack's Harbour, Indian Harbour, Emily Harbour, Cape Harrison, Ragged Islands, Turnavick Islands, Windsor's Harbour, Hopedale, Nain, and Ramah. The last three are stations of the Moravian missions. The missionaries stationed here are Germans, but most of them speak English, and all are well educated, and excellent men. They willingly receive and entertain strangers. A fortnight may be agreeably spent at Hopedale or Nain awaiting the return of the steamer. An opportunity is afforded of seeing the christianized Eskimo who live around these stations and have been taught by the missionaries not only in a knowledge of Christianity, but in useful industrious arts. Visitors usually return laden with Eskimo curiosities made from tusks of the walrus, and also articles of clothing made from the skins of seals and reindeer. All visitors are favourably impressed with the noble self-denying labours of the Moravian Missionaries.

MEDICAL AID FOR THE FISHERMEN: MISSION TO DEEP SEA FISHERMEN—DR. GRENFELL.

The *Windsor Lake* carries a doctor who is paid by the Government and supplied with medicines. He brings medical and surgical aid to the fishermen, at the different ports of call, in cases of sickness and accident. When it is taken into account that in the fishing season there are from 20,000 to 25,000 persons, many of them women and children, living for three and a half or four months in rude temporary huts on shore, or on board the floating fishing crafts going far north, exposed to the vicissitudes of the weather and in constant peril, it will be seen how little one medical man, moving up and down the coast in the mail steamer, and having but an hour at each port, could do to help such a multitude in cases of sickness. Some benevolent persons brought under the notice of the Managers of the *Mission to Deep Sea Fishermen* in England the hardships and sufferings of the Labrador fisher-folk, and their great need of medical and surgical assistance, and in many instances of warm clothing. The result was that the Mission Ship *Albert* was sent there in 1892, in charge of Dr. Grenfell. His report led to her return in 1893. With assistance obtained here and in England two excellent hospitals, fully equipped, were erected, one at Battle Harbour and one at Indian Harbour much further north. A doctor and a trained nurse were placed in charge of each. The *Albert* cruised along the coast during the fishing season, Dr. Grenfell ministering to the sick and relieving the poor with donations of clothing, and in some cases of food. The severe cases were carried to the hospitals. A large amount of good was accomplished. No less than 2,493 cases, medical and surgical, were treated.

The benevolent and liberal Sir Donald Smith, of Montreal, was so impressed with the value of these services that he presented this year to the Labrador Mission a beautiful steam yacht 80 feet long, to be employed in visiting the different fishing stations, in charge of Dr. Grenfell, and carrying to them medical and other relief, and conveying the sick to the hospitals. With such a vessel the good work will be greatly enlarged.

THE GRAND FALLS OF HAMILTON RIVER, LABRADOR.

Rigolet is the only port of call for the steamer in Hamilton Inlet. Hamilton River, which flows from the interior of Labrador, discharges its waters into the head of this inlet. The *Grand Falls* on this river were re-discovered in August 1891 by Mr. Henry G. Bryant, of Philadelphia, a noted traveller, and Prof. Kenaston, of Washington. These explorers, after a most perilous and toilsome journey of 250 miles up the river, in a boat, reached the Falls. Mr. Bryant has described his experience during this journey in an article contributed to *The Century Magazine*, and beautifully illustrated by pictures taken from his photographs of the various scenes. Recently he has published a small volume describing their adventures, and the appearance of the falls which is also illustrated. He describes the spectacle as most magnificent, amply rewarding the long and difficult journey. The river leaps from a rocky platform into a huge chasm. The roar can be heard at a distance of twenty miles. An immense column of mist rises to a great height, showing a beautiful rainbow. The height of the falls was found, on accurate measurement, to be 316 ft., that of Niagara being 150 to 164 ft. The canon into which the river plunges below the falls is 25 miles in length, the cliffs along its banks being 400 to 500 feet high at the entrance. At a short distance above the falls the river is of considerable width, but the banks gradually narrow till where it makes its final plunge the stream is not more than 200 feet across, the water being pent up and forming an arch and rushing on with extraordinary swiftness. The first white man who saw these falls, 30 years before, was a Scotchman named McLean, an official of the Hudson Bay Company. No one is known to have visited them since that time. Mythical stories regarding them were in circulation, and some writers represented them to be 2,000 feet high, so that sober-minded persons began to question their existence. Nothing would induce a Labrador Indian to approach the falls which they believe are haunted by evil spirits of extraordinary malignity, bent on the destruction of all intruders. A half-breed Indian who had the temerity to approach them, told Mr. Bryant that under the falls are witches constantly engaged in washing, and that he saw their long white arms and streaming hair as they tried to grasp and drag him into the foaming abyss. Gold he said would not induce him to go near them a second time. Ordinary tourists are not likely to visit the Grand Falls till a more practicable route is opened. A party lead by officials of the Canadian Geological Survey crossed Labrador last winter coming out at Hudson's Bay, and this summer they are traversing the great peninsula in another direction and will visit the Grand Falls. They found the country far better timbered than was previously believed, and much richer in animal life, especially reindeer.

It may be mentioned that Mr. Bryant, the discoverer of the Grand Falls, is now engaged in Arctic work, in connection with Peary's Greenland Expedition. He left St. John's on July 7th, 1894, in the steamer *Falcon*, as leader of the Peary Auxiliary Expedition, to bring home Peary and his party. He had it in view to spend a month in exploring and charting 350 miles of unknown coast in Jones's Sound previous to the return of the Greenland Expedition.

EXCURSIONS BY RAILWAY.

St. John's to Harbour Grace : distance, $83\frac{1}{2}$ miles ; time, five hours. First class fare, $2.50 ; second class, $1.70 ; one through train daily. During the summer months the regular daily train leaves St. John's at 10 a. m. and Harbour Grace at 11 a. m. There are extra trains running for shorter distances during summer, and frequent excursion trains. See time-table for information regarding "round trip tickets," excursion parties," "extra trains," etc. For fares and distances to intermediate stations see advertisements at the end of the volume.

The Newfoundland Railway Station is in the east end of St. John's. It is far from being an imposing structure; but in due time a more creditable and convenient station will take its place. The train runs at first towards the west and soon reaches Topsail (15 miles) where Conception Bay with its islands (Great and Little Belle Isle and Kelley's Island) and its beautiful scenery, comes into full view as the train reaches the station. Topsail is a pretty village—"the Brighton of Newfoundland"—a favourite summer and bathing resort for the people of St. John's, where comfortable boarding houses can be found, and the air is pure and health-giving. The scenery, as the train winds along the shores of the bay, in a bright summer's day, is rarely surpassed. Holyrood, at the head of the bay, presents some striking scenery, especially along the sea-arms which extend inland for some distance. After rounding the head of the bay the line runs inland, and Brigus Junction (47½ miles), the station for the thriving little town of Brigus (1,541 population), seven miles distant, on the north shore of Conception Bay, is then reached.

WHITBOURNE.

At Whitbourne (named in honour of the brave Captain Whitbourne, see page 14), a fine thriving village has sprung up, having saw-mills, railway work-shops and other industries. The land here is excellent, and farming operations are extending. There is a fairly good hotel. More and more Whitbourne is becoming a favourite resort for excursion parties; and as the numerous ponds in the neighbourhood are swarming with the finest trout, anglers make it their head-quarters.

HARBOUR GRACE.

Harbour Grace (83½ miles), the terminus of the line, (6,466 population) is a clean well laid out town. Its site is excellent;

and a walk down the shore eastward, or over the hills behind, where beautiful views of the bay are obtained, is charming. All visitors are much pleased with Harbour Grace, and its kindly hospitable inhabitants. Its supply of the purest water from a neighbouring lake is abundant. It is deeply interested in the Labrador fisheries to which large numbers of its people as well as of the various towns and villages on the north shore of the bay, resort in summer. The large fishing establishment of John Munn & Co. is well worthy of a visit. Here are seen the immense stores where dried codfish are piled and prepared for exportation; and the machinery for the manufacture of seal oil. The process of preparing and packing the "boneless codfish" tinning caplin; manufacturing the finest glue from the skins of codfish, and guano from their bones and other refuse; and of making refined cod-liver oil by the freezing process (an immense improvement) can be seen here in full operation. In all these new departments this enterprising firm have led the way. The firm of John Patterson & Co. is another supplying house doing a large trade.

In 1889, the beautiful Roman Catholic Cathedral was unhappily destroyed by fire. It was a gem of architecture, and an ornament of the town. Its restoration is now approaching completion under the zealous and skilful supervision of Bishop McDonald.

No visitor should fail to make a trip by railway to Harbour Grace. Comfortable accommodation can be had at *The Gordon House*, (fare $1.20 per day), and in other boarding houses.

HARBOUR GRACE TO HEART'S CONTENT.

The trip to Harbour Grace may be profitably completed by a carriage drive of 16 miles to Heart's Content *via* Carbonear. It can easily be accomplished in one day, leaving several hours to be spent in the world-famous western terminus of the Anglo-American Telegraph Co. The drive itself, in a fine day, over the breezy hills, is enjoyable; and the village of Heart's Content, with its surrounding scenery, is peculiarly striking. The spacious building used for telegraphic purposes cannot be mistaken, as it looms up like a Colossus over the low dwellings of the fishermen. The visitor may reckon on receiving a cordial welcome. The officials of the Company are most courteous and attentive to strangers, and ready to explain all the mysteries of telegraphy. The eye is at first bewildered looking at the complicated apparatus by which cable messages are sent or received. Keys, keyboards, jars, wires, wheels and other telegraphic paraphernalia seem to the uninitiated a mass of inextricable confusion. But the operator now seats himself before the "Recorder," the famous instrument invented by Sir William Thompson, which has quite superseded the older instrument known as the "Reflector," and made a new era in sub-marine telegraphy. He inquires of the operator at Valencia, Ireland, 1,700 miles away, what kind of weather they have. The last movement in sending the message has hardly ceased when the brass rollers begin to move and the reply commences to be received. As the paper tape passes perpendicularly between the rollers, a delicate syphon, hung in a little reservoir of electrified ink, is seen marking it; and the marks are the record of the message which has started from Valencia. The characters are traced on the tape about as fast as a slow penman copies a letter, and are read off at once by the practised eye of the operator. A small magnetic coil which is positively or negatively electrified by the working of two keys manipulated by the sender of the message, swings the syphon point now to one side, now to the other, along the tape, marking out a delicate line, which, to the uninitiated, looks like a minature tracing of the summits of a mountain range. Here is a high elevation on the line, there a depression; then a single notch, or two or three notches are traced. The keen eye of the telegrapher glances along this waving line, and every peak, depression or elevation is to him an alphabetical symbol. The curves correspond with letters and numerals, and thus he rapidly translates them into words. This is the wonderful "Recorder."—a machine of the most delicate fineness and flexibility, so as to minimize to the utmost the electric strain needed for working the cable. What a world of thought must have been expended in the construction of such an instrument, which with the little wire which unites two hemispheres, has made the crystal dome of the Atlantic a whispering gallery between the Old World and the New.

HOW BREAKS ARE DETECTED.

Another wonderful instrument shown to the visitor is the delicate machine by which a break or flaw in the cable is quickly located, and accurately determined within a few yards. The following explanation will convey some idea of the method by which this wonderful feat is performed: "The whole electric potency of the cable, when fully charged is known; and the same can be quickly ascertained of the two parts created by a break. A delicate instrument, adjusted to the nicest fractions, discloses the electric units or "ohms" in each part; and as the number of ohms to the mile is known, the miles and fractions of miles in both parts can be found out at each end of the cable. In the case of a clean break the locating of it takes about fifteen minutes. But a very angular break, or a flaw makes perturbations of the measurement which it, now and then, takes some hours to rectify."

FEAT OF THE S. S. "MINIA."

Almost as wonderful is the process by which the broken ends of the cable are picked up with ease and certainty and the injury repaired. The famous cable ship *Minia*, Captain Trott, a few years ago, picked up an injured cable of the Anglo-American Company, without trouble, at a depth of two and a quarter miles near the middle of the Atlantic.

NEW CABLE OF 1894.

Wonderful improvements in the manufacture of the modern cable have been made; and each new cable seems to surpass its predecessors. The duplex system of sending or receiving messages doubles the capacity of every new cable that is laid. The working life of a cable is now about 20 years. While this page is going through the press, the laying of a new cable by the Anglo-American Company has commenced at Heart's Content. It is described as far surpassing any previously laid. It is claimed for this new cable that it will possess twice the capacity of any existing cable, its conductor being 1200 lbs. per mile; the average of other cables being less than half this weight. The present cables at Heart's Content,—four in number—transmit about twenty words per minute in each direction, on the duplex principle, or forty in all. The new cable is expected to transmit 120 words per minute. The "Recorder" is to be superseded by the "Wheatstone Automatic" instrument, which will surpass the "Recorder" as far as it surpassed the now obsolete "Reflector." Such are the rapid strides made in ocean telegraphy.

THE OFFICIAL STAFF.

The station at Heart's Content gives employment to between 30 and 40 persons. The community made up of the electricians and operators, many of whom are married, constitutes a pleasant, refined society. They are picked men in their profession, well educated, intelligent and courteous. Superior talent is needed, and the salaries paid are liberal. Such compensation for the lonely isolated life passed in this retired spot is surely called for.

There is a romantic interest attaching to this spot where the possibility of wedding two hemispheres in electric bonds was first demonstrated. Mr. Frederick N. Gisborne has the high honour of being the originator and the first practical prime mover in the great enterprise which first established telegraphic communication between the Old World and the New. But it was the heroic perseverance, the dauntless courage and indomitable energy of Mr. Cyrus Field that, after thirteen long years of effort, won the final triumph in 1866, and completed the work. The services rendered to the cause of civilization by these two men are incalculable. From that date till the present hour thought has been flying on the lightning's pinions between east and west. In this secluded spot these men carry on the work, summer and winter, day and night, interpreting the mystic hieroglyphics scrawled on the slender strip of paper. The messages make a brief pause here, and are then flashed to their destination east and west. What tales of joy and woe; of "battle, murder and sudden death;" of the crash of empires; of the triumph or downfall of statesmen; of tempest and shipwreck; of fortunes won or lost; of events that rend the heart with grief, or brighten the eye with gladness, have been recorded on this paper tape as it rolls on laden with its burden of world history. But of the contents these operators are as silent as the recording syphon itself.

DILDO COD HATCHERY.

In returning to St. John's by the Newfoundland railway, the tourist can leave the railway at Broad Cove Station, and a drive of three miles will take him to Dildo, on Trinity Bay, now famous for its Cod and Lobster Hatchery, which has achieved such triumphant success. It is on an island about half a mile from the shore. Should it be the hatching season Mr. Nielson, Superintendent of Fisheries, will be found there, and the visitor may calculate on a warm and courteous welcome. The arrangements for hatching the cod and lobster ova; the different stages of the growth of the young fry, and the process of "planting," are full of interest. A visit here will be well repaid.

ST. JOHN'S TO PLACENTIA BY RAILWAY.

Distance, 84½ miles; time, 4 hours; fare, 1st class, $3. No tourist should fail to pay a visit to Placentia—the old French capital—one of the most interesting places in the island, not only on account of its historic associations, but for the exquisite beauty of its scenery, especially along the arms of the sea, one of which runs ten miles inland and the other six miles. In July they abound in sea-trout of the finest quality, which help to make the place a paradise to the angler. In addition, there are countless streams and lakelets in the neighbourhood, where he will find abundant opportunities of pursuing his favourite sport. The walks and drives around to places of interest are delightful. The artist will find much to interest him in the scenic beauty of many spots. Placentia is one of those places of which all visitors speak well, and from which no one returns disappointed. A week can be spent here very pleasantly.

OBJECTS OF INTEREST IN PLACENTIA.

The route is the same as to Harbor Grace as far as Whitbourne Junction (57½ miles). The Placentia Branch is 27 miles in length. Leaving St. John's at 10 a. m. the traveller arrives at 2 p. m. There are four hotels—Bradshaw's (near the station), Verran's, Ryan's and Sinnot's in the town on the opposite side of the harbour. They are though unpretending clean and comfortable. The town (563 inhabitants) has a quaint appearance, being built along a shingly beach. It was founded and fortified by the French, and held by them till 1713 (see Historical Sketch). Objects of interest are the Roman Catholic church—a handsome structure, and the remains of the oldest Protestant church (Church of England) in the island, but in a most dilapidated and neglected condition. William IV.,—the "Sailor King,"—visited Placentia when in command of the *Pegasus* (a ship attached to Nelson's fleet in the West Indies), and afterwards presented to this church a handsome silver communion service of five pieces, which is carefully preserved and is shown to visitors at the house of Mr. Bradshaw who has charge of it. It bears the inscription, "Given by His Royal Highness Prince William Henry to the Protestant Chapel at Placentia, Newfoundland, 1787." There are strong reasons for believing that this church was built soon after the treaty of Utrecht (1713), so that this humble wooden structure has braved the storms of probably 170 years. It merits more care and attention than it has yet received.

OLD TOMBSTONES.

The ground around it was used as a burying ground long before the erection of the Church, the dates on the ancient tombstones plainly proving this. Most of these stones have been broken across and are now placed within the church for preservation. The most interesting is one with the following inscription: "Dahemen Hilai—, May 1st, 1676." Two letters are effaced, so that the name of the occupant of the grave probably was "Dahemen Hilaire." Then came words which have completely puzzled antiquarians : "Canus de Tale le Araus anno nenego Semea." A copy of this inscription was sent to the late Professor Robertson Smith, of Cambridge, one of the Editors of the Encyclopædia Britannica, who pronounced some of the words to be Basque. Curiously enough the inscription is on both sides of the stone. The next oldest stone (1694) is that of a captain of a French King's frigate who rejoiced in the Breton name of " Johannes de Sulgaraichipi." He was good enough, however, to shorten it into "Croisic" for every day use. Another stone records the departure of a certain Richard Walsh in 1770, " who carried on a most extensive trade in this harbour with the greatest credit, and died in the 53rd year of his age feelingly lamented by his Planters and Dealers,"—which in those days was not often the case with deceased merchants. Some one has scratched on the stone " May he rest in Pace." At the top is a rude carving, in relief, of the cross, of the crucifiction, with all the attendant symbols, including the nails, pincers, sponge, dice.

CURIOSITIES AND RELICS.

On a door inside the church is the escutcheon of George III.; and in the quaint old Court House, which is close by, is the baton of office, bearing the quarterings of the House of Hanover. It is curious to find these relics of Basques, Bretons, French and the House of Hanover in such a spot on the shores of Newfoundland. Many interesting relics of the French occupation are preserved among the people. One of these is an old French brevet signed by Louis XIV., and counter-signed by his prime minister, Phelypeaux, granting to Le Sieur de Costebello the ownership of the small peninsula of Point Verte near Placentia. The brevet is dated 1709, and is written on parchment in the most crabbed of old French. Many other grants are preserved bearing the autograph of the Grand Monarque. An old French china bowl has been found and preserved, in which, no doubt many a goodly measure of punch had been brewed.

SITUATION OF PLACENTIA.

The situation of Placentia is most picturesque, nestling low on a sea-formed beach, encircled by hills on all sides except towards the bay. Castle Hill is an object of interest. On it the French built a formidable fortress which rose over the narrow entrance of the splendid harbour, and so completely commanded it that the English were never able to capture the town, though repeated attempts were made. On the opposite side is Flagstaff or Signal Hill. Its first name was Plaisance afterwards transformed into Placentia. Point de Verde is three miles distant. Lilly White Pond, famous for its trout, is five miles distant. On the shores of the Bay are La Manche Lead and Silver Mine, also Silver Cliff Mine. A small mail steamer plies on the bay. In fine weather charming trips can be made in her around the shores of this noble bay. A most beautiful drive to Salmonier—an arm of St. Mary's Bay, some 25 miles distant—affords many varied and picturesque views. In the season, excellent salmon fishing can be had at Salmonier. There is there fair accommodation for travellers.

THE FUTURE OF PLACENTIA.

Though the ancient glories of Placentia have departed, brighter prospects await it in future days. It is now a thriving little town, having an air of comfort. No signs of poverty meet the eye. It is one of the best centres for the Bank fishery. It is a port of call for two mail steamers and has become a trade centre for the southern and western shore. Now that the railway has reached it and brought it within four hours of the capital, and that the new line of railway will make it, when finished, accessible from Port-aux-Basque, multitudes of tourist and visitors from the United States and Canada, will make it a summer resort to enjoy its splendid scenery and health-giving air, and to ply the rod in its lakes, rivers and sea-arms. It has only to be known to be appreciated.

RICHARD BROTHERS—THE MAD PROPHET.

There is another memory connected with Placentia which has a curious interest. It is the birth-place of a singular personage called Richard Brothers—a religious fanatic—who created no small stir in London more than a century ago. He laid claim to the gift of prophecy, had visions and revelations, and scattered his predictions broadcast. His followers were numbered by thousands, and some of them were learned men and many moved in fashionable circles. He announced himself as being of Jewish descent, though separated from that race by 1500 years, and that he had come to restore the Jews which event was to take place in the year 1798. He was, he declared, of the tribe of Judah and a descendant of King David. On several of his more distinguished followers and patrons he conferred a similar distinction, and assured them he had learned by special revelation that they were Hebrews, one in particular being a descendant of Aaron, the High Priest.

HE REACHES NOTORIETY.

It seems scarcely credible to us in these days that such absurd ravings made a profound impression no longer ago than the reign of George III., and that in fashionable circles in London the excitement about the new Prophet Brothers was intense. "His house" we are told "was daily filled with persons of quality and fortune of both sexes; while the street was crowded with the great folks' carriages. Learned divines entered the field as his opponents. Scores of pious enthusiasts wildly testified in his favour. Thousands trembled at his denunciations of woe." One distinguished Oriental scholar named Halhed, who was also a member of Parliament, defended him in learned dissertations in the press, and also in parliamentary speeches.

BROTHERS' GREATEST WORK.

Exactly a hundred years ago (in 1794) Brothers published his greatest work entitled "A Revealed Knowledge of the Prophecies and Times." It is now ranked among the rare books, and its name appears occasionally in the catalogues of old books at a high price. It is said to be a tissue of the wildest ravings; once it was admired as an inspired production. Among other things he informed George III. that he would shortly have to surrender his Crown to himself as Prince of Israel and Governor-General of the world.

SAD END OF THE PROPHET.

The madness of poor Brothers now became more pronounced. He went to the House of Commons to prophesy to its members of coming wars and convulsions, but was summarily ejected. Soon after he was placed in a Lunatic Asylum where he ended his days. Numbers still believed in him and regarded him as a martyr, for

"Faith, fanatic faith, once wedded fast
To some dear falsehood hugs it to the last."

BROTHERS'S EARLY LIFE.

It is somewhat of a shock to find that this announced descendant of King David was the son of an Irishman who came out from the old land to better his condition; settled in Placentia; married a Harbour Grace lady named Jewer, by whom he had four sons, this Richard being the eldest. By some means or other his father managed to get him a place as midshipman on board a British man-of-war where he rose to be a lieutenant. On a reduction of the navy taking place he was retired on a pension of three shillings a day, and went to live in London where he developed into a prophet. There are numbers of the descendants of the Brothers's family now living in Newfoundland—industrious respectable people—who all cherish proudly the memory of their learned and distinguished relative, who attained greatness in such a remarkable way. It seems he did not forget his Newfoundland relatives. He sent £100 at one time to be divided among his brothers; also the present of an enormous cheese—the recollections of which are still vivid among those of the family who partook of it. A niece of the Prophet—Mrs. Mary Young, over seventy years of age—is, or was lately, living in Upper Island Cove, Conception Bay. There are also several other nieces and nephews—some in Fermeuse. Richard was not a conscious imposter; he was an honest enthusiast and a believer in his own prophecies. He must have had considerable ability and some learning. "A bee in his bonnet" did the rest; but Placentia will hardly erect a monument to the memory of her only prophet. That such a man should only 100 years ago have set fashionable London in a blaze with his delusions, and won a large following, having among them shrewd, intelligent and educated men, is a remarkable phenomenon even in the history of religious fanaticisms.

FROM ST. JOHN'S TO EXPLOITS BY THE NORTHERN AND WESTERN RAILWAY—DISTANCE 257½ MILES.

By far the most interesting railway excursion is by the Northern and Western Railway now under construction and which has been completed and is now operated to the Exploits River, a distance from the capital of 257½ miles. No tourist will omit this trip to Exploits which affords a view of the interior; of its largest rivers and lakes; of its best lands and forests; and some of its finest scenery. Along this line, at different points, salmon and trout fishing to any extent can be had; and after September 15th ptarmigan (willow grouse) and deer shooting. Some of the finest localities for deer-stalking can be reached by this line. Non-residents of the Colony, however, have to pay $100 for a license to kill deer, and not more than five stags and three does can be killed per season. A stop can be made at any of the intermediate stations for sport or for artistic purposes. The scenery is fresh and novel. At all the principal stations hotel accommodation either has been or will be provided shortly. The carriages are most comfortable, and the road admirably built. There are as yet only two through trains weekly, on Tuesdays and Fridays. Leaving St. John's on these mornings at 10 o'clock, by the ordinary train, Whitbourne is reached in three hours, where connection is made by the N. & W. Train which reaches its destination at Exploits in about 12 hours. Fare to Exploits from Whitbourne—1st class, $6; 2nd class, $4. For a full account of this railway—the stations, character of the country, scenery, fishing, etc., see page 61 to 76. The time-table will be found among the advertisements. The following is a Table of Distances for this railway when completed to Port-aux-Basque :—

TABLE OF DISTANCES — NEWFOUNDLAND NORTHERN AND WESTERN RAILWAY,—MILEAGE APPROXIMATE.

FROM ST. JOHN'S TO		FROM ST. JOHN'S TO	
Whitbourne	57½	Badger Brook	296½
Placentia Junction	64½	Lake Bond	304
Chapel Arm and Long Har. .	77½	Skull Hill Lake	309½
Tickle Har. and Pinch Gut .	82½	Mary March River	323
Rantem	89½	Summit White Hill Plain ...	330½
La Manche	91½	Falls, Kitty's Brook ...	349½
Arnold's Cove	99½	Grand Lake, Sandy Pond Rr.	362
Come-By-Chance	107½	Junction Brook	366½
Northern Bight	119½	Head of Deer Lake	377
Clarenville	132½	Fort	392½
Shoal Harbour	136½	Riverhead, Bay of Islands ...	405½
Thorburn Lake	146½	Corner Brook	408
Port Blandford, Clode Sound	154½	Birchy Cove	411½
Terra Nova	167½	Spruce B'k, St. George's Pond	429
Alexander Bay Station ...	184½	Seal Rocks, St. George's Bay	463
Gambo...	192½	Robinson's Head	481½
Benton, Soulis Brook ...	207½	Crabb's	486
Glenwood, Gander River ...	233	Falsh Gulch	496
Burnt Bay	245	Codroy River	526½
Ouinette, Norris' Arm ...	257½	Little Codroy River ...	530½
Bishop's Falls	268½	Cape Ray	542½
Opposite Grand Falls ...	279	Port-aux-Basques	550½

HOTELS IN ST. JOHN'S.

The best time for tourists to reach St. John's is the middle of June. This will give them three months of the best summer weather. Custom House Officers are in attendance on the arrival of each steamer to examine and pass the passengers' luggage. Cabs also meet the steamers. Fare to the hotels, luggage included, 50 cents.

"THE CITY HOTEL," Duckworth Street, near Prescott Street, has been recently enlarged and improved, and now contains from 35 to 40 rooms. It is well managed, clean and comfortable; table excellent; attendance good. From the balcony in front a fine view of the harbour and city is obtained. Charges:—for a front room with board, $2 per day; for other rooms, $1.50 per day. Travellers speak highly of the City Hotel. (See advertisement.)

"TREMONT HOTEL," 293 Water Street, has 19 rooms, is centrally situated and very comfortably fitted up. Travellers will find excellent accommodation here, every attention being paid to their comforts. Charges, from $1 to $2 per day acccording to the room occupied. (See advertisement.)

"THE CENTRAL HOTEL," Water Street, was destroyed in the great fire of 1892. The proprietor, Mr. Crosbie, secured temporary premises in George's Street, which though unpretentious in appearance are always well filled with guests—a proof of his attentions to their comforts. He is now erecting a large new hotel to be opened in November next, in Duckworth Street, a little west of Prescott St. The site is excellent. (See advertisement.)

"THE ATLANTIC HOTEL," a large and very fine building, was burned in the fire of 1892. It has been rebuilt on a smaller scale, but is not as yet opened.

"THE GLOBE HOTEL," 454 Water Street West, has 18 rooms, and is well conducted. Fare, from $1 to $2 per day.

Those who prefer private lodgings and board can readily obtain such.

CONSULS IN ST. JOHN'S.

German Empire—Robert H. Prowse; Italy—Consul-General for Newfoundland and Canada—W. J. Fisher; United States—T. N. Molloy; Brazil—A. O. Hayward; Portugal—T. R. Smith; Spain—Don Antonio Singala; Sweden and Norway—Robert H. Prowse; Belgium—H. E. Hayward.

CURRENCY.

An Act of the Legislature passed in 1887 renders it imperative that all accounts be kept and all moneys paid and received in dollars and cents; and provides that silver shall be a legal tender up to $10. It legalizes as current coin of the Colony, British and foreign coins, viz.: the British Sovereign and all its multiples, which shall pass current for $4.80; the Gold Eagle of the United States and all its multiples, which shall pass current for $9.85; British silver coins after the rate fixed for British gold coins.

ST. PIERRE AND MIQUELON—TRAVEL ROUTES.

The French Islands of St. Pierre and Miquelon can be reached from Halifax fortnightly by the steamer *Pro Patria*, carrying the mails. Agents in Halifax—Cunningham & Curren. This steamer does not call at any Newfoundland port.

The steamer *St. Pierre*, as already stated, plies fortnightly between Halifax and Placentia, calling at St. Pierre, and sailing through the beautiful Bras d' Or Lakes, C.B. Tourists who wish to visit St. Pierre can go by this route from Placentia and spend a week in St. Pierre; or from Halifax can reach St. Pierre, and after a short stay land at Placentia. The steamer *Harlaw* from Halifax also calls at St. Pierre, and afterwards at ports on the western coast of Newfoundland.

POSITION OF THE ISLANDS.

We have seen already under what circumstances these islands were ceded to France "as a shelter for her fishermen," in 1763. They are situated at the mouth of Fortune Bay, about 13 miles from the peninsula of Burin the nearest point of Newfoundland, and about equi-distant (135 miles) from Cape Race and Cape Ray. The Island of St. Pierre is seven and a half miles long, five and a half miles wide, and 26 miles in circumference. It contains several lakes, the largest of which is Savoyard, a mile in length. It has several small islands dependent on it, the principal being Isle au Chiens, at the mouth of St. Pierre harbour, on which the fish merchants have built their establishments. Owing to its rocky surface there is but little cultivation. There are a few farms of an inferior grade on the south coast; but its excellent harbour where the capital is built renders it by far the most important of the two islands.

DIMENSIONS.

Grand Miquelon, about 12 miles in length, was formerly separated from Petite Miquelon, or Langlade (commonly Langley); but of late years a sand bar has formed between them and has been the scene of many shipwrecks. The latter is more adapted

DIRECTIONS FOR TOURISTS.

for farming, and has 13 farms in a fair state of cultivation ; but neither has a safe harbour.

IMPORTANCE TO FRANCE.

These islands are of immense importance to France as the basis of her great Bank Fishery. The resident population has increased considerably. The census taken in November, 1892, showed the population of St. Pierre to be 5,703 : that of Miquelon 544 ; total 6,247. Of these 3,195 are males and 3,052 females.

The average export of fish for eight years ending 1892 was : Dried cod, 6,504,429 kilos ; green cod, 24,766,014 kilos.

The following figures show the rapid increase in the trade of St. Pierre :—

Date.	Value of Exports.	Value of Imports.
1847	$976,113	$509,092
1857	770,755	699,293
1867	1,718,037	1,462,521
1877	2,121,442	1,661,383
1887	3,375,986	2,545,654

Synopsis of shipping for 1887 :

	No. Vessels.	Tonnage.
From France	802	124,447
Provincial ports	225	15,807
Total	1027	140,254

The town of St. Pierre lies on the east side of the island. It is the seat of the Governor of the Islands. Two Atlantic cables are landed here. During the fishing season it presents a very busy aspect ; its roadstead often containing hundreds of fishing vessels, while thousands are temporaily added to its usual population. The chief buildings are the Governor's House ; the Court of Justice ; a large Church, Convent and schools, the Treasury, Post Office, Government Provision Store, and Printing office. There are also some handsome private dwellings. The hotels are the *Joinville, Pension Hacala,* and *International House.*

There is a College, three schools taught by the Brothers, and a girls' school taught by nuns. The sisters are of the Order of St. Joseph of Cluny, a Nursing and Educational Order. All the hospital nursing is under their charge.

Altogether St. Pierre is a highly interesting little town—unique in character, and the tourist will find much to attract him, not only in the place itself but in the customs and manners of the residents and the fishermen.

CHAPTER XVI.

SPORT IN NEWFOUNDLAND.

A GOOD FIELD FOR SPORSMEN.

It is not necessary, for the purposes of this book, to discourse at any great length on Sport in Newfoundland, beyond what has been already said incidentally in previous chapters.

That Newfoundland presents to the lovers of sport attractions such as few other countries possess is admitted by all who have given it a trial. Its countless lakes and lakelets abound with trout of the finest description, and are the abodes of the wild goose, the wild duck and other fresh water fowl. The willow grouse or ptarmigan (*Lagopus albus*) the rock ptarmigan, the curlew, the plover, the snipe are found, in the proper season, all over the island, on the great "barrens," or in the marshy grounds in immense numbers. The sea-pigeons and guillemots, or "murrs" or "turrs" as they are called in the vernacular are seen all around the shores and islands. The large Arctic hare, and the North-American hare, called erroneously by the natives a "rabbit," are to be met with,—especially the latter—in great abundance. The American hare is not indigenous, but some twenty years ago, a few pair were brought from Nova Scotia and let loose. They have thriven and spread to such a wonderful extent that they have reached nearly every part of the island, and in the fall and winter form an important item in the food of the working classes. Above all, the noble caribou or deer, in vast herds, traverse the island in periodical migrations from south to north, and furnish the highest prizes for the sportsman. Finer salmon streams than those of the island naturally are—or rather were—could not be found elsewhere; but as described in the chapter on the fisheries, they have been left unprotected, and ignorant and reckless greed has almost destroyed rivers that once abounded in the "Monarch of the brook." Already, under the restorative measures introduced by the Department of Fisheries and the protective rules and regulations enforced by wardens, a marked improvement has taken place, and in a few years the streams will recover their former abundance. Even now there are places where the salmon-fisher may find excellent sport. For more adventurous sportsmen there are the black bear and the wolf in the interior ; while the beaver and otter are found there around the lonely lakes and ponds. Now that these sporting regions are rendered accessible to some extent by railways, sportsmen are arriving in increasing numbers from other lands.

PTARMIGAN ABUNDANT.

The finest sport perhaps is ptarmigan—shooting which commences September 15th—before which date it is illegal, and terminates January 12th. These fine birds are quite equal to the Scotch grouse, and resemble them so closely that it is difficult to make out any specific difference between the red grouse, gorcock or moorcock of Scotland and those of Newfoundland. As a table bird they are unsurpassed in richness and delicacy of flavour. In September, after feeding on the wild berries, they are in excellent condition. In certain localities, and at some distance from settlements, they are very plentiful. In winter they become pure white.

WILD GEESE AND DUCKS, CURLEW, ETC.

The wild goose breeds in the most secluded ponds and brings her young ones down the brooks early in July, when they are full grown. The black duck, the finest of all table birds, is abundant in certain localities. The plover and curlew are so plentiful that sportsmen only fire at them when a shot at a flock can be obtained. They are bred on the shores of Labrador, and after feeding on the wild berries they arrive in Newfoundland almost balls of fat and in flavour peculiarly delicious. The wild goose is a remarkably fine bird, easily domesticated but does not breed when tamed. It crosses readily with the tame goose, the result being the mongrel goose so esteemed by epicures.

DEER STALKING.

The caribou or reindeer are finer than those of which Norway and Lapland can boast, being much larger and carrying far finer antlers. Stags have been often shot which weighed from 500 to 600 lbs. The antlers of the stag are palmated, sweeping backward and of magnificent proportions, the brow antlers meeting over the nose, like a pair of hands clasped in the attitude of prayer. These horns are shed in November. Their migrations are as regular as the seasons, from the south where they pass the winter to the north-western portions of the island where they feed and bring forth their young. When the October frost begin to nip the vegetation they turn toward the south and repeat their long march. September and October are the months for deer-shooting. Some knowledge of the country and the assistance of Mic-Mac Indians are requisite. There are favourite hunting grounds known to the initiated and to the Indian guides, where deer stalking can be enjoyed to perfection. One of the best of these is the "barrens" overlooking Grand Lake, opposite the northern end of the island. Here they collect in large herds before setting out on their southern migration. The "White Hills" in the neighbourhood of Hall's Bay, an arm of Notre Dame Bay, is another favourite stalking-ground. Inland from various settlements on the southern shore, in the late autumn and early winter, great numbers of deer are slain. At times the St. John's market is over-stocked in winter with carcases of venison brought by the steamer from this quarter. The quarters are often sold for five to ten cents per pound. Formerly deer-stalking was expensive sport as it was difficult to reach the interior; but railways as they open up the country will aid the sportsman in reaching the desired locality and lessen the expense. Indians are almost indispensable in these excursions.

LORD DUNRAVEN.

Lord Dunraven in "The Nineteenth Century for January, 1881," gave an account of a deer-shooting excursion he made in this island. He found it "a good field for exploration and sport." He said "the caribou are plentiful, and the Newfoundland stags are finer by far than any to be found in any portion of the North-American Continent." "Fur is pretty plentiful; wild fowl and grouse abundant; and the creeks and rivers are full of salmon and trout." In "Forest Life in Acadia," by Captain Hardy, R.A., the author says:—" I know of no country so near England which offers the same amount of inducement to the explorer, naturalist or sportsman as Newfoundland. To one who combines the advantages of a good practical knowledge of geology with the love of sport the interior of this great island, much of which is quite unknown, may indeed prove a field of valuable and remunerative discovery, for its mineral resources are unquestionably of vast importance." "The caribou are scattered more or less abundantly over an area of some 25,000 square miles of unbroken wilderness."

APPENDIX No. I.

ATLANTIC CABLES.

ERRATUM.

Page 278, line 3, for "1,200 lbs. copper to the mile in the new Anglo-American Cable," read "650 lbs." The number of words per minute transmissible over this cable has yet to be determined by actual experiment. While some anticipate 120 words on the duplex principle, or 60 each way, the less sanguine reckon on 90 per minute, duplex, or 45 each way per minute. The latter calculation is more likely to prove correct. The cost of the new cable is about half a million of dollars.

STOCK EXCHANGES.

Perhaps the most wonderful feat yet performed on the Anglo-American Cables is the transmission of intelligence between the Stock Exchanges of New York and London while business is proceeding. A special cable is appropriated to their use during five hours each day. The prices of stock are flashed both ways, so that a broker in New York can buy stock in London as readily as if he were one of the shouting crowd in the Exchange, and *vice versa*. Answers are received in from two to four minutes, so that instructions to brokers on either side are transmitted in this brief interval, while the auction is proceeding, and fortunes won or lost in a few seconds. Nine-tenths of this exchange business is transacted over the Anglo-American cables,—a fact which sufficiently attests their superior accuracy and speed.

THE IMPROVED GRAPNEL.

A grapnel is now in use on board the Cable Ship *Minia*, Capt. Trott, for picking up cables requiring repairs, which would seem to be endowed with almost human intelligence. The moment the cable is caught the grapnel rings a bell on board the ship, intimating "I have got him." At the same time, by an ingenious arrangement, it cuts the cable and firmly grasps the end that is wanted, leaving the other to be picked up afterwards. Then the hauling in process begins, and from the depth it may be of two miles, the grapnel soon appears at the surface of the water, holding in its death-like grip the end of the cable. Armed with such an implement Captain Trott the ablest cable engineer now living, is able to perform marvellous feats.

LENGTHS OF CABLES.

The following figures show the lengths of the cables :—

The Anglo-American Co's Cables.

Laid.	Between.	Nl. ms.	
1873	Ireland and Newfoundland	1,881	
"	Newfoundland, *via* St. Pierre & Cape Breton	293	
			2,174
1874	Ireland and Newfoundland	1,840	
1873	Newfoundland and Sydney, C. B.	343	
			2,183
1880	Ireland and Newfoundland	1,886	
"	Newfoundland, *via* St. Pierre & Cape Breton	360	
			2,246
1869	France and St. Pierre	2,648	
"	St. Pierre and Massachusetts, U. S.	759	
			3,407

The Direct United States Co's Cables.

1874	Ireland and Nova Scotia	2,423	
"	Nova Scotia and New Hampshire, U. S.	560	
			2,983

Compagnie Francaise Paris a New York Cables.

1879	France and St. Pierre	2,242	
"	St. Pierre and Cape Breton	188	
"	St. Pierre and Massachussets, U. S.	827	
			3,257

APPENDIX.

The Western Union Co's Cables.

1881—England and Nova Scotia	. . .	2,531
1882—England and Nova Scotia	. . .	2,576

The Commercial Co's Cables.

1884—Ireland and Nova Scotia	. . .	2,350
" —Nova Scotia and New York, U. S.	. .	841
		——3,181
" —Ireland and Nova Scotia	. . .	2,388
1885—Nova Scotia and Massachussets, U. S.	. .	519
		——2,907

1894—Commercial Cable : Duplicate of the previous one.

	Share—Capital of Companies.	
Anglo-American .	. $35,000,000— Each line .	$8,750,000
Direct United States	. 6,400,000 " " .	6,400,000
Compagnie Française	. 8,400,000 " " .	8,400,000
Western Union .	. 14,000,000 " " .	7,000,000
Commercial . .	. 8,000,000 " " .	4,000,000

APPENDIX No. II.

SCENERY OF THE BAY OF ISLANDS.

A lady tourist who last year visited the Bay of Islands in the s. s. *Harlaw*, wrote as follows of the scenery :—" As we approach this romantic bay, the magnificent scenery of the coast can scarcely be described in terms to do even faint justice to its merits. Great cliffs tower up above the ship, which the deep soundings allow to approach and steam for hours not a cable's length from the shore. Hundreds of small bays indent the coast, while some take a majestic sweep inland, unveiling innumerable isles and lovely beaches. Hour after hour we pass scenes and landscapes which gradually unfolded themselves to our delighted vision as very glimpses of fairy-land; but there were grander to come. Early next morning we were on deck, and words cannot describe the glorious sight presented. Before us was the Bay of Islands robed in all the magic colouring of an early summer morning—a vista of mountains capped with snow, fantastic peaks, cliff on cliff rising sheer from 2,000 to 2,500 feet, great chasms between columns of rocks which looked like the walls of some vast temple. From some of the precipices waterfalls, formed by the melting snow away up, tumbled in foaming beauty down the steep."

Advertisements.

AYRE & SONS,

WHOLESALE AND RETAIL

IMPORTERS

DRY GOODS,

BOOTS & SHOES,

GROCERIES,

PROVISIONS,

and HARDWARE.

WE keep one of the largest stocks in the Island and can always submit a good assortment. Our prices are low and cannot be beaten. Visitors and travellers will find it advantageous to purchase from us.

Fishing Tackle & Sporting Goods

Water Street, St. John's.

EVERY ONE KNOWS WHERE.

Advertisements.

JOHN STEER,

IMPORTER AND DEALER IN

General Dry Goods,

Provisions, Groceries,

Fish and Oil.

Our Special Lines

CHOICE BONELESS BEEF,
CHOICE BEEF CUTTINGS,
CHOICE FAMILY FLOUR.

WONDERFUL VALUE IN TEAS!

Orders by Letter have careful and prompt attention.

379, 381, and 383, WATER-ST.,

ST. JOHN'S, NEWFOUNDLAND.

Advertisements.

JOB BROS. & CO.,

GENERAL IMPORTERS,

Water-St., St. John's, N.F.

DEPARTMENTS:

Dry Goods, Groceries,

Hardware, Store Goods,

And Naval Stores.

*Exporters of Fish, Cod and Seal Oil,
Seal Skins, Lobsters,
AND GENERAL PRODUCE.*

Agents "Royal" Insurance Company,

(OF LIVERPOOL).

JOB BROTHERS,

Mersey Chambers, Old Churchyard, Liverpool.

Advertisements.

COLIN R. CAMPBELL.   GEORGE SMITH.

CAMPBELL & SMITH,

(FORMERLY McDOUGALL & CAMPBELL,)

BROKERS, COMMISSION MERCHANTS & AUCTIONEERS,

St. John's, - - Newfoundland.

Special attention paid to shipping and forwarding Goods of all kinds. Sale and purchase of Bread Stuffs and Provisions.

➤FRUITS---Dry and Green◄

Codfish and Oils, Lobsters, Salmon Herring, Etc., etc.

CATTLE, HORSES,

and all kinds of P.E.I. Produce.

Advertisements.

SHEA & CO.

General Commission Merchants

STEAMSHIP AGENTS.

AGENTS FOR

✳ Allan Line Steamers ✳

SAILING EVERY FORTNIGHT BETWEEN THIS PORT AND BRITAIN.

AGENTS FOR

Ross & Dobell Lines Steamers,

SAILING THROUGHOUT THE SEASON BETWEEN MONTREAL, CHARLOTTETOWN, P. E. I., AND THIS PORT.

Advertisements.

New York, Nfld., and Halifax
STEAMSHIP COMPANY.

Red Cross Line

S. S. SILVIA, S. S. PORTIA,

Sailing at intervals of about ten days from New York, calling at Halifax, St John's, Nfld., and occasionally, Pilley's Island, Nfld.

Attractive Tourist Route!
First Class Passenger Accommodation.

For information regarding freight or passage, apply to

C. F. BOWRING & Co. .... *Liverpool.*
BOWRING & ARCHIBALD, *New York.*
F. D. CORBETT & Co. .... *Halifax.*
HARVEY & Co. ...... *St. John's, Nfld.*
BOWRING BROS. ..... *St. John's, Nfld.*

Advertisements.

Black Diamond S. S. Company.

STEAMERS:

Bonavista,
    Coban,
        Louisburg,
            Cacouna,
                Cape Breton.

STEAMERS of this Line sail from Montreal at intervals of a week, calling at Charlottetown, P. E. Island, Sydney, C. B., and St. John's, N. F. The St. Lawrence route affords tourists one of the most delightful trips in the world. While enjoying the advantages of a sea voyage, the traveller is out of sight of land only a few hours between Montreal and St. John's, N. F.

For information regarding freight or passage, apply to

PEAKE, BROTHERS & Co.,   Charlottetown, **P. E. I.**
DOMINION COAL COMPANY,   Sydney, **C. B.**
HARVEY & Co.,   St. John's, Newfoundland.

Advertisements

N. F. Coastal Steamship Co.,
(LIMITED).

S. S. "GRAND LAKE,"
S. S. "VIRGINIA LAKE,"
S. S. "WINDSOR LAKE,"

Under Contract with the Government for the Conveyance of Mails.

SUMMER SERVICE, 1894.

S.S. *Virginia Lake* & *Windsor Lake* will leave St. John's for Northern Outports.

| Tuesday, April 24. |
| Tuesday, May 8. |
| Tuesday, May 22. |
| Tuesday, June 5. |
| Tuesday, June 19. |
| Tuesday, July 3. |
| Tuesday, July 17. |
| Tuesday, July 31. |
| Tuesday, Aug. 14. |
| Tuesday, Aug. 28. |
| Tuesday, Sept. 11. |
| Tuesday, Sept. 25. |
| Tuesday, Octr. 9. |
| Tuesday, Oct. 23. |
| Tuesday, Nov. 6. |
| Tuesday, Nov. 20. |
| Tuesday, Dec. 4. |
| Tuesday, Dec. 18. |
| Monday, Dec. 31. |

S. S. *Grand Lake* will leave St. John's for Western Outports.

| Saturday, April 21. |
| Saturday, May 5. |
| Saturday, May 19. |
| Saturday, June 2. |
| Saturday, June 16. |
| Saturday, June 30. |
| Saturday, July 14. |
| Saturday, July 28. |
| Saturday, Aug. 11. |
| Saturday, Aug. 25. |
| Saturday, Sept. 8. |
| Saturday, Sept. 22. |
| Saturday, Oct. 6. |
| Saturday, Oct. 20. |
| Saturday, Nov. 3. |
| Saturday, Nov. 17. |
| Saturday, Dec. 1. |
| Saturday, Dec. 15. |
| Saturday, Dec. 29. |

* On these trips the Steamer goes as far as Battle Harbor, connecting with Labrador Steamer.

Advertisements.

NEWFOUNDLAND RAILWAY—STATIONS AND FARES.

From	To	Miles	1st Class	2nd Class
St. John's to	Dunnsmere	7	$0 35	$0 20
"	Irvine	10	0 50	0 30
"	Topsail	15	0 60	0 45
"	Manuels	18	0 70	0 50
"	Kelligrews	24	0 60	0 60
"	Seal Cove	27	1 00	0 75
"	Duff's	28	1 00	0 75
"	Holyrood	33	1 20	0 90
"	Woodford	36	1 35	1 00
"	Salmon Cove	38½	1 50	1 10
"	Brigus Junction	47½	1 80	1 30
"	Hodge Water		1 90	1 40
"	Whitbourne	57½	2 00	1 50
"	Blaketown	62	2 25	1 65
"	Broad Cove	66¼	2 50	1 70
"	Span'd's Bay R'd	76	2 50	1 70
"	Triton	79	2 50	1 70
"	Harbor Grace	83½	2 50	1 70

Children under 12, half-price; children under 5 (one child only and in arms), with parent or servant, free.

Excursion rates: one single first-class fare.

NEWFOUNDLAND NORTHERN AND WESTERN RAILWAY—STATIONS AND FARES.

From	To	Miles	1st Class	2nd Class
Whitbourne to	Placentia J'ction	7	$0 40	$0 30
"	Long Harbor	14	0 60	0 40
"	Tickle Harbor	25	0 75	0 55
"	Rantem	32	1 00	0 70
"	La Manche	34	1 05	0 75
"	Arnold's Cove	42	1 25	0 80
"	Come-by-chance	50	1 50	1 00
"	Northern Bight	62	1 85	1 20
"	Clarenville	75	2 25	1 50
"	Shoal Harbor	79	2 35	1 55
"	Thorburn Lake	89	2 65	1 75
"	Clode Sound	87	2 90	1 90
"	Terra Nova	110	3 30	2 20
"	Alexander Bay	127	3 80	2 50
"	Gambo	135	4 05	2 70
"	Benton	149	4 47	2 98
"	Gander River	175	5 25	3 50
"	Ouinette	190	5 70	3 80
"	Exploits	200	6 00	4 00

Children under 12, half-price; children under 5 (one child only and in arms), with parent or servant, free.

PLACENTIA RAILWAY—STATIONS AND FARES.

From	To	Miles	1st Class	2nd Class
Whitbourne to	Placentia J'ction	7	$0 40	$0 30
"	Ville Marie	7	0 70	0 60
"	Dunnville		1 00	0 75
"	Placentia	27	1 00	0 75

Children under 12, half-price; children under 5 (one child only and in arms), with parent or servant, free.

Advertisements.

ANGLO-AMERICAN TELEGRAPH COY.

OFFICE HOURS: 8.30 A. M. TO 9 P. M.

STATIONS.

St. John's, Central Station: Foran's Exchange Buildings.
" Post Office Station.
" Hoylestown Station.

LOCAL TARIFF.

Bay Bulls, Cape Broyle, Ferryland, Caplin Bay, Renews, Fermeuse, Trepassey, Brigus,	} 10 words 25 cts.	Bay Roberts, Harbor Grace, Carbonear, Heart's Content, Whitbourne, Placentia, Rantem, } 10 words 25 cts.
Black River, Long Harbor, Conn River, Bay-du-Nord, White Bear Bay, Burgeo,	} 10 words 50 cents.	Rose Blanche, La Poile, Channel, Trinity, Catalina, Bonavista, } 10 words 50 cents.

FOREIGN TARIFF.

	10 words.	Add'l word.
Cape Breton, Nova Scotia and New Brunswick ...	$1 00	and 9 cts.
Ontario and Quebec	1 05	" 10 cts
Maine	1 15	" 11 cts.
New England States, P. E. I. and New York City ...	1 25	" 11 cts.
Great Britain and France	25 cts. per word.	
Germany ...	25	" "
Spain (Barcelona via France and Marseilles Cable)...	38	" "
Spain (all other places)	40	" "
Portugal	39	" "
Italy, Sicily, Sardinia	32	" "
Norway	35	" "
Pernambuco	1 55	" "
Rio de Janeiro	1 66	" "
Bahia	1 66	" "

To calculate the cost of a message to Barbadoes, multiply $2.21 by number of words, and add 75 to total. If over ten words, add eight cents to the 75 for each word over the ten.

NOTE.—Words over ten letters count as two words.

Advertisements.

Union Bank of Newfoundland.

FORTIETH ANNUAL REPORT.

THE Directors have pleasure in submitting to the Proprietors the Fortieth Annual Report and the Abstract Statement of the affairs of the Bank, for the year ending 31st May, 1894.

The net Profits for the year, after all deductions for expenses of management, rebate on local bills discounted not yet due, computed interest on deposit receipts outstanding, and allowing for all bad and doubtful debts, are $86,475.16 ; making, with $9,244.63 balance at credit of Profit and Loss Account last year, a total for distribution of $95,719.79, which your Directors have appropriated as follows, viz. :—

For Dividend of 6 per cent. paid in December last	$27,360 00
For Dividend of 6 per cent. to be paid on 20th instant	27,360 00
For a Bonus of $3 per share to be paid on 20th instant	13,680 00
To Reserve Fund	20,000 00
Leaving a balance at credit of Profit and Loss Account of	7,319 79
	$95,719 79

GENERAL STATEMENT.

LIABILITIES.

To Proprietors' capital		$456,000 00
" Reserve Fund		320,000 00
" Profit and Loss (undivided profit)		7,319 79
" Bank Notes in circulation		616,080 00
" Due by Bank, including deposits at interest, payable in Jan'y and July only on receiving 15 days' notice		3,015,305 59
" Dividend No. 78, of 6 per cent. for half-year ending 30th November, 1893	$27,360 00	
" Dividend No. 79, of 6 per cent. for half-year ending 31st May, 1894	27,360 00	
" Bonus No. 36, of $3 per share, for half-year ending 31st May, 1894	13,680 00	
	$68,400 00	
Less Dividend to 30th November last paid	27,360 00	41,040 00
		$4,455,745 38

ASSETS.

By Specie in Vault of the Bank	$196,974 82
" Notes of other Banks	517 00
" Bills discounted, loans, &c.	2,881,671 72
" Balances due by Banks and funds available in 15 days	1,360,581 84
" Bank premises, iron safes and furniture	16,000 00
	$4,455,745 38

C. S. PINSENT, *Pro Manager.*

St John's, 31st May, 1894.

Advertisements.

Commercial Bank of Nfld.

ST. JOHN'S, NEWFOUNDLAND.

Established 1857.   [Incorporated 1858.

Capital - - - *$306,000*

(In Shares of $200 each).

Reserve - - - *$110,000*

Unap. to Cr. of P. & L.   *12,116*

Collections made on favorable terms.

Agents :—*London*—The London and Westminster Bank, (Ltd). *Liverpool*—The Bank of Liverpool, (Limited). *New York*—The National Bank of the Republic; *Boston*—The Atlas National Bank; *Montreal*—The Merchant's Bank of Canada; *Quebec*—The Merchant's Bank of Canada; *Halifax*—The Union Bank of Halifax; *St. Pierre, Miquelon*—Banque des Iles.

HENRY COOKE, - - - Manager.
H. D. CARTER, - - Chief Accountant.

Advertisements.

WILLIAM J. CLOUSTON,
[East Corner Market House Hill.]

WATER STREET, - - ST. JOHN'S, N. F.

MANUFACTURER OF AND DEALER IN

All kinds of Tinware, Iron, Stoves, Enamelled Wares, &c.

JOBBING PROMPTLY ATTENDED TO.

HEARN & CO.

COMMISSION MERCHANTS
AND WHOLESALE DEALERS
IN PROVISIONS AND SPIRITS.

———AGENTS FOR———

COLGATE'S STERLING SOAP.

AND MANUFACTURERS

FINEST
QUALITY
BUTTERINE.

Advertisements.

Central Hotel!

George Street,

(Near the General Post Office).

G. G. CROSBIE, - - - **Proprietor.**

EXCELLENT accommodation to travellers guaranteed, and the utmost attention paid to their comforts. Rooms well furnished and commodious. Near the busiest part of the city. ☞ The New CENTRAL HOTEL, Duckworth-St., near Prescott-St., is in course of erection, and will be the largest and finest Hotel in St. John's.

City Hotel!

DUCKWORTH STREET, ST. JOHN'S.

Mrs. G. WALSH, - **Proprietress.**

THIS Hotel has been enlarged and refitted, and is now considered the best in Newfoundland. It is lighted by electricity; with hot and cold water baths; smoking and reading rooms; is near the business places; and commands a picturesque view all over the city. It is within three minutes walk of all Passenger Steamships. The "CITY" is known as the "House" of Commercial Travellers. Gentlemen visiting St. John's would do well to stay at this Hotel. A branch of the General Post Office is also kept in the same building.

Advertisements.

M. MONROE

GENERAL MERCHANT,

St. John's, - Newfoundland.

All descriptions of British, American and Foreign

kept in stock in our various departments.

Codfish, Cod Oil,

Salmon, Herring,

Lobsters, &c., &c.,

PURCHASED AT HIGHEST CURRENT RATES.

INSURANCE:

Advertisements.

Telephone Address: "LEDINGHAM."

Terra Nova Foundry, Engine and Boiler Works.

WATER STREET EAST.

ENGINES and Boilers, of all descriptions, for marine and land purposes, on stock and made to order.

Heavy smith-work executed with powerful Steam Hammers. Castings of all descriptions, in Iron or Brass, got up on the shortest notice. Mill work of every description executed. Shafting, Pulleys, Hangers, Leather and Rubber Beltings, Iron Piping, and Fittings in Iron or Brass, kept in stock. Public and Private Buildings heated by Steam or Hot Water. Repairs to Hulls and Machinery of disabled Steamers a speciality— executed afloat or on Dry Dock, to which the Subscribers has full access for such work.

☞ *Competent Engineers, Boilermakers and Coppersmiths, always on hand to attend Steamship, Mill and Factory Repairs.*

Advertisements.

W. & G. Rendell,

Water Street, St. John's, Newfoundl'd.

Property and Commission Agents,

——AGENTS FOR THE——

Phœnix Fire Assurance Company

OF LONDON.

Importers of, and Dealers in, all descriptions of

Paints, Oils, & Roofing Material.

Advertisements.

WEST END DRUG STORE!

M. CONNORS, PROPRIETOR.

A large and varied stock of
Drugs, Medicines and Perfumery, Paints, Oils, Varnishes, &c.,
constantly on hand.

Newest Garden Seeds in Stock.

Prescriptions carefully compounded, and their preparation receives personal and prompt attention. Medicine Chests supplied and re-fitted at shortest notice.

358 - WATER STREET WEST. - 358

WILLIAM COOK,

278   WATER STREET, ST. JOHN'S, NEWFOUNDLAND.   278

HOUSE AND SHIP BUTCHER.

Vegetables, Meats, and Ships' Stores.

*** Ships' letters addressed to my care delivered immediately on arrival.

SATISFACTION GUARANTEED.

Z. COX,

347 - WATER STREET, ST. JOHN'S, NEWFOUNDLAND. - 347

GENERAL IMPORTER of Provisions, Groceries, etc.— FLOUR, BEEF, PORK, TEAS, JAMS, BISCUITS, SYRUPS and FANCY GROCERIES ; FRUITS and VEGETABLES, when in season.

OUTPORT ORDERS RECEIVE PROMPT ATTENTION.

Advertisements.

JOHN ANDERSON.

GENERAL IMPORTER.

Largest importer of Ready-made Garments in the Colony.

The Universal Provider to the Workingmen of the City and Fishermen of the Country, the great Bargain House of St. John's.

Killer of Big Profits!

Dry Goods, Groceries & Provisions.

371 - Water Street - 371

ST. JOHN'S, NEWFOUNDLAND.

Advertisements.

Tremont Hotel!

WATER-ST., - ST. JOHN'S, N.F.
(O'DWYER'S BLOCK).

Mrs. McGRATH, - Proprietress.

TRANSIENT and permanent boarders accommodated upon reasonable terms. The TREMONT HOUSE contains large well-ventilated, nicely furnished rooms, also commodious bath-rooms, and is centrally situated, being near the business places of the city. The patronage of the travelling public is respectfully solicited. Every satisfaction guaranteed, and all orders attended to at the most reasonable rates.

"NEWFOUNDLAND: THE OLDEST BRITISH COLONY."
Price $2.50. - Pp. 490.
BY JOSEPH HATTON AND REV. M. HARVEY, LL.D.
London: Chapman and Hall, 1883.

An admirable account of the oldest British Colony.—*Fortnightly Review.*

No more interesting work has ever come under our notice than this.—*European Mail.*

By far the most complete account of Newfoundland that has yet appeared.—*London Daily News.*

The story of Newfoundland is told so attractively and completely that we doubt if it will ever require retelling. It may be supplemented but not superseded.—*Land and Water.*

An admirable book.—*London Academy.*

An interesting and well-written work.—*Pall Mall Gazette.*

The best account of Newfoundland ever printed.—*New York Herald.*

"TEXT-BOOK OF NEWFOUNDLAND HISTORY."
Price Fifty-five cents.
BY REV. M. HARVEY, LL.D.
(Second Edition.)
London and Glasgow: W. Collins & Co., 1890.

"WHERE ARE WE AND WHITHER TENDING?"
Price Fifty cents.
BY REV. M. HARVEY, LL.D.
London: Trubner & Co., 1886.

While admitting that the pessimist can readily find a certain justification of his views in the many dark and discouraging facts of human existence, the author still believes that there are ample grounds for holding human progress to be a grand reality.—*Westminster Review.*

Cheerful in tone and popular in style.—*Saturday Review.*

The question is discussed with much point and acumen.—*Scotsman.*

The author is the happy possessor of a well-furnished mind. He displays an acquaintance with ancient and modern history, with literature and philosophy, with science and statistics, which would be creditable in any man, and is somewhat surprising in a citizen of St. John's, Newfoundland. The result is an eminently readable book.—*Glasgow Herald.*

A fresh vigorously written book.—*United Presbyterian Magazine.*

The lectures well repay perusal.—*Liverpool Courier.*

The work displays great scholarship.—*Kirkudbright Advertiser.*

The lectures are brilliantly written.—*New York Churchman.*

"UNDER THE GREAT SEAL."
A thrilling History of Newfoundland in the days of the Fishing Admirals.
BY JOSEPH HATTON;
Author of "By Order of the Czar," "Clytie," etc.
London: Hutcheson & Co., 1893.

www.ingramcontent.com/pod-product-compliance
Lightning Source LLC
Chambersburg PA
CBHW021207230426
43667CB00006B/597